Mastering FreeSWITCH

Master the art of advanced VoIP and WebRTC
communication with the most dynamic application
server, FreeSWITCH

Anthony Minessale II

Giovanni Maruzzelli

[PACKT] open source*
PUBLISHING   community experience distilled

BIRMINGHAM - MUMBAI

Mastering FreeSWITCH

Copyright © 2016 Packt Publishing

All rights reserved. No part of this book may be reproduced, stored in a retrieval system, or transmitted in any form or by any means, without the prior written permission of the publisher, except in the case of brief quotations embedded in critical articles or reviews.

Every effort has been made in the preparation of this book to ensure the accuracy of the information presented. However, the information contained in this book is sold without warranty, either express or implied. Neither the authors, nor Packt Publishing, and its dealers and distributors will be held liable for any damages caused or alleged to be caused directly or indirectly by this book.

Packt Publishing has endeavored to provide trademark information about all of the companies and products mentioned in this book by the appropriate use of capitals. However, Packt Publishing cannot guarantee the accuracy of this information.

First published: July 2016

Production reference: 1260716

Published by Packt Publishing Ltd.
Livery Place
35 Livery Street
Birmingham B3 2PB, UK.

ISBN 978-1-78439-888-0

www.packtpub.com

Credits

Authors

Anthony Minessale II

Giovanni Maruzzelli

Reviewers

Ayobami Adewole

Brian West

Commissioning Editor

Amarabha Banerjee

Acquisition Editors

Neha Nagwekar

Rahul Nair

Content Development Editor

Kajal Thapar

Technical Editors

Pramod Kumavat

Mohita Vyas

Copy Editors

Dipti Mankame

Safis Editing

Project Coordinator

Shweta H. Birwatkar

Proofreader

Safis Editing

Indexer

Tejal Daruwale Soni

Graphics

Disha Haria

Production Coordinator

Arvindkumar Gupta

Cover Work

Arvindkumar Gupta

About the Authors

Anthony Minessale II is the primary author and founding member of the FreeSWITCH Open Source Soft-Switch. Anthony has spent around 20 years working with open source software. In 2001, Anthony spent a great deal of time contributing code to the Asterisk PBX and has authored numerous features and fixes to that project. In 2005, Anthony started coding a new idea for an open source voice application. The FreeSWITCH project was officially open to the public on January 1 2006. In the years that followed, Anthony has been actively maintaining and leading the software development of the FreeSWITCH project. Anthony also founded the ClueCon Technology Conference in 2005, and he continues to oversee the production of this annual event.

Anthony has been the author of several FreeSWITCH books, including *FreeSWITCH 1.0.6*, *FreeSWITCH 1.2*, *FreeSWITCH Cookbook*, and *FreeSWITCH 1.6 Cookbook*.

I'd like to thank my wife Jill and my kids, Eric and Abbi, who were in grade school when this project started and are now grown up. I'd also like to thank everyone who took the time to try FreeSWITCH and submit feedback. I finally thank my coauthor Giovanni Maruzzelli for working on this book.

Giovanni Maruzzelli (`gmaruzz@OpenTelecom.IT`) is heavily engaged with FreeSWITCH. In it, he wrote a couple of endpoint modules, and he is specialized in industrial grade deployments and solutions. He's the curator and coauthor of *FreeSWITCH 1.6 Cookbook* (Packt Publishing, 2015).

He's a consultant in the telecommunications sector, developing software and conducting training courses for FreeSWITCH, SIP, WebRTC, Kamailio, and OpenSIPS.

As an Internet technology pioneer, he was the cofounder of Italia Online in 1996, which was the most popular Italian portal and consumer ISP. Also, he was the architect of its Internet technologies (`www.italiaonline.it`). Back then, Giovanni was the supervisor of Internet operations and the architect of the first engine for paid access to `www.ilsole24ore.com`, the most-read financial newspaper in Italy, and its databases (migrated from the mainframe). After that, he was the CEO of the venture capital-funded company Matrice, developing telemail unified messaging and multiple-language phone access to e-mail (text to speech). He was also the CTO of the incubator-funded company Open4, an open source managed applications provider. For 2 years, Giovanni worked in Serbia as an Internet and telecommunications investment expert for IFC, an arm of the World Bank.

Since 2005, he has been based in Italy, and he serves ICT and telecommunication companies worldwide.

I'd like to thank all people who made writing this book a challenging journey for me, all who helped, all who supported, all who gave me obstacles to overcome. This book has been brought to you by the knowledge that was socially cumulated by humans through the centuries, let's praise them. I finally want to thank my coauthor Anthony Minessale II for being so patient and "Always See Everything."

About the Reviewers

Ayobami Adewole is a software engineer and technical consultant with experience spanning over 5 years. Ayobami has worked on mission critical systems; these include solutions for customer relationship management, land administration and geographical information systems, enterprise-level application integrations, and unified communication and software applications for the education and business sectors.

Ayobami is very passionate about VoIP technologies, and he continues to work on cutting-edge PBX solutions built on FreeSWITCH. In his spare time, he enjoys experimenting with new technologies. His blog is at http://ayobamiadewole.com.

> My unending gratitude goes to my parents for instilling in me the culture of discipline and hard work.

Brian West is a founding member of the FreeSWITCH team. He has been involved in open source telephony since 2003. Brian was heavily involved in the Asterisk open source PBX Project as a Bug Marshal and developer. In 2005, Brian joined the initiative that eventually lead to the FreeSWITCH Open Source Soft-Switch. Today, Brian serves as the general manager of the FreeSWITCH project and keeps the software moving forward. Brian has countless skills as a developer, tester, manager, and technologist, and he fills a vital role in the FreeSWITCH Community.

Contributors

Moises Silva wrote the entire 6th chapter, *PSTN* and *TDM*.

The following people contributed substantially to this book:

- Darren Schreiber
- Benjamin Tietz
- Russell Treleaven
- Seven Du (Du Jinfang)
- Muhammad Naseer Bhatti
- Florent Krieg
- Michael Jerris
- Iwada Eja
- Martyn Davies
- Charles Bujold
- Christian Bergamaschi
- Alexandr Dubovikov
- Lorenzo Mangani
- Dan Christian Bogos

www.PacktPub.com

eBooks, discount offers, and more

Did you know that Packt offers eBook versions of every book published, with PDF and ePub files available? You can upgrade to the eBook version at www.PacktPub.com and as a print book customer, you are entitled to a discount on the eBook copy. Get in touch with us at customercare@packtpub.com for more details.

At www.PacktPub.com, you can also read a collection of free technical articles, sign up for a range of free newsletters and receive exclusive discounts and offers on Packt books and eBooks.

https://www2.packtpub.com/books/subscription/packtlib

Do you need instant solutions to your IT questions? PacktLib is Packt's online digital book library. Here, you can search, access, and readPackt's entire library of books.

Why subscribe?

- Fully searchable across every book published by Packt
- Copy and paste, print, and bookmark content
- On demand and accessible via a web browser

Table of Contents

Preface

Real Time Communication (RTC) is a huge sector, in perennial growth. It spans from VoIP to FAXes, from VideoConferencing to CallCenters, from PBXes to WebRTC, using many interworking technologies to connect the past with the future, legacy applications to new users and markets, creating and developing new ways for saving time and money, fostering collaboration, and enjoying leisure.

FreeSWITCH covers it all; it is the most reliable, scalable, and flexible open source foundation, and is used to build services and products worldwide.

This book adopts a professional approach and attitude, making available a wealth of cumulated actual industry experience in each aspect of FreeSWITCH implementation.

Written for professionals, each chapter contains the knowledge needed to frame and understand its domain, and a thorough explanation of FreeSWITCH wheels and knobs, best practices, and real-world solutions.

What this book covers

Chapter 1, Typical Voice Uses for FreeSWITCH, gives an overview and analyzes each sector where FreeSWITCH is in production.

Chapter 2, Deploying FreeSWITCH, shows best practices in FreeSWITCH installation and management.

Chapter 3, ITSP and Voice Codecs Optimization, suggests what to look for when choosing an Internet Telephony Service Provider, and how to get the best from DIDs, terminations, T38, and voice traffic.

Chapter 4, VoIP Security, exposes specific measures and tools used to keep FreeSWITCH protected from unwanted attention and hostile behavior.

Chapter 5, *Audio File and Streaming Formats, Music on Hold, Recording Calls*, covers all that is related to audio manipulation with FreeSWITCH, from prompts optimization to call center barge in, from playing live streams to HD codecs.

Chapter 6, *PSTN and TDM*, happens to be the first published, thorough explanation of all possible interactions between FreeSWITCH and Sangoma, Digium, and other compatible hardware for interfacing traditional and legacy telephony networks.

Chapter 7, *WebRTC and Mod_Verto*, provides a detailed overview of what WebRTC is and what techniques it entails, and then follows the development of a complete FreeSWITCH implementation.

Chapter 8, *Audio and Video Conferencing*, delves into the intricacies of setting and managing FreeSWITCH multiuser conferences both via SIP and WebRTC, with chatting, screen sharing, moderation, and advanced techniques for videocomposing the screen.

Chapter 9, *Faxing and T38*, explores all facsimile transmission aspects, and how to reliably fax via VoIP, send office documents, and integrate with mail.

Chapter 10, *Advanced IVR with Lua*, proves that it is not your average code snippet or more of the same example. Starting from the thoroughly described script techniques, it will be possible to build your industry-grade applications.

Chapter 11, *Write Your FreeSWITCH Module in C*, describes exactly what is needed to add or modify FreeSWITCH functionalities at the most fundamental level: interfacing your custom hardware, or your legacy OSS, or whatever.

Chapter 12, *Tracing and Debugging VoIP*, shows the art of SIP packet tracing, using the latest open source tools.

Chapter 13, *Homer, Monitoring and Troubleshooting Your Communication Platform*, walks through the operation of the most advanced VoIP/WebRTC monitoring and data warehousing solution: Homer. Once implemented, your support staff will reach Nirvana!

What you need for this book

For implementing the same solutions described in this book, you will need a (virtual) machine with Debian 8 (Jessie) 64 bit, and some Linux admin and networking knowledge.

Who this book is for

This book is for skilled professionals who want to jump right into the depths of FreeSWITCH, such as system administrators, programmers, and telephony technicians who want to augment their ability to create real-world VoIP and WebRTC products and services.

Conventions

In this book, you will find a number of styles of text that distinguish between different kinds of information. Here are some examples of these styles, and an explanation of their meaning.

Code words in text, database table names, folder names, filenames, file extensions, pathnames, dummy URLs, user input, and Twitter handles are shown as follows: "Several built-in modules exist to assist in this, such as mod_lcr and mod_nibblebill, but the real beauty of FreeSWITCH's handling of calls in a wholesale scenario is due to four core building blocks."

A block of code is set as follows:

```
<?xml version="1.0" encoding="ISO-8859-1" ?>
<!DOCTYPE scenario SYSTEM "sipp.dtd">
<scenario name="FreeSWITCH: call extension 1001">
<!-- we send the intial INVITE -->
<send retrans="500" start_rtd="mer">
<![CDATA[
```

When we wish to draw your attention to a particular part of a code block, the relevant lines or items are set in bold:

```
<?xml version="1.0" encoding="ISO-8859-1" ?>
<!DOCTYPE scenario SYSTEM "sipp.dtd">
<scenario name="FreeSWITCH: call extension 1001">
<!-- we send the intial INVITE -->
<send retrans="500" start_rtd="mer">
<![CDATA[
```

New terms and **important words** are shown in bold.

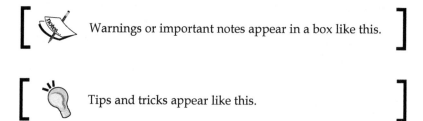

Warnings or important notes appear in a box like this.

Tips and tricks appear like this.

Reader feedback

Feedback from our readers is always welcome. Let us know what you think about this book—what you liked or may have disliked. Reader feedback is important for us to develop titles that you really get the most out of.

To send us general feedback, simply send an e-mail to feedback@packtpub.com, and mention the book title via the subject of your message.

If there is a topic that you have expertise in and you are interested in either writing or contributing to a book, see our author guide on www.packtpub.com/authors.

Customer support

Now that you are the proud owner of a Packt book, we have a number of things to help you to get the most from your purchase.

Downloading the example code

You can download the example code files for this book from your account at http://www.packtpub.com. If you purchased this book elsewhere, you can visit http://www.packtpub.com/support and register to have the files e-mailed directly to you.

You can download the code files by following these steps:

1. Log in or register to our website using your e-mail address and password.
2. Hover the mouse pointer on the **SUPPORT** tab at the top.
3. Click on **Code Downloads & Errata**.
4. Enter the name of the book in the **Search** box.
5. Select the book for which you're looking to download the code files.
6. Choose from the drop-down menu where you purchased this book from.
7. Click on **Code Download**.

You can also download the code files by clicking on the **Code Files** button on the book's webpage at the Packt Publishing website. This page can be accessed by entering the book's name in the **Search** box. Please note that you need to be logged in to your Packt account.

Once the file is downloaded, please make sure that you unzip or extract the folder using the latest version of:

- WinRAR / 7-Zip for Windows
- Zipeg / iZip / UnRarX for Mac
- 7-Zip / PeaZip for Linux

The code bundle for the book is also hosted on GitHub at `https://github.com/PacktPublishing/Mastering-FreeSWITCH`. We also have other code bundles from our rich catalog of books and videos available at `https://github.com/PacktPublishing/`. Check them out!

Errata

Although we have taken every care to ensure the accuracy of our content, mistakes do happen. If you find a mistake in one of our books—maybe a mistake in the text or the code—we would be grateful if you could report this to us. By doing so, you can save other readers from frustration and help us improve subsequent versions of this book. If you find any errata, please report them by visiting `http://www.packtpub.com/submit-errata`, selecting your book, clicking on the **Errata Submission Form** link, and entering the details of your errata. Once your errata are verified, your submission will be accepted and the errata will be uploaded to our website or added to any list of existing errata under the Errata section of that title.

To view the previously submitted errata, go to `https://www.packtpub.com/books/content/support` and enter the name of the book in the search field. The required information will appear under the **Errata** section.

Piracy

Piracy of copyright material on the Internet is an ongoing problem across all media. At Packt, we take the protection of our copyright and licenses very seriously. If you come across any illegal copies of our works, in any form, on the Internet, please provide us with the location address or website name immediately so that we can pursue a remedy.

Please contact us at copyright@packtpub.com with a link to the suspected pirated material.

We appreciate your help in protecting our authors, and our ability to bring you valuable content.

Questions

You can contact us at questions@packtpub.com if you are having a problem with any aspect of the book, and we will do our best to address it.

1
Typical Voice Uses for FreeSWITCH

FreeSWITCH (FS) is one of the world's most robust **Real Time Communication (RTC)** switching tools. It packs a rich feature set, and its modular approach allows it to stay ahead of the curve as new technologies emerge in the marketplace.

With this strong foundation, FreeSWITCH has matured into a product which is in use in a multitude of environments. However, FreeSWITCH can also be complex and overwhelming because of its rich feature set.

This book unravels some of the ways FreeSWITCH can be utilized.

In this chapter, we will cover "traditional" Voice over IP usage. See other chapters for video, conferences, RTC, and so on. We will also cover the following:

- Routing calls
- Products and services
- Development
- Billing

Understanding routing calls in FreeSWITCH

Routing calls is the very essence of FreeSWITCH. Moving calls around can assume very different meanings and use very different techniques, depending on the scenario and with which aims it is done. You don't use the same tools and interaction level for an enterprise PBX, a telemarketing dialer, and a provider-to-providers minutes exchange.

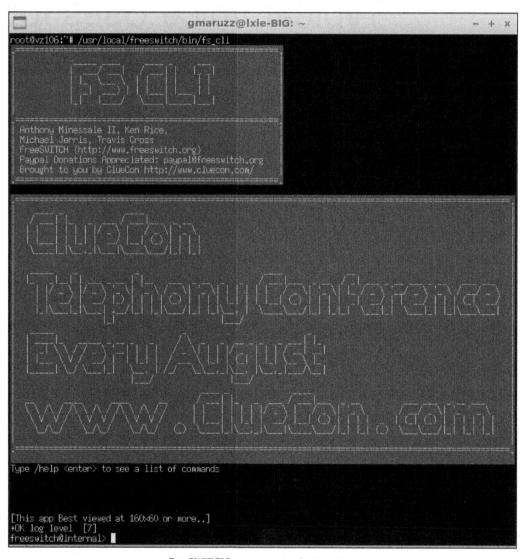

FreeSWITCH's remote console at startup

Wholesale (provider to providers)

FreeSWITCH supports a multitude of useful features for call routing services. When we describe call routing, we are referring to connecting Party A with Party B. These routing scenarios are generally heavy on logic regarding cost analysis, interconnections with other carriers, and user permissions. These routing scenarios also typically exclude features the user directly interacts with (such as voicemail or auto attendants).

FreeSWITCH can be utilized as a powerful wholesale routing engine. Several built-in modules exist to assist in this, such as mod_lcr or mod_nibblebill, but the real beauty of FreeSWITCH's handling of calls in a wholesale scenario is due to four core building blocks:

- The ability to remain in the audio path or get out of the audio path, as needed
- The ability to transcode, which helps correct problems between pieces of VoIP equipment which aren't compatible
- The ability to maintain information about caller and callee in variables, and to manipulate those values as the call is progressing (such as tracking how much money someone has left in their account, or what the per-minute rate of the call is)
- The ability to bridge calls and handle failures and retries when calls don't connect, using a variety of call progress monitoring and failure handling routines which are built-in to FreeSWITCH

FreeSWITCH's flexible design aids in providing a tremendous amount of customization and capabilities as well. Examples include the ability to add transcoding support for codecs at any moment during the call in a way that will automatically and inherently work with any other codecs which are installed, and the ability to add custom handling for failures in a way that suits your environment.

Wholesale services typically represent high-volume customers who want to:

- Configure a client for making calls and associate monetary value with each individual client ("current balance" or "amount spent" are examples)
- Allow a client to attach phones, PBXs, other switches, or ancillary equipment
- Track a client's usage of said service based on what they connected, where they called, and how long they talked, and potentially apply discounts or premium fees based on time-of-day, destination, or other variables
- Detect fraud, abuse, or lack of funds automatically, both at call start and mid-call

- Allow for prompts and menus to automatically add funds or "top-up" services
- Allow for reporting

FreeSWITCH is capable, out of the box, of providing all of these services with simple dial plan configuration. Additionally, FreeSWITCH can be attached to a web, mobile, or legacy user interface to allow for users to manage their account, services, and monetary assets.

Residential uses of FreeSWITCH

FreeSWITCH stands as one of the best open source class 4 (and class 5) switch options, and is often the undisputed champ in many different roles because of the number of features offered by the many ready-made modules. It is definitely an excellent choice for the **Internet Telephony Service Provider** (**ITSP**), but let's not forget one of its simplest use cases: Residential service.

Some residential options include things like **Network Address Translation** (**NAT**) when configuring end-user devices like **Analog Telephone Adapters** (**ATA**). This can be challenging when working with disparate networks and client devices residing on LANs behind residential gateways and firewalls.

FreeSWITCH has configurable options for its **Session Initiation Protocol** (**SIP**) stack (called Sofia) especially designed to overcome these hurdles and provide a viable solution for residential service.

Some reasons why FreeSWITCH makes a good choice for residential service are:

- It is easily embeddable in low power devices
- It has easy configuration of end-user devices for home networks
- It had standard voicemail services via `mod_voicemail`
- It has advanced voicemail options using an **Interactive Voice Response** (**IVR**) enabled audio navigation system
- It has custom scripting options for things like Unified Communications

Routing with federated VoIP

Federated VoIP is a distributed Voice over IP network composed of autonomous systems.

Federated VoIP is to telephony what internet e-mail is to messaging. Particularly, it allows for the free flow of traffic without depending on a central exchange (or exchanges), just like e-mail does not depend on a central post office. It works by exchanging mail messages directly between organizations' (or even personal) Mail Servers that have the authority and capability of managing their own traffic.

Let's continue with the example of e-mail (of note, SIP was based on SMTP and HTTP protocols, that is, the protocols that orchestrate mail and the Web). So, here's the trick: no central authority is involved, it's all peer-to-peer exchange of messages in a worldwide network that works with extreme overall reliability day in and day out for billions of people and trillions of communication exchanges.

Exactly the same criteria can be applied to Voice over IP (SIP) and Instant Messaging (SIMPLE or XMPP), basing all communication exchanges around the concept of a personal address like an e-mail address, which is used both by SIP and IM, and often exactly the same for both clients. The example address `joe.bloggs@overthetop.com` could be used for all unified communications with Joe.

Initially, VoIP had been popularized as a better and cheaper way to manage traditional telephony traffic and to connect to traditional voice carriers. Then it was adopted by the carriers themselves because of its better suitability to modern digital networks and compatibility between hardware providers. So, today's approach to VoIP often brings an unnecessary prejudice about dependency from carriers.

Federated VoIP gets rid of this, having autonomous servers exchanging their communications, finding each other via DNS (queries about destination address) without the need for central authority and/or carriers, just like the e-mail system. Around this core concept has grown an ecosystem of encryption, mapping, and resolving traditional telephone numbers via DNS (ENUM) and other additional services. It should be noted that there is no technical requirement for encryption in Federated VoIP.

FreeSWITCH has all the features needed by Federated VoIP:

- Full encryption support: TLS and STCP for signaling, SRTP and ZRTP for media
- DNS SRV query support
- ENUM mapping support
- NAT traversal support

- Full codec support and transcoding
- IM support via SIP's SIMPLE (can be gatewayed by an XMPP server like Jabberd)
- Presence support via SIMPLE (can be gatewayed by an XMPP server like Jabberd)
- FreeSWITCH can act as an inbound and outbound gateway with PSTN and cellular networks (for example, GSM, etc), offering ENUM termination service to calling parties

FreeSWITCH is able to work as a complete, self-sufficient autonomous system or as a part of a bigger composite system with one or more SIP proxies, like Kamailio or OpenSIPS, taking care of routing, proxying, load balancing, and so on.

Dialers/telemarketing

The subject of dialers and telemarketing often makes system administrators and telephony switch operators queasy with anxiety when they are considering the limitations of their networks, hardware capability, and other system resource implications with the onslaught of marketing campaigns directed to their customers. This certainly does not stop FreeSWITCH from being a great choice when writing dialer and telemarketing applications, and not all dialer and telemarketing systems should have negative connotations.

FreeSWITCH is a natural front-runner when choosing a softswitch for writing dialer and telemarketing applications because of the small learning curve needed to develop applications in a variety of programming languages, and the excellent community support.

A developer can create a custom dialer application in FreeSWITCH utilizing a core switch database data in real-time to drive the logic. They can utilize modules like mod_event_socket to connect to the switch and perform API functions like initiating calls and managing IVRs for things like credit card payment, billing and collection, or opt-in and opt-out campaign functionality.

Not all telemarketing and dialer applications are used for marketing. Some ways FreeSWITCH is currently being utilized for dialers and telemarketing are:

- Delivering inclement weather school-closing notification recordings to telephone lists
- Auto-dialing church congregation members to connect them to IVR applications for surveys and volunteering
- Notifying political constituents of party meetings and gatherings

- Live agent outbound calling for fundraising or event coordination

```
                          gmaruzz@lxle-BIG: ~                    _ + x
freeswitch@internal> help

Valid Commands:

...,,Shutdown,mod_commands
acl,<ip> <list_name>,Compare an ip to an acl list,mod_commands
alias,[add|stickyadd] <alias> <command> | del [<alias>|*],Alias,mod_commands
banner,,Return the system banner,mod_commands
bg_system,<command>,Execute a system command in the background,mod_commands
bgapi,<command>[ <arg>],Execute an api command in a thread,mod_commands
break,<uuid> [all],uuid_break,mod_commands
cdr_csv,parameters,cdr_csv controls,mod_cdr_csv
chat,<proto>|<from>|<to>|<message>|[<content-type>],chat,mod_dptools
coalesce,[^^<delim>]<value1>,<value2>,...,Return first nonempty parameter,mod_commands
complete,add <word>|del [<word>|*],Complete,mod_commands
cond,<expr> ? <true val> : <false val>,Evaluate a conditional,mod_commands
conference,              list [delim <string>]|[count]
                xml_list
                energy <member_id|all|last|non_moderator> [<newval>]
                volume_in <member_id|all|last|non_moderator> [<newval>]
                volume_out <member_id|all|last|non_moderator> [<newval>]
                position <member_id> <x>,<y>,<z>
                auto-3d-position [on|off]
                play <file_path> [async|<member_id> [nomux]]
                pause [<member_id>]
                file_seek [+-]<val> [<member_id>]
                say <text>
                saymember <member_id> <text>
                stop <[current|all|async|last]> [<member_id>]
                dtmf <[member_id|all|last|non_moderator]> <digits>
                kick <[member_id|all|last|non_moderator]> [<optional sound file>]
                hup <[member_id|all|last|non_moderator]>
                mute <[member_id|all]|last|non_moderator> [<quiet>]
                tmute <[member_id|all]|last|non_moderator> [<quiet>]
                unmute <[member_id|all]|last|non_moderator> [<quiet>]
                deaf <[member_id|all]|last|non_moderator>
                undeaf <[member_id|all]|last|non_moderator>
                relate <member_id> <other_member_id> [nospeak|nohear|clear]
                lock
                unlock
                agc
                dial <endpoint_module_name>/<destination> <callerid number> <callerid name>
                bgdial <endpoint_module_name>/<destination> <callerid number> <callerid name>
                transfer <conference_name> <member id> [...<member id>]
                record <filename>
                chkrecord <confname>
                norecord <[filename|all]>
                pause <filename>
                resume <filename>
                recording [start|stop|check|pause|resume] [<filename>|all]
                exit_sound on|off|none|file <filename>
                enter_sound on|off|none|file <filename>
                pin <pin#>
                nopin
                get <parameter-name>
                set <max_members|sound_prefix|caller_id_name|caller_id_number|endconf_grace_time> <value>
                file-vol <vol#>
                floor <member_id|last>
                vid-floor <member_id|last> [force]
                clear-vid-floor,Conference module commands,mod_conference
console,loglevel [level]|colorize [on|toggle|off],Console,mod_console
console_complete,<line>,,mod_commands
console_complete_xml,<line>,,mod_commands
create_uuid,<uuid> <other_uuid>,Create a uuid,mod_commands
db,[insert|delete|select|exists|count|list]/<realm>/<key>/<value>,db get/set,mod_db
db_cache,status,Manage db cache,mod_commands
domain_exists,<domain>,Check if a domain exists,mod_commands
echo,<data>,Echo,mod_commands
```

Some rows from FreeSWITCH's remote console help

FreeSWITCH Products and Services

Another way to see what FreeSWITCH can do is to think in terms of what services it will give its users. Here, too, different technologies and techniques are deployed to cater to different kinds of users, looking for a different set of features.

Business PBX services (hosted and on-premises)

FreeSWITCH's scalability and feature set lends itself naturally to being used as the basis of an extremely powerful business PBX phone system. Successfully deployed in both on-premises environments for small SOHO businesses while scalable to hundreds of users, or utilized as the foundation for hosted PBX services hosting hundreds of thousands of users, the system lends itself naturally to powering these types of solutions.

Out of the box, FreeSWITCH includes basic PBX modules which provide powerful functionalities. These modules include features such as:

- Ring groups (simultaneous and sequential)
- Call forwarding
- Presence
- Text to speech
- Call queues
- Caller ID blacklists
- Caller ID name delivery
- Privacy features / anonymous calling
- CDRs / Call logs
- Eavesdrop / whisper
- Voicemail
- Music on hold (w/ streaming sources)
- Usage limiting
- Call pickup / group pickup / call intercept

We could go on further, but this is a good general idea of the building blocks that are provided. Most of these modules can be activated by adding four to six lines of XML to a dial plan configuration file. The power of dial plan combined with modules should not be underestimated - this is powerful stuff with very little work to get it going!

Additional components exist for expanding into:

- Chat
- Messaging / SMS
- HTTP services

Customer demands will sometimes lead to more complex requirements that might not be handled by default modules. However, ready-made building blocks combined with the ability to run your own custom scripts within FreeSWITCH allows for providing quick time to market services even for the most demanding customer base.

Call centers

Any company doing substantial business in any market segment will attest that support is a cornerstone of a business's success. A robust and comprehensive telephony platform is crucial, and FreeSWITCH allows for a configurable, scalable and maintainable solution suitable for call centers of any size.

There is no shortage of flexibility with FreeSWITCH. If your solution requires a custom application, FreeSWITCH provides a host of development options for your call control and routing. Although you are free to use any supported language to "roll your own" solution, FreeSWITCH comes complete with robust call center modules that are being utilized in production environments in literally thousands of deployments all over the world.

Mod call center includes features like:

- Multi-tenant capability
- Multiple agent call-distribution strategies, such as :
  - Longest idle agent
  - Round robin agents
  - Agent with least talk time
  - Agent with fewest calls
  - Top-down tier position escalation
- Time-based scoring escalation strategies like:
  - Total time in system
  - Time in current queue

- Caller configuration options:
  - Maximum wait time
  - Maximum wait time with no agent

- Tier rule configuration options:
  - Wait time
  - Skip tiers with no agents
  - Discarded abandoned callers
  - Resumed abandoned callers

- Recurring announcements with time frequency interval settings

With IVR trees easily integrated into your call center solution and full access to databases for CRM and Knowledge Basis, your ability to create call center applications is almost limitless.

If your requirements do not dictate the granularity of complex configuration options, then there are other options available with an alternative FreeSWITCH module called Mod FIFO. As the name implies, it serves as a first in, first out call-queuing mechanism, with many features and strategies, music on hold, and announcements, that's easy to integrate in custom or third-party applications.

Value added services and games, prizes, and polls

Value Added Services (VAS) are services that offer something on top of pure voice transport.

Some examples include:

- Real time translations (for example, three-way calls with an interpreter)
- Party lines (for example, multiple-way calls)
- Virtual meetings (for example, conferences with or without moderator)
- Cooperative Environments (for example, audio-video-screensharing-whiteboarding)
- Fax-on-demand
- Call screening-whitelisting-blacklisting
- SMS feed subscriptions (news, traffic, special interests, and so on)

Interactive entertainment and polling is a business that fits perfectly with the ease of programming and integrated messaging capability of FreeSWITCH.

Here are some examples of what has been realized in this field:

- Radio and TV live talk shows that allow for the public to ask questions and vote on issues, both through voice calls and via SMSs

- Voice menu trees that ask questions to customers, giving them prizes after a number of correct answers (for example, product awareness and loyalty)

- Redeem-the-code types of campaigns, where customers or the public can enter a code they found on your documentation or advertising to be awarded a bonus, both via SMSs and voice calls with DTMF

- Incoming calls statistics (comparative ROI analysis on multiple channel advertising campaigns, for example, what they call the most, the number advertised on radio, TV, Internet, or the one in the press?)

"Class 4" vs "Class 5" operations (and SBCs)

FreeSWITCH is a softswitch. That is, it is a software that handles and interconnects calls, like the manual switchboards where operators answered and distributed calls by moving jacks and cables in old black and white movies.

Softswitches in telco jargon are often categorized as pertaining to a "class," and "Class 4" and "Class 5" are the only two classes you will hear about.

Because those are fuzzy terms, almost marketing terms, you will never find the exact demarcation between Class 4 and Class 5 features and capabilities; a lot of them overlap (anyway, it's mostly the same technology).

An arbitrary rule of thumb can be to use Class 4 when talking about large volume, wholesale switching of call minutes between different carriers, ITSPs, CLECs, with minimal meddling in the audio streams (apart from transcoding, if needed). The term "Class 5" applies to audio or text-based services where end user interaction is in focus and where sophisticated logic is required.

FreeSWITCH is widely used in both contexts.

A typical Class 4 usage would be to interconnect many providers of international voice routes and sell voice minutes based on algorithms about least cost route and/or route quality. Here, the sheer volume of signaling that can be managed per second and the availability of very efficient ways to lookup which route to connect to is of paramount importance. FreeSWITCH with "bypass media", `mod_lcr`, `mod_easyroute`, some Lua scripting or custom C code is a perfect platform, easy to use and modify on the fly, without service interruption.

Typical Class 5 usages would be an enterprise or SOHO PBX, a call center system, a fax server with mail2fax and fax2mail, an airport IVR to query flights' arrival times, and so on. Here, FreeSWITCH offers prized features like audio quality (that is, no glitches, distortions, and so on), programmability (how easy it is to implement complex services and business logic), capability of interfacing different media (PSTN to WebRTC, SIP to Skinny, TDM to Skype, SMS to XMPP, and so on) and different audio formats (alaw, ulaw, High Definition Audio, Silk, Siren, G729, Opus, mp3, wav, raw, and so on). Easy integration of Text To Speech and Automatic Speech Recognition, manipulation of audio prompt libraries, and easy ways to gather and interact with user pressed DTMFs are the highlights in FS Class 5 operation.

"SBC" is another very vague marketing buzzword. A **Session Border Controller (SBC)** is a softswitch that sits on the edge of your own telecommunication network and acts as a point of demarcation and interconnection with the external world. Let's say an SBC is a softswitch with an emphasis on security, NAT traversal, media proxying, network connectivity, manageability, audio transcoding, protocol gatewaying (connecting with different protocols), and protocol adaptation (being the compatibility layer between different "interpretations" of the same protocol). FreeSWITCH excels in those areas, as we have seen before in the two "Classes", while it sports specific SBC features like the most advanced NAT traversal, so smart that it can connect endpoint (that is, user phones) behind residential ADSLs and firewalls, or form a federation between the many international offices of a company, each SBC sitting on different NATed LANs. Also, as security goes, FreeSWITCH is one of the reference implementations for ZRTP media encryption, as well as TLS and SIPS.

WebRTC / web services / Internet-only services

FreeSWITCH's unique modular approach made it an easy choice for extending integration into WebRTC and other web-based services which need a bridge between different types of technologies. As an example, web-based communications are useful but are often hindered by their inability to connect to the rest of the established world, causing adoption to be slow. As an example, users will be reluctant to get rid of their desk phone when their browser-based replacement can't call phone numbers but only other browsers. Best of all, WebRTC support follows the same ease-of-installation and global compatibility standards that FreeSWITCH has become known for in the VoIP world. Users can make calls where one side of the conversation is WebRTC and the other is the PSTN, or WebRTC to SIP and so on. FreeSWITCH does all the hard work of normalizing the audio and signaling services between the two services and bridging any gaps that may exist when connecting from one type of service to another.

Mobile "over-the-top" SIP

As mobile services become more pervasive in the telecommunications industry, mobile network operators have responded by increasing data speeds. In this process, many service providers are now investigating "over-the-top" services which utilize data communication services to transmit and receive voice and video. These services often link to messaging or social applications and provide both real-time, semi real-time, and recorded communication services via data connections. In many cases, the user experience simulates phone technology even though it is not using traditional telephony services provided by the underlying communications service provider. In these cases, there is added complexity for handling such services.

Over-the-top services face a number of challenges, which include:

- The ability to adapt to rapidly changing network performance characteristics
- The ability to "hand off" calls as different networks which have better qualities come into range (that is, moving from 3G to 4G or 3G to WiFi)
- Selecting appropriate codecs which match available capacity and bandwidth
- Having sufficient buffering and audio stream management strategies to allow for quality communication while being resilient to issues in network consistency
- Providing feedback to the user to allow her to understand what is happening during these complex shifts
- The ability to track device configuration and usage information as customers roam to various locations, change devices, and so on.
- The ability to adapt to networks which block or restrict some kind of traffic
- Integrating with various types of physical hardware on the user's device
- Being able to debug issues when it's unclear if they're caused by the device, the mobile network, or the softswitch

Despite the various unique challenges over-the-top apps pose, the attractive promise of cheaper phone calls integrated into social, e-mail, or other methods of communication remains a popular target for many companies.

With these goals and issues in mind, where does FreeSWITCH fit in? It should come as no surprise that FreeSWITCH is a great match for solving these challenges. While less discussed within the FreeSWITCH community, FreeSWITCH contains hidden gems for features such as:

- Managing a jitter buffer manually, where you can account for non-standard network environments

- Support for STUN, TURN, ICE, and alternate signaling ports and methods (such as UDP and/or TCP), and the ability to bridge between endpoints using different methods

- The ability to select codecs on the fly on a per-call basis, which is useful in conjunction with a mechanism to detect current network conditions

- The ability to handle unexpected events gracefully (such as dropped calls) where strategies can be taken to reconnect a caller automatically without dropping both sides

- Rich statistics and RTCP feedback implementation providing real-time information to both caller and callee about the quality of the transmission

These are just some of the building blocks that make FreeSWITCH unique when attempting to solve these over-the-top problems. Make no mistake, over-the-top applications are still a challenge. But FreeSWITCH gives you a huge head start in tackling these problems.

Skype to SIP call, seen from FreeSWITCH's remote console

Development

FreeSWITCH is often considered the perfect development tool, particularly in enterprise, startup, and telco environments.

Strict on output, broad on input

The philosophy underlying FS architecture lends itself perfectly to interface legacy, commercial, and proprietary hardware/software: FS output is very, very strict in its adherence to the letter of the standards (SIP and related RFCs), so it's able to make itself understood by whatever it's trying to communicate with, but it is also very, very flexible for what it accepts as an input, for example, core developers embedded into FS, all the quirks, and the workarounds, to let it accept the often non-standard (or plain wrong) "interpretation" and "extensions" of SIP standards that have been pushed on the market by the various generations of VoIP software and hardware providers (often with the "unintended" side effect of locking in their customers).

Very structured, very reusable techniques

FS is built around mainstays of modern technology: XML, message queues, JSON, RPC, and standard libraries. Developers don't have to learn new ad hoc "languages" to fully exploit the power of FS: All of its configuration, dialplan, upstream and downstream endpoints and gateways — all of its features and behaviors are completely defined by XML standard documents that can also be created in real time dynamically by tried and true XML generating applications and languages. Given a basic knowledge of communication fundamentals, a wealth of pre-existing, in-house knowledge of structured information management can be reused.

Polyglot by vocation and destiny

All kinds of programming languages can be used to interact with FS. This is due to the fact that we're dealing with two main paradigms, XML and message queues (and also XML exchanged back and forth via message queues). All computer languages, both scripted and compiled ones, have very efficient, stable and performing ways to interact with XML structured information, from C to Basic, from Perl to PHP, Python to Lua, Erlang to C# to .NET, Java and all the others in between. Interacting with the message queues governing and reporting FS behavior is done through a simple API that is the same for all languages covered by SWIG: In each language you'll find the same "objects" with the same "methods" (or "functions") and "attributes" to interact with.

Extreme scalability, from embedded to big irons

Different tasks are best performed by different devices, with different price points, power consumption, sets of hardware interfaces: From WRTG routers to Raspberry PIs (for example, for residential CPE, or as WiFi VoIP, or as a portable communication gizmo), from desktop PCs (as a personal or callcenter softphone) to multisocket multicore massive servers (capable of delivering high call per second origination and termination) and powerful DSP blades (for high capacity call transcoding, Text To Speech generation, Automatic Speech Recognition and media management). For all of those roles we can use the same FreeSWITCH software, that behaves and is managed in the same way.

Born internationalist

Using the same foundation system library as the ubiquitous Apache Web Server, FS runs at full efficiency on Linux, Windows, FreeBSD and Solaris, on Xen, AWS, KVM, and VMWare. DevOps people often prefer to use their own deployed, stable, and known operating systems and managing tools.

Telcos internal integration ("FreeSWITCH is the Perl of VoIP")

Telcos, telecommunication companies, both the old Bells and the new CLECs or VMOs, are a fascinating patchwork of legacy, proprietary, in-house developed, partner-provided, stakeholder-imposed hardware and software. With all kinds of database engines (Oracle, DB2, SQL Server, SAP, MySQL, PostgreSQL, and so on), directory systems (LDAP, Active Directory), AAA mechanisms (Radius, Diameter, and so on), SIP and SS7 equipment (some of which nobody knows how to operate anymore, "so please don't touch it"), and many different functions and departments barely interacting with each other, there can be huge return time for even the smallest feature request or bug turnaround.

In a complex environment like this, FS can be introduced as universal filter and glue, allowing incompatible systems to communicate (as protocol translator and adapter), transcoding to and from all audio formats (ulaw to mp3 to High Definition Opus, Siren, Silk, etc), manipulating signaling and log generation for billing, accounting, tracking, charting, debugging purposes (additional and optional SIP packet headers injection and parsing, CDR generation, mediation, reconciliation, and so on), and database interfacing (native, odbc, REST, SQL, NoSQL, and so on).

FreeSWITCH is accepted into telco environments because of its known stability and "industrial grade" structure, and because it does not carry any "hobbyist" or "hackerish" fame.

Starting from resolving specific problems with "ad hoc", Swiss army knife solutions, FreeSWITCH can then expand its internal reach to prototype new features and services, substitute unwieldy legacy systems (for example, IVRs, fax servers, and so on), and quickly become the poster boy of Sales and Marketing departments for quick implementation and flexibility, while gaining the Operations respect and love for its stability, performances, and manageability.

Rapid new services prototyping

Standard, real programming languages give FreeSWITCH a fast pace of implementation for any kind of features and services: What is simple stays simple, and what is complex becomes possible, without crashes, instabilities, or performance bottlenecks.

Programming languages bring with them all their wealth of libraries, both standard, open source, commercial, and in-house developed. So, all kinds of objects, systems, procedures are within reach, both bleeding edge external services and internal, legacy, proprietary, prehistoric leftovers.

Real business logic can be crafted without compromises, accessing each call in real time, at the desired abstraction level, from the most abstracted down to the detail of the single SIP packet.

WebRTC will allow entire new classes of applications and services, using the ubiquitous web browser as a communication endpoint, while FS modules exist for managing any kind of content, from real-time broadcast to video, from conferencing to queuing calls and managing call center operators.

Click-to-Call, database interaction, SMS sending and receiving, website complementing and synergy, full CMR integration, marketing campaigns, media redemption analysis, dynamic real-time events, horizontal scalability via tried and true load-balancing, cloud leveraging—all that and much more is what FreeSWITCH can be used for to speed up the time to market and implement convergent media multi-pronged strategies.

A debugging session, seen from FreeSWITCH's remote console

Accounting and billing

In telecommunications (and probably everywhere), accounting and billing are two separate logical entities, although there are cases (for example, real-time prepaid accounts) where they happen together and are strictly intertwined.

Accounting is keeping a tab on who gets what, for example, what metered services a user accessed, when the user accessed them, for how much time, and so on. Particularly, in telephony, which calls were made to what numbers, for how long, for each customer. This process involves generating and managing **Call Detail Records** (**CDRs**) for each and every call, where all the above details and much more are stored and can be retrieved. CDRs are also a precious source of debugging and troubleshooting information, allowing for the identification of which problems affected failed or low quality calls.

On the other hand, billing involves operating on the customer account, adding or subtracting "credits" related to the cost of the services accessed, with costs calculated based on unitary prices that can depend on multiple variables (from which prefix to which prefix a call was made, how long it lasted, at which time of day it was made, which route was chosen to connect it to the remote party, and so on). Also, in the case of prepaid credits and calling cards, there is often a requirement to not allow customers to access services after their credits expire, for example, if they have 10USD on account and the call costs 2USD/min, then after 5 mins the call has to be interrupted (perhaps with a message about how to top up the account). Cost calculation is often referred to as "rating," while the gathering of CDRs and their conversion into a uniform format ready to be rated is called "mediation."

Call Detail Records (CDRs)

FreeSWITCH has plenty of flexibility for CDR generation, in subtle and varied ways so as to accommodate all kind of operations, and provide this foundation layer for every business model.

Default CDRs are generated by FS's `mod_cdr_csv` as rows in files containing Comma Separated Values (CSVs). We can choose to keep track of the caller side (A leg), the callee side (B leg), or both (AB). For each leg we can have a row in the `Master.csv`, one in the specific caller CSV file, and/or one row in the specific callee CSV file.

The format and contents of those rows are defined by templates that allow us to record whatever mix of variables is suitable for our operation and business model, from any kind of timers (total duration, duration after answer, billable duration, and so on), to origination and destination numbers, time of day / day of week, individual account ID, company account ID, and so on.

There are various templates ready made in the FS distribution, among them one that generates CDRs in the same format generated by Asterisk (so to leverage legacy billing systems), and another one that generates files containing rows of SQL inserts, ready to be piped to a database client for further usage.

Another possibility for CDR generation (instead of or in addition to CSV files) is implementing mod_cdr_xml. Using XML allows for much more structured information to be put in the records, and can be sent real live via POST or GET to an HTTP server (which may itself enter rows into various database tables).

Mod_nibblebill / CGrateS

FreeSWITCH contains built-in modules to assist in real-time rating and credit management. Unique to FreeSWITCH is the ability to provide these services real time in a lightweight manner. With its multi-threaded design, billing and rating can be done on each leg of a call easily with different rates for each party, in addition to rates which might vary based on the selected carrier, time of day, number of calls currently active, or other such data.

One such module within FreeSWITCH that assists in this process is mod_nibblebill. A simple module at its core, nibblebill hooks into the heartbeat features FreeSWITCH provides for every leg of a call. On each heartbeat, nibblebill provides quick mathematical calculations about whether there are enough funds remaining to continue the call and logs to a database that the call has continued and to immediately deduct additional credit. This module is fairly lightweight for small to medium system capacity and can be expanded in larger systems by using basic database technologies already available. In addition, anyone who can program a database can program an interface to manage adding, subtracting, and tracking monetary value from a customer's account in conjunction with mod_nibblebill. This makes implementing the basics of a billing system easy. You can find many more details about mod_nibblebill in another Packt Publishing book, *FreeSWITCH 1.2*.

When combined with CDRs, you can also pair accounting and historical data with each call. This allows for a complete picture of billed services to a customer.

Other real-time tools exist such as **Carrier-Grade Rating System**, **CGRateS**, which links to FreeSWITCH and watches calls real time as they progress. Using FreeSWITCH's powerful event system, CGRateS monitors and manages calls as they happen and records data about the calls for reconciliation. CGRateS is an independent, open-source project, but is linked closely to the FreeSWITCH system for real-time handling of events happening on the switch, both as billing, anti-fraud, LCR, and thousands other features. CGRateS project developers are available for custom installation and implementation of complete solutions. On top of CGRateS engine, VoIPtology has developed CGRBilling, a commercial packaged solution with Web interface.

Other billing options (open source - commercial)

Many rating and billing systems exist out there, designed for the whole telecommunication market, or specifically for FreeSWITCH. That's because the entire telecom industry, since inception, has been the buyer and the research sponsor on billing systems. You can say that many computer advancements as a whole where targeted to advance telecom's billing systems.

Most of the industry relies on offline management of CDR files that are normalized, inserted into a database, and then massaged following business rules to obtain the single customer's bill for the period. With the advent of web interfaces that allow the customer to verify their own account in almost real time, the management flow cycle for CDRs has been shortened to be almost instantaneous, albeit still file-based. An open source, mature, and industrial grade example of this approach is JBilling.

On the other side, real-time billing open source applications are, in addition to the aforementioned CGRateS, ASTPP (complete solution, billing, rating, crm, lcr, and so on), Vbilling (complete solution, integrated with switch management), Viking (expanded from wholesale to cover retail too).

All of these open- source solutions are available with commercial support and backing, and by the time you're reading this book, a billing solution will probably be available for FusionPBX, the open source GUI for the management of FreeSWITCH.

Many pure commercial solutions and services are available, both as software install and as cloud services. Please check FreeSWITCH online documentation for an updated list.

Summary

In this chapter we have covered some of the many different use cases for FreeSWITCH, and we have seen how the different technologies that compose FS can be deployed using various techniques.

The key here has been the concept of toolset: FreeSWITCH is a focal point of real-time communication technologies that span the entire field, from billing to transcoding, from interactive voice attendant to least cost route management.

Also, we've seen how there are many ways to harness this power, to make FreeSWITCH cater to our own kind of users and business goals, using different tools for different aims, from XML to scripting languages, from databases to external services.

In the next chapters we will go deep into the rabbit hole, beginning with *Chapter 2, Deploying FreeSWITCH*, about production deployment best practices, that will show how to end up with a system that is reliable, manageable, robust, and performing.

2
Deploying FreeSWITCH

FreeSWITCH is deployed in production on a range of hardware platforms from BeagleBoards and RaspBerryPIs, to big iron, telecom-grade servers. FS will happily work as a little appliance on a customer's premises and will merrily chug millions of calls in the datacenter. The trade-off between hardware cost, power consumption and form factor depends on use case. Obviously, the more cores and CPUs you throw at it, the more the RAM, and the faster the hard disks; the more concurrent calls you can get.

Here we focus on best deployment practices to obtain the most reliable service from your FreeSWITCH server. In this chapter, we will cover:

- Network requirements
- Testing
- Logging
- Monitoring
- **HA (High Availability)** Deployment

Network requirements

Quality of audio perceived by the user will first and foremost be affected by the network performance. Delays, jitter, and loss of packets can severely degrade end user experience, to an unacceptable level. There are several key components that can enable FreeSWITCH to operate more securely and efficiently: MPLS or dedicated peering connections can greatly enhance the network reliability, while **Quality of Service (QoS)** packet tagging and differentiating settings between your local LAN and the public WAN infrastructures will let you find the sweet point between infrastructure costs and audio quality.

Understanding QoS

QoS is a mechanism for guaranteeing that certain types of communication can be ranked for importance of delivery to ensure quality. There are multiple types of QoS that can be achieved in most network environments. Generally, QoS can be done on the physical layer (for example, guaranteeing that all phones are connected on a network that has its own cables, separate from any web browsing or data networks), the virtual network layer (by creating a VLAN which splits all voice traffic from data), and on the packet layer (by tagging individual VoIP packets for importance and priority over others).

Properly planned out physically separated networks or networks where voice operates on a VLAN and a dedicated network uplink on the WAN side have the highest chance of success and improved quality. Simply put, if data and voice aren't mixing, and you have sufficient bandwidth for times when everyone is on the phone at the same time, you should have a reliable experience without much extra work because every device has all the capacity it needs. Unfortunately, in today's world, customers aren't often willing to invest in such scenarios.

While VLANs and separated networks are great concepts and should be implemented where possible, they're not practical in many network setups. This leaves packet-based QoS, often nicknamed as *packet tagging* or *QoS tagging*. In this method, every IP packet that leaves FreeSWITCH can be tagged as to its priority level. This priority level is supposed to be used by all associated network equipment to guarantee timely or priority delivery. As an example, if a router is receiving requests to service two different websites at the same time, but packets for one site are marked as higher priority, and the Internet link is saturated, the high priority packets will be sent before the low priority packets. The assumption is the lower priority application can handle loss of packets while the higher priority application cannot, or is more sensitive to such losses and will have a degraded experience for the user.

Enabling QoS is a *weakest link* network design. Simply tagging packets as important won't do anything unless all the equipment on the path looks at the tags and processes them properly. This means your network gear at all sections of your network must be of sufficient quality to support QoS properly. Assuming that's the case, enabling QoS on the FreeSWITCH server is relatively easy if you're using Linux and have the ability to setup IPTables.

It's important to note that, very often, people who know SIP typically run it on port 5060, mistakenly believing that setting up QoS tagging on port 5060 will somehow result in improved call audio. This is *not* the case because 5060 is used for signaling, not media. Instead, media is done over a range of ports (on FreeSWITCH this defaults to 16384-32768). This port range is defined in the `switch.conf.xml` file in the `autoload_configs/` directory. These are the ports which you should be tagging with QoS if you're seeking improved audio quality.

In the following example, we provide the IPTables command which will tag audio packets as high priority. `# Mark` RTP packets with EF:

```
iptables -t mangle -A OUTPUT -p udp -m udp --sport 16384:32768 -j DSCP
--set-dscp-class ef
```

This command will change the `DSCP` tag in the IP header to indicate a class of `ef` or Expedited Forwarding.

Once this command is executed, all audio packets sent out from the network will be tagged as high priority. If the network infrastructure supports this, those packets are more likely to be sent (even on a saturated link) than other packets, leading to better quality audio.

LANs, WANs, and peering

FreeSWITCH has some powerful configuration capabilities when being utilized in an environment where multiple LAN, WAN, or other peering engagements exist. Specifically, FreeSWITCH allows for multiple interfaces to be defined, in the form of bindings. This allows you to send and receive data on a specific IP and port combination, and treat all packets on that port and IP with specific settings and handling.

A sample scenario of how to utilize FreeSWITCH's multi-interface capabilities to take advantage of LAN, WAN, and peering arrangements is as follows.

In this scenario, we simulate a high-traffic office environment with demanding call quality requirements.

The specific objectives are as follows:

- Route all LAN traffic over a specific network card which is physically connected to the corporate LAN and has physical guarantees of sufficient bandwidth
- Route all WAN signaling traffic over a medium-quality network link to the public Internet
- Route all WAN audio traffic over a high-quality network link to the public Internet
- Route all traffic destined for our upstream VoIP provider's gateway over a specific network card which links to an MPLS and connects directly to that VoIP provider

The preceding scenario would have the following benefits:

- Calls from LAN phones to the PSTN would traverse only the MPLS link and the corporate LAN, making the call more secure while guaranteeing call quality over dedicated links
- Calls from LAN phones to non-PSTN numbers or that route via Internet gateways or peers would traverse high quality network paths for audio and standard quality links for signaling
- Calls from roaming WAN users which utilize the system remotely would also have audio routed via high-quality links and signaling routed via standard quality links
- As a side benefit, a security benefit would be that an attacker attempting to DoS the WAN network might only know the signaling IP addresses, so any DoS attack would have no impact on call quality for already established calls

To achieve this, you would set up:

- A network interface with a local IP address for your corporate LAN
- A network interface with a public IP address for signaling, which maps to your medium quality network
- A network interface with a public IP address for audio, which maps to your high quality network
- A network interface with an IP address for your MPLS and VoIP carrier gateway

In the end, you will end up with four IP addresses. You would attach those four IP addresses to three SIP interfaces within FreeSWITCH. We'll call them `corp`, `Internet` and `voip_gateway` for simplicity. `Corp` and `voip_gateway` would carry signaling and audio on the same IP address, while `Internet` would actually consist of two IP addresses, one for audio and one for signaling.

The preceding scenario would be set up in your FreeSWITCH SIP Profiles. This would result in the highest quality possible for any type of common call traversing this environment.

Testing with SIPp

Testing is an important task when you are working on a new service and you want to check everything before deploying it in a production environment. For **Session Initiation Protocol** (**SIP**) one key testing tool is definitely SIPp, open source software that can be used for testing purposes. It is able to behave as SIP **User Agent Client** (**UAC**) as well as **User Agent Server** (**UAS**) hence you can use it these ways:

- SIPp is used as UAC and calls FreeSWITCH (IVR, voice applications, and more)

- SIPp is used as UAS and is the endpoint being called (by another FreeSWITCH extension for instance)

- SIPp is used on both sides of a single call (the caller and the callee) to build completely automated tests

Running scenarios

One of the strengths of SIPp is that it is highly customizable: the user writes scenario files in XML format that details all communication steps. An XML scenario file basically describes every SIP message the tool has to send and every response it is supposed to get. Some variables are also available so you do not have to take care of things like `tags` and `call-id` stuff. This flexibility in building scenarios means you can simulate many different things: from a basic call to elaborated services such as IVRs, voicemail calls (with user authentication and message recording), and so on.

Let's see a simple scenario with SIPp as UAC. In a vanilla FreeSWITCH setup, call extension `1001` as user `1000`. The scenario file would look like the following (please note that SIP messages after first `INVITE` have been deleted to make the XML content shorter):

```
<?xml version="1.0" encoding="ISO-8859-1" ?>
<!DOCTYPE scenario SYSTEM "sipp.dtd">
<scenario name="FreeSWITCH: call extension 1001">
```

```
<!-- we send the intial INVITE -->
<send retrans="500" start_rtd="mer">
<![CDATA[

        INVITE sip:1001@203.0.113.100 SIP/2.0
        Via: SIP/2.0/[transport] [local_ip]:[local_port];branch=[branch]
        From: 1000 <sip:1000@[local_ip]:[local_port]>;tag=[pid]
SIPpTag00[call_number]
        To: 1001 <sip:1001@203.0.113.100:[remote_port]>
        Call-ID: [call_id]
        CSeq: 1 INVITE
        Contact: sip:1000@[local_ip]:[local_port]
        Max-Forwards: 70
        Subject: Test_call
        Content-Type: application/sdp
        Content-Length: [len]

        v=0
        o=user1 53655765 2353687637 IN IP[local_ip_type] [local_ip]
        s=-
        c=IN IP[media_ip_type] [media_ip]
        t=0 0
        m=audio [media_port] RTP/AVP 0
        a=rtpmap:0 PCMU/8000

    ]]>
</send>
<!-- we expect to receive a trying -->
<recv response="100" optional="true" rss="true"/>
<!-- the FreeSWITCH server should ask us to auth your request -->
<recv response="407" auth="true" rss="true"/>
<!-- we ack the 407 message -->
<send crlf="true">
    [...]
</send>
<!-- we send again the INVITE with the auth field -->
<send retrans="500">
<![CDATA[
    [...]
      [authentication username=1000 password=1234]
    [...]
    ]]>
</send>
<!-- we expect to receive a trying -->
```

```
<recv response="100"/>
<!-- we expect to receive a provisional 180, but it's not sure yet -->
<recv response="180" optional="true"/>
<!-- we expect to receive a provisional 183, but it's not sure too -->
<recv response="183" optional="true"/>
<!-- we expect 1001 to pick up the call -->
<recv response="200" rtd="mer" rss="true"/>
<!-- we ack the 200 OK SIP message (if the call has been picked up)
-->
<send crlf="true">
    [...]
</send>
<!-- we pause, but we could instead send media here by playing a pcap
file -->
<pause milliseconds="1000" crlf="true"/>
<!-- we hang up the call -->
<send retrans="500">
    [...]
</send>
<!-- FreeSWITCH should reply 200 OK -->
<recv response="200" crlf="true"/>
<!-- various scenario parameters -->
<ResponseTimeRepartition value="100, 200, 500, 1000, 1500, 2000, 5000,
10000"/>
<CallLengthRepartition value="10, 100, 500, 1000, 5000, 10000,
20000"/>
</scenario>
```

To run such a scenario is an easy task to accomplish, you only need to run the `sipp` binary:

```
./sipp -sf call_1001.xml -i 192.168.1.10 -m 1 203.0.113.100
```

Here the parameter `-sf` specifies the scenario file, `-i` specifies the local IP address, `-m` specifies the number of test calls to start (here, only one) and the last address represents the FreeSWITCH server, but many other parameters are available. A complete report is printed out at the end.

SIPp provides a command-line user interface that displays real-time information about the scenario being run so the user can check if everything is running as expected even if the tests are not finished. The command line interface can be used to increase/decrease the frequency and the number of **calls per second** (**cps**) to start, if more than one is set with the `-m` option.

In addition to signaling, SIPp is able to handle media traffic/RTP packets, so even voice QoS testing can be done with it, such as evaluating the **MOS (Mean Opinion Score**) of a test call. To implement it in the previous scenario, the following instruction could be introduced once the call is established:

```
<nop><action><exec play_pcap_audio="scenario/test.pcap"/></action></
nop>
```

If you want to use SIPp as a UAS (as per the last two use cases mentioned in the introduction), meaning the SIPp instance receives a call made by your SIP server, you will need to register SIPp to FreeSWITCH (pretending SIPp is a phone) to make it reachable from a SIP server point of view. This can be done with a dedicated scenario; several such examples are available on the Internet.

Load testing

SIPp is handy for load testing. Indeed, the tool is able to start as many concurrent instances as the hardware can handle so it is very easy to simulate hundreds or even thousands of simultaneous calls. For instance, two hosts can each run a SIPp instance with a simple call scenario: one starts a call towards the FreeSWITCH server that itself creates the leg towards the second host that finally picks up the call for x seconds. Instances and calls of this scenario can be slowly increased, and the tester can then find the limit of the hardware hosting FreeSWITCH when the results start to deviate from the expectations (because of too many dropped packets for instance). Moreover, it is possible to enable time trackers, an important SIPp feature during load test because it displays how long the duration was between two (or more) steps (for example between the moment when the call is initiated and the moment when it is answered).

If you decide to run such tests, make sure the hosts running the SIPp instances are not the bottleneck though.

Logging with FreeSWITCH

Logging is an integral part of any properly managed communication operation. The capability of tracing the minimal details of protocol exchanges and the paths through the internal software mechanisms can be invaluable for pinpointing the intermittent problem of a customer.

There are two main media for logging in FreeSWITCH: the console, for example the `fs_cli` application, and the `log` file. Both options use the same mechanism to show or save information.

By default, FreeSWITCH logs all information into one `log` file at the `DEBUG` level (the highest detail, producing the most quantity of information). The `log` file is created and managed by module `mod_logfile`, configured through `logfile.conf.xml`. By default, that single log file is called `freeswitch.log` and is located in `freeswitch/log/`.

The general format for the log lines is: `call-uuid YYYY-MM-DD hh:mm:ss:nnnnnn [LEVEL] source_file_name:line_numberfunction_name() <log data>`.

Log levels go from `EMERG` (Level 0) to `DEBUG` (Level 7), each progressive level enabling recording of more information than the preceding, to culminate with `DEBUG` that allows for a tremendous quantity of information on the internals of each FreeSWITCH function, useful both to FS core developers, but in some cases also to determine what is going wrong with a call.

It is possible to generate multiple log files containing information at different levels, and also files tracing the inner working of just one function. That can be managed by creating different logging profiles in `logfile.conf.xml`.

Using profiles, you can build a mapping that will record `ERROR`, `CRITICAL` and `ALERT` information for all modules (default) while specifying higher levels for specific internal functions and the maximum `DEBUG` level for a particular module. The profile also contains the name and place of the `log` file, while rotation can be specified as activated by HUP signal and/or by reaching a configured size (defaults to 10 MB).

`Debug` loglevel is very verbose, and you don't want it to be activated all of the time, because on a busy server it would quickly fill an inordinate amount of disk space and because disk I/O operations would exact too much in terms of context switches and wait states.

You would normally run FS with loglevel 3 or 4 (`error or warning`), and you would notch up to loglevel 7 from FS console only when needed, with:

```
fsctl loglevel [loglevel]
```

Don't forget to lower the loglevel, after gathering the information you're looking for. To modify loglevel only for a particular channel (`uuid`), from FS console you use:

```
uuid_loglevel [uuid] [loglevel]
```

While in dialplan you can use `session_loglevel` app:

```
<action application="session_loglevel"
data="loglevel "/>
```

The FreeSWITCH logging system is much more flexible than this. Actually you can specify in `logfile.conf.xml` a different loglevel for each single C source file and/or for each single C function. This is almost never useful in a production environment, but is very useful when debugging the source code itself (for example to FreeSWITCH project developers). You can find full instructions and explanation for this finer loglevel mapping in the comments embedded at the head of the vanilla distributed `console.conf.xml` (console uses the same mapping method as logfile).

All of the aforementioned methods and techniques apply to console logging too, configured by `console.conf.xml`. On console, the FreeSWITCH administrator will see all the same information we've listed scrolling by, smartly colorized for an intuitive interpretation. It is possible to change in real time and live, both the level of console logging and the source of it, for example global, modules, or functions.

Another important tool related to logging and debugging FreeSWITCH operation is the capability of `mod_sofia` to show (and optionally log to a specified level) all of the SIP and SDP packets for a call, or for an interface (SIP profile), or globally. This is extremely useful both at setup time and for debugging problems and malfunctions. You can rely on it instead of going back and forth with `ngrep` and/or `wireshark`.

As a FreeSWITCH administrator you will deal with logging all the time, be it reading the log output that scrolls on the FS console in real time *as it happens*, or by perusing and analyzing the debug logfile to identify what problem lead to a failed call, or by collecting durations, destinations, originator, and monetary costs of each and every call from CDRs.

Logging is what gives FreeSWITCH administrators the information on which to base most of their activity.

Call Detail Records

Each call will generate one or more **Call Detail Record (CDR)**. CDRs are written after the call ends, and contains all information needed for accounting and billing that call. As an example, an outbound call (outbound is most critical for accounting and billing) the CDR would contain information such as date/time, caller account, caller device, destination, and duration. As an added bonus it can contain all kinds of details about the call itself, such as codec used, outbound route or gateway, and/or the status of the system.

So, in CDRs you can store and gather any kind of info you deem useful on a per-call basis. A complete call is often composed of an A leg (caller) bridged to a B leg (callee). In the FS console, the show calls command shows that each call is composed of two channels (A leg and B leg). You can choose to write a CDR for A leg, B leg, or both.

There are two main kinds of CDRs FreeSWITCH is able to generate: **Comma Separated Value (CSV)** files, and XML files. CSV files are easier for humans to read, and can be parsed quite simply with regular expressions and spreadsheets. XML CDRs are able to better describe complex information, and can be processed by advanced XML and XSLT libraries.

From their respective configuration files (`cdr_csv.conf.xml` and `xml_cdr.conf.xml`) you can define which call legs you want to write CDRs about. By default, like in normal practice, only A legs generate CDRs.

CDRs are built following a template that can be constructed to contain any kind of variable available in the channel, and in any format you may deem useful. For example, there is a template that mimics the Asterisk CDR format, that you can use for compatibility with legacy accounting and billing software, and another template that would generates files with SQL `insert` rows, that can then be used to directly populate a database.

CDRs will then be kept as traffic documentation, and/or further processed: inserted in a database, for example, where each call will be given a cost, and that cost added to the caller account bill.

XML or CSV — the best practice in any case is to have files written to the disc, that can be used to reconcile accounting and billing in case of database or network malfunction. Also, at the end of each individual call, all of the variables that were associated with the leg (many more variables than you suspect!) can be automatically dumped in the file, so allowing for later debug and troubleshooting.

An advanced technique that can be useful in special or corner cases: CDRs can be generated real-time by a custom application that listens to FS events and do whatever is needed to record, rate, and/or bill each single call while it happens, interfacing whatever systems your operation and business model requires (AAA, Radius, Diameter, Databases, The Spanish Inquisition, and more).

 In a high volume environment, it is considered best practice to do the further massaging of CDRs on a different machine to the FreeSWITCH server. This is so you don't have the CPU and Disk load degrade the performance and the audio quality delivered to customers.

Monitoring

When deploying one or more FreeSWITCH servers in a production environment, it is essential to set up some monitoring mechanisms. Monitoring is more than a best-practice, it is a must-have to maintain a reliable, highly-available, powerful VoIP softswitch. It is necessary in order to be quick to react in case of critical issues and various emergencies. Setting up monitoring mechanisms is easy to say, but a good question would be 'what should we monitor, and how?' You would probably want to keep an eye on several aspects of a running server, for instance:

- Check if everything is fine at a system level, for example:
    - Is the FreeSWITCH service up and running?
    - Are all the IP ports that are supposed to be listening actually listening?
    - Is my host too loaded or is it just fine?

- Check more specifically if the FreeSWITCH service is sane
- Check very specific aspects of the operation, for example:
    - Does my IVR behave like it should?
    - Are the conference rooms working?
    - Is the voicemail service working?
    - And so on...

SNMP

If you look for monitoring tools on the Internet, a lot of what you find will be related to **SNMP (Simple Network Management Protocol)**. SNMP is a widely used protocol on networks all around the world that provides a simple way to retrieve the status of a particular host. It exposes a lot of information local to the host, so that a remote machine can gather it and then can show the data in a fancy way to administrators. Usually, the remote machine is said to be a management host and it retrieves data from lots of different hosts and devices. To be strict, SNMP is read/write and can therefore also be used to set parameters on the managed host. It exists in three versions, SNMPv3 being the last version but SNMPv2 still being largely used.

SNMP and FreeSWITCH

You can visualize SNMP as a tree with a root node (.1) and branches, each of them storing at different levels, information about the host, the network interfaces, the processes running on it, and so on. The structure of the tree exposed by SNMP is defined by **MIB** (**Management Information Base**), which are highly extensible descriptions. For instance, if you want to know the hostname of an SNMP client, it is provided at the following leaf (called OID, for object identifier) in SNMPv2: .1.3.6.1.2.1.1.5 (or SNMPv2-MIB::sysName, because a MIB maps OIDs to human-readable strings, like in DNS, network addresses are translated to names).

SNMP is defined in detail in RFC3418. FreeSWITCH has an SNMP module called mod_snmp which exports a few very relevant internal attributes, such as:

- Service uptime
- Currently active sessions
- Peak sessions
- Current session attempts per second
- Peak sessions per second

These attributes are available at a specific OID (registered as FreeSWITCH at IANA):

```
.1.3.6.1.4.1.27880
```

Installation and configuration (on Linux)

On Debian 8 (Jessie), the preferred Linux distro for running FreeSWITCH, you must first install all snmp related server, clients, and utilities. As root:

```
apt-get install snmp snmp-mibs-downloader snmpd
download-mibs
```

For FreeSWITCH and its mod_snmp to be able to connect to snmpd (SNMP daemon) as a subagent, add the following instructions to the SNMPd configuration file (located at /etc/snmp/snmpd.conf):

```
####
#  Run as an AgentX master agent
master          agentx
#  Listen on default named socket /var/agentx/master
agentXPerms     0755 0755 freeswitch daemon
```

Once started, the SNMP client will start to listen on dedicated ports (basically 161/udp). And after starting FreeSWITCH, if everything works as expected you will see this in the main log file:

```
[NOTICE] switch_loadable_module.c:496 Adding Management interface 'mod_
snmp' OID[.1.3.6.1.4.1.27880.1000]
```

Now you are able to query FreeSWITCH stats over the SNMP interface. The quickest way to test it is using a tool called snmpwalk or snmpget (the first will extract everything it can from a branch, the latter will get you the value associated with a leaf), but make sure you use the right version and the right community configured in snmpd.conf:

```
#snmpwalk -v2c localhost .1.3.6.1.4.1.27880.1.2

SNMPv2-SMI::enterprises.27880.1.2.1.0 = Timeticks: (41794715) 4 days,
20:05:47.15

SNMPv2-SMI::enterprises.27880.1.2.2.0 = Counter32: 1

SNMPv2-SMI::enterprises.27880.1.2.3.0 = Gauge32: 0

SNMPv2-SMI::enterprises.27880.1.2.4.0 = Gauge32: 3000

SNMPv2-SMI::enterprises.27880.1.2.5.0 = Gauge32: 0

SNMPv2-SMI::enterprises.27880.1.2.6.0 = Gauge32: 0

SNMPv2-SMI::enterprises.27880.1.2.7.0 = Gauge32: 100

SNMPv2-SMI::enterprises.27880.1.2.8.0 = Gauge32: 1

SNMPv2-SMI::enterprises.27880.1.2.9.0 = Gauge32: 0

SNMPv2-SMI::enterprises.27880.1.2.10.0 = Gauge32: 1

SNMPv2-SMI::enterprises.27880.1.2.11.0 = Gauge32: 0
```

If FreeSWITCH's mod_snmp was unable to connect snmpd during startup initialization, you will see this:

```
SNMPv2-SMI::enterprises.27880 = No Such Object available on this agent at
this OID
```

Getting more information

If the information provided by mod_snmp does not fit your needs, you may want to look for another SNMP feature: the exec or extend instruction. Basically, it allows you to export the result of any local script on the host to a specific OID.

Imagine you have a gateway called `gw1` defined on the FreeSWITCH external profile. You want to be able to know at any time how many inbound/outbound calls are going in and out of this specific gateway, a simple way to do it would be to create a script `check_gw1.sh` on your system. This script would merely run the `sofia status gateways` FreeSWITCH CLI command with a few system commands to isolate the relevant part of the result:

```
#!/bin/bash
if [ "$1" == "in" ]; then
        /usr/local/freeswitch/bin/fs_cli -x 'sofia status gateways' | grep
gw1 | awk '{print $4}'
else
        /usr/local/freeswitch/bin/fs_cli -x 'sofia status gateways' | grep
gw1 | awk '{print $5}'
fi
Then, you have to extend both values:
extend gw1_in  /etc/snmp/check_gw1.sh in
extend gw1_out /etc/snmp/check_gw1.sh out
```

And restart the SNMP daemon.

Now, you can test your export using `snmpwalk` again:

```
#snmpwalk -v2c localhost NET-SNMP-EXTEND-MIB::nsExtendOutputFull
NET-SNMP-EXTEND-MIB::nsExtendOutputFull."gw1_in" = STRING: 0/0
NET-SNMP-EXTEND-MIB::nsExtendOutputFull."gw1_out" = STRING: 0/0
```

At any time, from any authorized host, you are now able to query your FreeSWITCH servers for those very specific variables: inbound/outbound failed and total calls for gateway `gw1`. Of course this is a very simple example and there is no limit on what kind of data you can return using SNMP.

Monitoring tools

Now that we have an insight into what SNMP is and what it is useful for, it is worth mentioning the ecosystem of tools gravitating around monitoring to gain some clue of what can be done and have some examples of concrete applications. Among the most popular monitoring tools are Nagios and Cacti.

Monitoring with Nagios

Nagios is a tool used to monitor hosts on a network in real-time or near real-time. It gives an overview of a whole network and provides a simple way to check at a glance if everything is fine on a specific host and the processes and services running on it. Basically Nagios does two things:

- It starts monitoring tasks such as:
  - Ping hosts
  - Query hosts using SNMP
  - Run plugins (there are a lot available on the Internet)
  - Run custom scripts

- It provides a Web interface that gives a global overview of the infrastructure status (and emphasizes issues, if any)

The statuses of the hosts and processes can be OK, WARNING, CRITICAL or UNKNOWN, which offers a certain granularity in the way alarms are raised. Nagios also offers a reporting tool providing graphs such as alert histograms, availability reports or trends (here, since the 1st of January of the same year):

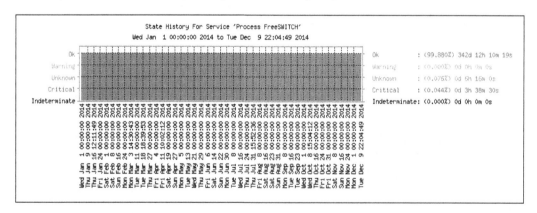

Nagios can do a lot of things, and is hard to provide a formula to satisfy every situation. However, when a new host is set up in a production environment, some sensors seem to be essential like pinging the host (to check its availability at a network level) or checking if the FreeSWITCH process is running.

Sometimes though, checking if the service is running and if the ports are indeed open is not enough because it does not give a feature-level view of the service's status. That's why more specific sensors can be implemented: a custom script that sends **SIP OPTION** messages to one or all ports of the FreeSWITCH server and checks the answered SIP message is as expected. Another test could be to call a forbidden extension or an unknown destination and check if the SIP response code is good (403, 404): this way it is easy to automatically check if the dialplan and features like call restrictions are working. These examples can be implemented very easily using tools like sipsak (available on Linux and Windows operating systems) or even using custom Perl/Ruby/Python scripts built by the community.

One of the most popular among them is the Ruby NagiosSIPplugin (https:// github.com/ibc/nagios-sip-plugin) which can be used to send **SIP OPTIONS** messages to check the availability of a SIP server. It returns one of the Nagios status codes, depending on the message received from the server:

- OK: The **SIP OPTIONS** response code matches the one expected
- WARNING: A reply has been received but the code does not match
- CRITICAL: No relevant reply had been received (for instance, the server is not available or not reachable so this can be a service or a network issue)

The plugin can be easily tested from the command line:

```
[root@telcodevsw]# ./nagios_sip_plugin.rb -t udp -s 203.0.113.1 -p 5060
-f "sip:friendlymonitoring@203.0.113.100" -r "sip:+33122334455@pstn" -T 3
-c 200

OK:status code = 200

[root@telcodev sw]# echo $?

0
```

Several parameters can be specified such as transport protocol, server address, SIP 'From' and `Request-URI` fields, timeout delay, and the response code expected (other parameters are available, you can check the help using -h). In the previous example the FreeSWITCH server is behaving as expected and the plugin return code is 0 (which means `OK` for Nagios as specified in the API documentation). However, if you test with an IP address where no FreeSWITCH instance is running or on a random port where no SIP profile is listening, a return code 2 is expected, meaning `CRITICAL` state:

```
[root@telcodev sw]# ./nagios_sip_plugin.rb -t udp -s 203.0.113.2-p 5060
-f "sip:friendlymonitoring@203.0.113.100" -r "sip:+33122334455@pstn" -T 3
-c 200

CRITICAL:Timeout receiving the response via UDP (Timeout::Error:
execution expired)

[root@telcodev sw]# echo $?
2
```

When the plugin is working it can be integrated into Nagios. To accomplish it, there are two main steps:

1. Declare a new Nagios `command` in the configuration file, referring to the Ruby NagiosSIP plugin previously downloaded:

    ```
    define command {
        command_name    check_sip_options
        command_line    $USER1$/nagios_sip_plugin.rb -t $ARG1$ -s
    $HOSTADDRESS$ -p 5060 -r "sip:$ARG2$" -f "sip:$ARG3$" -T 5 -c
    $ARG4$
    }
    ```

2. Declaring a new service referring to the new command:

    ```
    define service {
        service_descriptionCheck SIP availability (SIP OPTIONS)
        check_commandcheck_sip_options!udp!+33122334455@pstn!
    friendlymonitoring@203.0.113.100!200
    check_period                        24x7
    notification_period                 24x7
    hostgroup_name                      freewitch_servers
    contact_groups                      admins
    use                                 generic-service
    }
    ```

This service definition applies to the group of servers `freeswitch_servers` and inherits settings from a more generic template called `generic-service` here. A service definition can be way longer.

Another interesting Nagios add-on is `check_mk`, with its `logwatch` capability. It can parse system log files as well as other specific log files and apply regexes on them to find out if a message is present or not. This can be applied to a FreeSWITCH server by parsing the execution logs to search for failed calls, then an alarm can be raised if too many calls fail.

Monitoring with Cacti

Compared to Nagios which is designed to provide real-time alarms about the network and the hosts it contains, Cacti is a tool used to store data over medium/long periods and generate graphs about it. In the manner of Nagios, Cacti checks various aspects of a system and provides a Web interface to display the results in graphs generated with `rrdtool`. Cacti is a not a *proper* monitoring tool as it cannot be used for real-time purposes, however it is still useful for data analysis over medium, long, and even sometimes short periods (for instance, comparing usages between the day before and the current day). Cacti is largely designed to work with SNMP but it also enables administrators to gather data to graph using custom scripts.

Going back to the SNMP, we know we can export any data we like from the running FreeSWITCH service. Hence, coupled with Cacti, it is easy to get reports like:

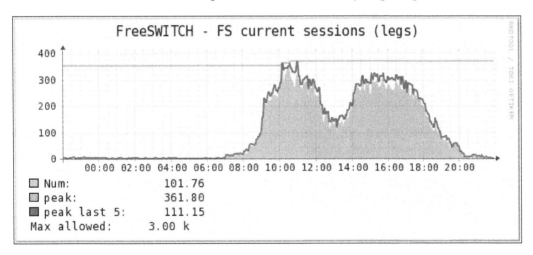

Here, four different variables (exported thanks to FreeSWITCH's mod_snmp) are displayed:

- Current number of sessions (SNMP OID: .1.3.6.1.4.1.27880.1.2.3)
- Peak number of sessions (SNMP OID: .1.3.6.1.4.1.27880.1.2.10)
- Peak number of sessions lasting five minutes (SNMP OID: .1.3.6.1.4.1.27880.1.2.11)
- Max number of sessions allowed (SNMP OID: .1.3.6.1.4.1.27880.1.2.4)

It is also possible to extract more specific data (per gateway current calls, per SIP profile active sessions, and so on) and export them in SNMP so that graphs can be generated with these distinctions making it easy for the administrator to understand uses and load distribution on FreeSWITCH servers.

HA deployment

"The contemporary form of Murphy's law goes back as far as 1952, as an epigraph to a mountaineering book by John Sack, who described it as an "ancient mountaineering adage": Anything that can possibly go wrong, does."

– Wikipedia

Like mountaineers, we survive because we respect the environment where we live and thrive: we know it is full of perils, and we know that ignoring those dangers can be deadly (at least for our business/career).

People are used to the concept of communication as a utility, you take the phone and you hear the line tone… Only in the case of major disasters will a user experience an interruption in the working of her voice calls. Barring a hurricane and the like, the telecommunication industry has an outstanding history of reliability, one of the very few fields where we can experience those magic figures of 99.999% uptime (the mythical five nines).

So, we have users with very high expectations when it comes to their capability to place a call and be reached from outside, completely the opposite to, for example, what they expect from their office PC operating system and applications, where crashes and malfunctions are known daily nuisances.

How can we cope with such expected reliability? We must plan for failures, not try to avoid them. Failures will come, that's certitude; we can lower their frequency, but we cannot avoid them. We need to ensure that each individual point-of-failure will not result in a system failure, for example we need to have multiple paths for everything: network connections, electrical power, disk storage, FreeSWITCH servers, and more.

As a bonus, when we design HA into our operation, we are almost there for achieving horizontal scalability, for example our operation will not only be unbreakable, but will grow linearly with the number of users, simply adding more of the base elements that compose our solution.

Storage, network, switches, power supply

As a rule of thumb, you must double each individual path, so it cannot become a *single point of failure*.

So, at wire level, you will have each machine with at least two different physical network cards in different PCI slots (for example, avoid a single card containing multiple adapters). You *bond* these two cards together as one *virtual* adapter for the same IP address(es), and you bring both network cables to a different switch. This way you also ensure physical connectivity in case of failure of a network card, switch, or cable (many failures are not caused by failed hardware, but by human errors like cutting a cable, or wrongful disconnections from patch panels).

You want to be connected by at least two routers bonded to at least two network carriers (so you hopefully survive the thrashing of the cable down the road), and then to two or more ITSPs.

Each physical machine will be built with double power supplies (PS are the most easily broken pieces of hardware, because of the fan) and double system (boot) hard disks in RAID 1 (mirroring) (hard disks will routinely break well before their Medium Time Before Failure, MTBF).

Storage (for common files, configurations, recorded prompts, voice mail, and more) will be preferable to a redundant SAN with redundant fiber connections, or alternatively (and way cheaper) to a Cluster Filesystem or an HA NFS server. A minimal but reliable HA NFS server is composed of two machines in an active-passive setup, accessed via a Virtual IP address that will be assigned by HeartBeat to the active machine. Each machine will have some disk space (typically many entire disks in raid 5 or 10) that mirrors the corresponding disk space on the other machine via DRBD. This solution (NFS + HeartBeat + DRBD + double network cards and switches) is well documented and effective. In case of a machine or filesystem failure, the Virtual IP address will be moved by HeartBeat on the other machine, and clients will continue to access the files that were mirrored real-time at block level by DRBD. The devil is in the details, so be sure to follow each step of a tried and true industry solution description (like the Linbit ones), not a page from a casual tech blog.

Virtualization

HA requires multiple machines, and more and more operations are using virtualization because of consolidation and manageability considerations. Let's have a look at FreeSWITCH virtualization best practices.

Real hardware machines (for example, non-virtual) running only FreeSWITCH on top of a clean operating system and a known kernel revision are the best solution for a reliable quality delivery. Voice and video operations are real-time operations. Delays of more than 150 milliseconds are perceived by users and jitter (variations in delay) will add complexity to delay management. Quality is all about constant timing of the transmitted and received packets.

Original source of timing are the IRQs of the physical machine, derived by BIOS from the motherboard's quartz oscillator. Those IRQs are the basis for the operating systems' timers, which allow for nanosecond formal accuracy, and millisecond actual accuracy. The vast majority of packets are 20 milliseconds long (while usage of packet duration - for example `ptime` – of 10 or 30 ms is much rarer) so accuracy in the millisecond range actually matters. Then the scheduler will decide at kernel level which process will get CPU access, and so the possibility to check the timers.

So far, the critical aspects are the timers and the scheduler in the kernel (so the need for a known kernel, preferably the same one on which FreeSWITCH is developed and tested by the core team). In an actual, physical machine that's complex but predictable and reliable. FreeSWITCH's core team goes to great lengths to ensure constant timing by automatically using the most advanced time source available from the kernel, and by deriving all internal timings from a single source.

Virtual machines were not designed for real time traffic: although it can serve millions of hits or queries, a web or database server is not time sensitive. As long as they deliver throughput, the exact millisecond one item is delivered and in which timing relation is with previous and later items is not important at all (in DB and Web operations there is no previous or later, each item is usually unrelated to other delivered items).

So virtualization builds an emulation of many virtual machines on top of one hardware machine, each virtual machine simulating a hardware running its own kernel, timers, scheduler, IRQs, BIOS, operating system, and more. This allows for the maximum saturation of CPU and I/O usage, maximum exploitation of the hardware, and minimization of power consumption and space filled in the datacenter, by multiplexing in a random order, CPU and hardware access to the various kernels, operating systems, and applications concurrently running on the *actual*, physical machine. It's enough of a statistically fair distribution. That's not good at all for real time communication quality.

Delivering decent real-time communication quality and traffic throughput from a virtual machine is more a black magic art than a science, and you can find on mailing lists, blog pages, and broscience, a quantity of incantations that can be of help.

You may succeed, and run a carrier class operation, but you need to be really careful and dedicated. The orthodox verb on this matter is: *don't*. No matter if Xen, KVM, Amazon EC2, or VMWare. Simply, don't do it for production systems with any sizeable load (as opposed to development and prototyping, where quality under load is not a concern, and virtualization is handy).

So, we're stuck with a correspondence of one FreeSWITCH server equal to one hardware machine? Not exactly, not at all.

In growing levels of overhead, you can, run multiple profiles with the same FS processes, run multiple FreeSWITCHes concurrently on the same operating system, and use containers to create various virtual environments in which to run various FreeSWITCHes.

The first two solutions will need to use separate IP ports for each profile or FS instance, and will share the same environment, for example `userspace`. The third solution, containers, allows for complete separation of execution environments, so each container will have its own IP address with a full range of ports in exclusive usage, and will be completely separated from other containers for security concerns.

From the admin point of view or feel, a container is like a virtual machine. But is actually a changeroot on steroids: there is one only kernel, one only scheduler, only one set of IRQs, one only set of timers, no emulation, no indirection, no contentions. All processes of all containers are just regular processes, and CPU and I/O access is given to them by way of a *quota* system. If all quotas are set to the same value, resources are distributed like all processes run on one only container, or in the native (host) environment.

So, containers are the most efficient and performing virtualization technology, because they take a completely different approach from *traditional* virtualization. Containers are a security group of related processes, which appear as a separate machine. This gives to each container direct access to timing, and performances indistinguishable from native, bare metal operating systems.

The drawback of containers versus other virtualization technologies is that you can run only Linux, and one only kernel revision (the one of the host, bare metal operating system). All the rest is possible: your distro of choice, multiple concurrent distros, multiple versions of the same distro, and more. You will choose the userland you prefer (for FS, you typically choose between Debian and CentOS). Then you can start, stop, backup, or migrate your container just as you would do with a traditional virtual machine.

The most mature technology in this field used to be OpenVZ, a series of patches to the regular Linux kernel and a set of tools to manage containers (for example that will appear as VMs to you). For ease of installation OpenVZ is also distributed as packages for RHEL-CentOS and for Debian. You'll add the repositories, and then add the packages. After a reboot you'll be ready to build your new containers. OpenVZ is the basis of Virtuozzo and Parallels Cloud Server, commercial virtualization solutions offered by Parallels, complete with a GUI for management, and ability to manage other kinds of VMs, like KVM.

LXC (**Linux Container**) is arguably the future of containers. It is actively developed and present in both RHEL-CentOS and in Ubuntu-Debian, but is clearly Canonical-Ubuntu the champion of LXC.

LXC can be leveraged also by installing Proxmox, a container and VMs management system that offers a complete open source solution, very well engineered, giving ease of use to all components of an HA virtualization platform: LXC, KVM, redundant storage, VM migration, and more. Proxmox offers a web based solution to all containers and storage administration, with redundancy and high availability. You can buy a support contract and be entitled to privileged access to the best tested repositories.

Load balancing and integration with Kamailio and OpenSIPS

You attain HA duplicating for (at least) your communication paths and your servers, by building a resilient system without a *single point of failure*. You want to eliminate the risk that a malfunction of an element can stop or degrade the functions of the whole system.

In the Web world

In standard HA web operations you run multiple web servers behind a load balancer that faces the clients. So, the flow is: client asks for a page to the web server at `http://www.example.com/` address. That server is actually not a real web server, but a load balancer, that proxies the request to one of the real web servers, and then proxies the answer from that web server back to the client.

The load balancer (proxy) is a light process, requiring little hardware to just move bits back and forth. The real web servers are beefy machines where actual, heavy lifting is done.

We have reached the goal of avoiding the risk of web service interruption (if one web server goes down, the load balancer will sense it and send the incoming traffic to the other web servers). Also, we achieved horizontal scalability: as traffic increases we just add more web server machines, the load balancer will, ahem, balance the load between them.

But we just shifted the *single point of failure* from a single web server to a single load balancer. If the load balancer goes down, service is interrupted, clients will have nobody to connect to and to receive answers from. Back to square one? Actually, no.

We've done the right thing shifting the single point of failure from a heavy and complex environment (a web server requiring lots of RAM, CPU power, connections to DBs, application logics, updates, and more) to a very light and lean entity (a load balancer that needs no intelligence, requires almost nothing in resources, uses a static configuration, kind of fire and forget service).

So, how do you duplicate your load balancer? You cannot load balance it (it would only kick the can forward, for example, you end up with a single point of failure located in the *balancer of load balancers*).

To duplicate the load balancer, you use a different strategy: you have a second machine with the same resources, software, and configuration like the first one (actually you can think of it as a *copy* of the first machine), running live side by side with the first machine, using a different IP address.

In normal operation, the first machine is on `http://www.example.com/` IP address and got all the traffic, in and out, while the second machine does nothing, just sitting there humming idle (the second machine is on a different IP address, so no traffic directed to `http://www.example.com/` will reach it). Remember that load balancing is a very light process, so it will be very cheap to have a second machine standing by idle, as a spare.

When the first machine malfunctions (because of a software or hardware failure), we shut it down, then change the IP address and identity of the second machine, and traffic begins to flow in and out of the second machine, that is now answering at the `http://www.example.com/` Internet address.

The last touch to our solution is to make the procedure of malfunction sensing, shutdown of failed machine, *impersonation* by second machine, and resumption of traffic flow, an automated, very fast, repeatable and reliable flow. This is usually done by accessory software called HeartBeat.

We reached our goal: we presented a unique address to our web users so to them a failure in our system will be transparent, only a delay of an instant in the display of the requested web page.

In the FreeSWITCH world

Building an HA FreeSWITCH service requires the same components as the previous web example, with some added complexity due to the dual nature of SIP calls: signaling and media (for example, audio).

SIP load balancer in our case will be provided by Kamailio or OpenSIPS open source software (using its `dispatcher` module).

In SIP, the establishment, tearing down, and modifications of the call are carried out by the exchanging of specific *signaling* network packets that describe who the caller is, who they are looking for, how the call has to be established, how to encode audio to be understandable by both sides, and also the actions of calling, ringing, answering, hanging up, and more. Those *signaling* packets (the *proper* SIP packets) are sent between known ports at known IP addresses, and define the communication flow in its entirety.

But this is only a flow description, for example packets contain no audio, only indications about how to exchange audio packets.

Audio is exchanged using a completely different protocol, auxiliary to SIP, called RTP. Those audio packets will use completely different and previously unknown IP ports (which ports to use is negotiated between caller and callee via SIP packets).

Of those two packet exchanges only the RTP (audio) stream is time sensitive. SIP signaling packets can be delayed by almost any amount of time without significant communication disruption. Maybe your call will be answered one whole second (1,000 milliseconds!) later, so what? On the contrary, a delay of more than 150 milliseconds is perceived as bothering, and can you imagine talking on the phone with audio that comes and goes with one second gaps now and then? Other than full gaps, other audio annoyances are delay, jitter, and packet loss in RTP, that can dramatically lower the quality in the resulting sound reconstruction.

Those two flows (signaling and media) are completely independent, and this often results in completely different paths taken by SIP packets and by RTP packets.

For example, caller and callee can have their SIP packets routed through a number of SIP proxies in between, while RTP packets go directly from caller to callee and vice-versa (that's very often what happens when calls are between phones connected to the same LAN). Or RTP can be routed by a single proxy between caller and callee, while SIP packets traverse a much more tortuous path (that's what often happens when caller and callee are in different LANs). Or any other mix and match of communication paths.

Let's see how we can build an HA FreeSWITCH service in the simplest (but real and robust) of topologies: all machines (load balancers and FreeSWITCH servers) are sitting on public IP addresses, directly reachable from the Internet. In our example we'll have the active load balancer assigned by HeartBeat with the public IP address corresponding to `sip.example.com` in addition to its own IP address (for example it ends up with two IP addresses). In case of active `lb` failure, HeartBeat will reassign `sip.example.com` IP address to the standby load balancer (again, in addition to its own IP address). For example, the standby machine will become the active one and traffic will begin to flow in and out of it.

SIP (signaling) packet will flow from caller to active load balancer. Load balancer will route the packet to one of the FreeSWITCH servers (chosen randomly, or by some algorithm).

All FreeSWITCH servers will be configured exactly the same way (they will only differ by their IP address), and will have their own *guts* (the internal data structures representing phones, calls, SIP details, and more) residing in a PostgreSQL database (this FreeSWITCH setup is called *PostgreSQL in the core*).

This will allow all FreeSWITCHes to be completely interchangeable: they will all know about where each registered phone is to be located (all registrar information will be on the database). Whichever server that phone has originally registered on, the registrar information will be common between all FreeSWITCHes.

So, SIP signaling packets coming from the caller will be routed by the load balancer to one of the multiple FreeSWITCHes. Each one of them will be able to connect the call to one of the registered phones, or to provide special services to the caller (voice mail, conferencing, and more).

FreeSWITCH answers to the incoming SIP signaling packets from the caller will first go to the load balancer (to FS the call is coming from LB). Then the load balancer will route to the caller the SIP signaling packet coming from FS.

SIP signaling path for a voicemail access will be: caller->LB->FS->LB->caller. For an outgoing call (for example PSTN) would be: caller->LB->FS->ITSP->FS->LB->caller. For an in-LAN call would be caller->LB->FS->callee->FS->LB->caller.

Audio (RTP) will instead always flow from the caller (and callee, if any) to FS, and from FS to the caller (and callee, if any). If the call is just to the FS box (as in voicemail access) audio packets will go directly back and forth between caller and FS. If there is actually a callee (for example if the incoming call will generate an outgoing leg toward another phone) audio packets will flow back and forth from caller to FS, and from callee to FS. FS will internally route those audio (RTP) packets between caller and callee, and between callee and caller, joining inside itself the two legs in a complete, end-to-end call.

SIP signaling packets will be routed from load balancer to an FS server, and that FS server will insert its own RTP port and IP address in the answer SIP packet part that defines the audio (RTP) path. That SIP answer packet containing the RTP address will go to the load balancer, and from it to the caller. The caller will then start sending audio (RTP) packets directly to that FS server, and vice versa (SIP signaling packets will continue to pass by the load balancer). In case of a two leg call, the four streams (caller to FS, FS to caller, callee to FS, FS to callee) will be cross routed (for example switched) inside FS itself.

Until now we left the database as our *single point of failure*. Fortunately, there are proven technologies to achieve database HA, master-slave, clustering, and many more. The most popular and simplest one is the active-passive configuration, similar to the configuration we applied to the load balancers and very similar to the one described earlier for DRBD NFS servers.

One machine is the active one and gets all traffic, while the other one is passive, sitting idle replicating the active machine's data on itself (so to contain at each moment an exact copy of the active machine's database data). The database is accessed to the published IP address, assigned by HeartBeat to the active machine. In case of failure, HeartBeat will reassign that *official* IP address to the standby machine, thus making it the active one.

This database HA topology has the advantage of being conceptually simple (you must just ensure that the standby machine is able to replicate the active machine's data). The main drawback is that the data replication process can fail or lag behind, and you end up with a standby machine that does not contain an exact copy of the active machine's data or that contains data that is not even consistent. The other big drawback is that for serving a big database, a machine needs to be huge, powerful, full of RAM and with multiple, big and fast disks. So, you will end up with a very costly big bad box just sitting idle almost all the time, passive, waiting to take over the tasks in case of failure of the active machine. A new solution to both those problems is being made available for PostgreSQL: **BDR (Bi-Directional Replication)**. BDR will allow the use of both machines at the same time, each machine to be guaranteed to be consistent within itself at any moment, and eventually consistent with the other machine. BDR also allows for database replication between different datacenters, to achieve geographical distribution and resiliency to datacenter failures.

We just described a very basic and easy to implement HA FreeSWITCH service solution. The main drawback of this FreeSWITCH HA solution is the exposition on the public Internet of the various FreeSWITCH servers' addresses, that will not be shielded, for example, by DDOS attacks and other security dangers.

Kamailio and OpenSIPS (software we use to implement load balancer) are particularly apt and proven in defending VOIP services from attacks, floods, and DDOS.

A different topology, and indeed one that's often used by Telecom Carriers, would be one that only exposes to the Internet the load balancers. LB will act as registrar too, and will use `rtpproxy` processes to route audio in and out of the system. In this topology, FreeSWITCH servers' addresses will be unreachable from the public internet (an example would be private addresses), and all RTP audio will flow via the `rtpproxy` processes.

DNS SRV records for geographical distribution and HA

So, we achieved a system without a single point of failure, we attained High Availability for our customer base. No calls will be dropped!

We got customers on both coasts of the USA, in Europe, and in Asia too. They are all accessing our solution hosted in a New York datacenter. Our customers in Philadelphia and London are getting perfect quality, while from Tokyo and San Diego they lament occasional delays and latency. Small problems, nuances of a well engineered, failure resistant service.

Then a flood, a power outage or another disaster strikes the datacenter that hosts our solution. The datacenter is no longer reachable from the Internet. Our entire service is wiped out, our customer base will be completely unable to make or receive calls until we find a different datacenter and we rebuild our solution from the most recent offsite backup media.

Ugh!

SRV records in a Domain Name System are used to describe which IP addresses and ports a service can be accessed from, and in which order those address/port couples will be tried by clients. SRV records are often used to identify which SIP servers a client needs to connect to in order to reach the destination desired.

The interesting property of SRV records is that, just like MX records for mail (SMTP) service, a DNS server can return multiple records to a query. Each of those records will have a *weight* associated with it, which will suggest to the client in which order those records would have to be tried. If the one with the lowest weight will not work, try the next higher weight, then the next, and so on. Two records can have the same weight; they would be tried in a random order.

We can manipulate SRV records to optimize traffic patterns and delays and for achieving datacenter disaster survival. Let's say we deploy our solution, load balancers, FreeSWITCHes, Databases and NFS servers, all on both coasts, in New York and in the San Francisco datacenter. We'll use a DNS server with a geolocation feature to answer European and East Coast customers with a lower weight at the New York datacenter address, while Asian and West Coast users will receive a set of records with the lowest weight assigned to the San Francisco datacenter address.

This will ensure both our goals: each one will use the closest site, and in case the closest site is unreachable or not answering, they will use the other one. Yay!

Summary

In this chapter we have seen how to deploy FreeSWITCH in an actual production environment. We reviewed the best practices for best service. A reliable network, both at LAN and WAN level, with QoS and MPLS. Functional and load testing services with SIPp. Debug and CDR logging for keeping track of what happens. Monitoring it all with Nagios and Cacti to alert us when things go wrong and analyze trends. We have seen how to offer *five nines* telecom grade availability with HeartBeat redundancy and Kamailio load balancing, and geographical distribution and disaster recovery with DNS SRV records. We don't let our users and customers down.

3
ITSP and Voice Codecs Optimization

This chapter reveals the most important things to consider when connecting voice traffic to FreeSWITCH — what you want to check out in an **Internet Telephony Service Provider (ITSP)** to get the best resulting quality and more bang for your bucks.

In a fiercely competitive market, many operators are floating different products and offers, targeted to the general public, to companies of a specific size, or to vertical markets.

Here you'll find an explanation of what can actually make a difference for you and your users and customers, apart from price points.

In this chapter, we will cover:

- ITSPs – what they do
- Routes (to numbers)
- DIDs (aka DDIs) — for example, numbers
- Quality
- Support
- Additional features (T38, Caller ID, Overlay)
- Integration APIs
- Codec gotchas
- High definition audio, stereo

ITSPs – what they do

An Internet Telephony Service Provider brings to its customers SIP trunking connections that allow for outbound and inbound calls to/from the **Public Switched Telephone Network (PSTN)**, to/from the **Public Land Mobile Network (PLMN)**, and to/from other SIP users.

ITSPs don't need to own a physical Internet backbone, nor the "last mile" of cables going from the backbone to their customers' premises. ITSPs connect to the public Internet and operate their own SIP servers and (optionally) their own gateways from SIP to PSTN (from now on we'll write only PSTN, for brevity's sake, meaning both PSTN and PLMN).

ITSP business is to sell minutes of PSTN communication to their SIP end users: Both communication coming from PSTN (a caller from PSTN wants to reach a number connected to the SIP device of an ITSP's customer) and communication going to PSTN (ITSP's customer from his/her SIP device wants to call a number connected to the PSTN).

In the real world, much SIP to SIP communication passes through PSTN: ITSPs' customers still call phone numbers (for example, +12125551212, instead of SIP addresses like sip:alice@atlanta.example.com). Because there is no established way for mapping phone numbers to SIP addresses, even if phone numbers ultimately lead to a SIP device (for example, to a customer of a different ITSP) the call will be treated by the caller's ITSP as a PSTN-bound call. Barring an ITSP to ITSP direct peering (or federation), and barring both ITSPs (or end customers) participating in the same collective effort like e164.org (public ENUM directory resolving phone numbers to SIP servers), SIP communication between customers of different ITSPs will be routed through PSTN (they're just phone numbers):

SIP_caller_A=>ITSP_SIP_A=>PSTN_GW_A=>(((PSTN_CLOUD)))=>PSTN_GW_ B=>ITSP_SIP_B=>SIP_callee_B

An ITSP needs to be aware of its customers connecting to its SIP servers, so as to allow users to make outbound calls, and to locate them when incoming calls are to be terminated to their devices: ITSPs must manage SIP registration of their customers. Some ITSPs manage registrations of all individual SIP devices of their customers, while other ITSPs register just the PBX server of their customers. Such servers will act as hubs for incoming/outgoing calls.

Those are all of the basic ITSP functions: Managing SIP registrations of customers, routing outbound SIP customers' calls to its own or third party-operated PSTN gateways, peers with other ITSPs that offer routes to other countries' PSTN gateways, routing incoming calls to its customers' SIP devices, optionally offering other ITSPs routing to its own PSTN gateways. A more or less complex operation and accounting system will allow for the management and billing of customers, and optionally for billing of peers.

Around this common core, each ITSP builds its own offering, adding features that allow customers to manage themselves through a web portal, to choose between various price points that balance cost against the quality of call routes, to query a **least cost route** (LCR) database, setup PBX features (voice mail, call transfers, follow me), conference services, local geographical numbers in various parts of the country or worldwide, fax inbound and outbound transmissions, text messaging gateways, automatic software integration (API) with services provisioning and management system, and so on.

Routes (to numbers)

The path from an ITSP to a destination phone number is called a (SIP) route. Often the ITSP (and major carriers and Telcos alike) has many routes it can choose from to connect the outbound call originated by its customer's SIP device. This exchange of routes minutes is a very big and complex business, and, if we include the big Telcos, is one of the major businesses on Earth.

As you can imagine, the ramifications of such a business depend on local regulations, international agreements, geopolitical situations, business alliances, economic development levels, and a thousand other factors.

In some countries and regions, origination (gathering and routing of outbound calls) and/or termination (providing PSTN gateways to inbound calls) is a legal monopoly of one or few companies; in other regions and countries, regulation requirements can set the bar of entering the business in a way that floods the market with pop and mom's shops or that makes it the exclusive preserve of companies worth billions.

Each ITSP chooses its own mix of different route providers, and there are many "meta-ITSPs" specialized in aggregating and arbitrating traffic from many different route providers and packaging it for other ITSPs that sell minutes to end customers.

DIDs (aka DDIs) – numbers

DID stands for Direct Inward Dialing, while DDI means Direct Dial In, and both acronyms refer to the same thing: A phone number that will lead incoming calls to a device. In our case, a call to that number will be ringing a SIP device.

Normally a customer will port his/her pre-existing PSTN number(s) to his/her ITSP (that is, the customer's number will not make the landline ring anymore, but will ring the end customer's SIP device passing through the ITSP SIP network). ITSPs often have a specific branch of their customer service assisting in the number porting procedures.

DIDs are sought by customers for many reasons: As a primary way to get incoming phone calls (for example, the main phone number of a person or a company, if they have no previous number, or don't want to port it), or as a means to be present in local, regional, or international markets, so as to allow the public to reach a company for the cost of a local call, or to be compliant with regulations that require a company to have a local phone number for customer support.

Also, for each country there are special kinds of numbers with special billing: They can be called for free (for example, toll-free numbers, "800" numbers) from national fixed lines or from both national fixed and national mobile lines, or conversely they can cost a premium fee to be called, a premium that goes in part to the assignee of the number (for example, for pay numbers, hot chatlines, special support lines, "900" numbers, and so on).

In a way, DIDs are the opposite of SIP trunking. A DID provider gets phone numbers assigned or reserved from the competent authorities, and routes inbound calls from those numbers to the SIP devices of its customers.

DID providers can have an agreement with Telco companies to have the numbers routed directly to their SIP servers. Alternatively, they can have special devices, physical gateways, that accept from one side, telephone lines (one at time, or more often T1 or E1 "trunks" composed of 30 voice channels multiplexed in one cable) or cellular network "SIM interfaces", and transform the incoming PSTN or PMLN calls into SIP calls which are then routed to the customer's SIP device.

Each DID is provided with a "capacity" measured in "channels", that is, how many concurrent calls can be incoming on that number (and routed to the customer) before the caller hears the busy signal. Capacity can be from one single voice channel to hundreds.

DIDs have a worldwide market, and multiple local phone numbers from any number of countries and regions can bring incoming calls to the same SIP device, SIP call center, or SIP PBX.

As for routes, DIDs in the same country or region are often offered by a multitude of operators, from first tier big Telcos, to illegal and shady groups, to inexperienced and temporary new companies, with very different inherent parameters of stability, continuity, reliability, audio quality, and so on.

Each ITSP can provide DIDs, at least in a state, country or region, and there are many different global DID providers able to offer regular, toll free and premium numbers from a multitude of countries. Those global providers often buy DIDs from smaller local providers and then resell to ITSPs (that sell to end customers).

Quality of routes

Routes manage the path of a customer's outbound calls, while DIDs bring inbound traffic to the customer. They both take care of the transit of a SIP audio call from caller to callee, and have many of the same challenges to their quality in common.

White, black, and grey

The technical barrier for providing termination services (routes to PSTN) and origination services (DIDs that get calls from PSTN) is so low that in countries and regions where VoIP is under monopoly, or where a cartel of big companies control the market imposing hefty prices, the business opportunity is so compelling that a plethora of independent operators, of widely differing reliability and regulation compliance (or which are outright illegal) discreetly populate the scene.

Talking about routes and DIDs to and from these destinations, it is often referred to by the term "grey" market. That's because one side (you, the end customer) is white in the open, regulation abiding, while the other end is black in the dark, possibly illegal, side of the business. And of course you have all the 50 shades in between.

A white route or DID will go to a first tier operator or to the monopolist, and will have a robust price tag, but its audio quality, continuity, reliability and stability will be mostly assured. A service you can count on.

On the opposite side, the various shades of grey will be offered to you with costs that reflect quality and reliability, and some of them can stop working completely and forever without warning.

Many ITSPs organize their offers using grey routes where quality is not of paramount importance, backed up from second tier and first tier routes in case of cheap route failures.

Some ITSPs let customers choose a customized mix of routes of different qualities to different destinations, and a custom procedure to react to failures (for example, try another cheap route, escalate to second tier, and so on)

Codecs and bandwidth

Each voice call using G711 codecs (that is, native non-compressed telecom formats) consumes around 80-100 Kbps for each direction, including network overhead (for a possible total of around 200 Kbps). The G729 codec results in roughly 30 Kbps usage per direction, and is currently the most adopted VoIP codec because of its favorable balance between payload compression (low bandwidth usage) and audio perceived quality.

Bandwidth utilization can vary greatly depending on various factors such as SIP header compressions, network fragmentation, silence suppression, period of sample, and other minor details.

The sample duration at which the audio is packetized at is mostly 20 milliseconds, and, while this value is the most adopted because of its robustness in the face of packet loss and delays, the ratio between overhead (headers contained in the packet) and payload (actual encoded audio) is very unfavorable.

So, in situations where bandwidth is costly (for example, satellite communication, developing countries, radio transmission, and so on) the sample duration is often brought to 30, 40, or 60 msec, and/or other much more compressed codecs are used (for example, G723, ilbc, Speex), sacrificing some audio quality.

The quality of a voice call is determined by the worst quality of its path (for example, an ilbc originated call cannot get better because it's translated to your receiving G711; on the contrary, each translation further degrades the audio quality of the call).

For the same reason, check thoroughly, your ability to actually enjoy the advantages of a High Definition Audio Codec. If your call transits even for a moment on the PSTN, any HD will be reduced to worse than G711 (because of translation degradation). So high definition audio is mainly for calls to other SIP users. But even if you use an HD codec and your ITSP accepts it, it will not necessarily (actually almost never), be accepted as it is on the path from your ITSP to another ITSP, even if that second ITSP claims to support the same one. You can have better luck calling other customers of your same ITSP.

A special case of high definition audio implementation would be if your ITSP has a direct connection with 4G and LTE cellular network carriers. Many first tier cellphone carriers are beginning to roll out high definition audio to their customers, so ask your ITSP if it supports HD audio calls with them. Cellular networks, while they have been known since the beginning for way lower audio quality relative to PSTN, are about to invert this proportion and be the showcase for mass HD audio adoption.

Infrastructure capability

A very important issue with ITSPs is their propensity to overbook their bandwidth, or even worse, their capability to manage SIP signaling, for example, call establishment.

You can encounter a situation where your ITSP is growing so fast that it is not able to deliver enough bandwidth to all of its customers, particularly during peak time.

But more often the problem arises from the sudden arrival of a specific new customer, for example, a new call center, that moves all of its traffic into routes and servers that until now provided much less throughput.

Worst of all is when a customer using predictive dialers or teleblasters comes online. The bandwidth usage can be compatible with the ITSP setup, but the call attempted per second (cps) can bring the ITSP's SIP servers to a crawl, because for each successful cold call they try to connect to 20 numbers in old and ineffective lists. This can hamper your ability to place and receive calls.

Another, sometimes overlooked, limitation (on the customer side, this time) that can damage call quality and completion rate is the "Asymmetrical" world of ADSL. Asymmetrical Data Subscriber Line's bandwidth is, um, asymmetrical, while VoIP is completely symmetrical. So an ADSL can be pretty fast in downloading a video at 2 Mbps, but its VoIP bandwidth (and the number of maximum concurrent audio channels) will be defined by the upload speed, which is often dramatically lower than the download speed.

Packet delay and, worse, jitter (a discontinuous variation in delay that cannot be easily compensated) can negatively affect audio quality and is relative to the physical distance between end points and to the propagation delay in the path between them.

So, you can be better served by an ITSP, which SIP servers are connected to your SIP devices through a high speed or dedicated network (for example, MPLS), whose infrastructure is directly connected to a first tier Internet backbone, and which has its own datacenters near your region and near the region of your highest traffic.

Various important features

Fax transmission has been designed and optimized to fully exploit the physical characteristics of traditional PSTN analogical copper lines, and has been the bête noire of VoIP for a long time. Even the best, uncompressed codecs (G711) are not able to guarantee a high success rate of T30 (for example, fax) transmissions. That's because of the hyperstrict timing requirements that were guaranteed by a real-time analogical transmission, but are practically impossible for an asynchronous digital transmission. We'll see this in a later section of this book, but the SIP solution to this problem is a protocol enhancement called T38. T38 works around the timing problems, but its implementation must be compatible end to end, and the eventual gateway to PSTN connected fax machines must be of high quality.

So, if you need faxes (inbound and/or outbound), choose an ITSP with well-known, good T38 support for routing this kind of traffic, and perform many tests before committing to a contract.

Another important feature is **911 and emergency calls**. You are probably required by law to ensure you are compliant with your country regulation in the matter of emergency calls (police, ambulance, firefighters, and the like) so, when in doubt, check with a lawyer. Roughly speaking, retail ITSPs often provide this kind of service as part of their standard offer, while wholesale providers almost never do. There are specific "wholesale" providers that specialize in emergency call services, and they can be used to complement the offer of "regular" wholesale providers.

One other thing to bear in mind is the **Caller ID Name (CNAM)** display and set feature — the alphanumeric string that is displayed on the callee's device. While CNAM information in SIP packets is part of the SIP standard, there is not (yet) a publicly accessible database that maps names to numbers and vice versa. This information is contained in proprietary databases maintained by major carriers, with bilateral agreements for access. Many initiatives and commercial providers exist that allow the querying of this information for a fee. If you are interested in this feature, be sure that your ITSP uses these services, and optionally give you the possibility of porting or setting your CNAM, and as always, run some actual tests before committing.

Messaging services, like SMS, MMS, and the like are starting to be deployed by some ITSPs. Often they are provided via some RESTful web API that, via their site, allows the use of some messaging provider service. The most SIP-compliant way to interface with messaging is via SIMPLE, part of the extended SIP standard, and very well supported by FreeSWITCH. If you can choose, choose SIMPLE.

Then there are **API and REST interfaces**. It can be very useful, depending on your specific needs, to integrate into your operation the management of your ITSP services. Adding a DID, a branch office, moving numbers between different departments, setting up redirection and follow me, integrating voicemail in a workflow, and so on: All those and many other different settings and procedures can be controlled automatically by your internal software, provided your ITSP gives you a way to interact with them. Check out how complete its API is, and how its "style" fits with your company programming practices.

Support, redundancy, high availability, and number portability

In this last section we accumulate all the "oh so obvious" issues that can make your life as an ITSP customer very unpleasant.

What is the support policy of your candidate ITSP? How long does it take to be connected with a knowledgeable person? How knowledgeable is that person? What about nights, weekends, holidays?

And also, what kind of monitoring and operation system do they have? Are they able to immediately come up with the SIP trace of the call you have a problem with? Or do they want you to provide the trace?

How are non-critical tickets serviced, like feature request or reconfiguration of features?

How does your potential ITSP handle their own infrastructure failure? What kind of High Availability architecture have they implemented? What if its datacenter got cut out from you or destroyed? Do they have a parallel datacenter? Do they depend on a single upstream provider for their connectivity? In case of an outage, you'll be glad you asked those questions.

This is a pitfall of number portability. Be aware that usually, as per your country regulation, your PSTN or mobile number is owned by you and you can port it to whatever other carrier or provider you like. This may not be the same with your ITSP-provided DIDs: They may just be leased to you, and you'll be unable to port them to another ITSP.

Also, porting numbers is not immediate, and, particularly for a large set of numbers, can require substantial time, perhaps weeks.

Again, for large sets of numbers, and when moving a substantial quantity of traffic to a new ITSP, try to be sure it is able to handle the new kid. Don't switch from zero to one hundred! Ramp it up slowly, constantly checking vital data, and be prepared to switch to a plan B if something turns out for the worse.

Summary

In this chapter we saw what to look for when making commercial choices about our upstream and downstream providers.

What is the mission of an ITSP? What kind of services do they sell? What technologies are involved in their operation? What should we be aware of? What questions should we ask? What are the hints that tell the good from the bad ones, and the features that define the one that is right for us?

We understood the differences between white and black routes to international destinations, their different pricing, reliability, quality. Then we saw the same with DID (DDI), the phone numbers we want people to call in order to reach us.

We closed the chapter with a reasoned laundry list of other features that can greatly affect our experience as Service Provider Customers.

4
VoIP Security

VoIP and FreeSWITCH security is a multi-layered area. You need to take care of all and each of those layers, because it is the weakest link that defines the strength of the chain.

We will not touch here on the issues related to general computer security. We will focus instead only on specific FreeSWITCH and VoIP best practices. Please note that if you have root access to your server via the Internet with a password "12345678", all the following specific measures will do little good.

In this chapter, we will cover:

- Best practices to secure and protect FreeSWITCH
- Fail2ban configuration
- Encryption of SIP signaling, fraud prevention
- Encryption of RTP audio, privacy, and confidentiality
- Certificates in WebRTC and WebSockets (DTLS, mod_verto)

Latest versions of it all

It's of paramount importance to update immediately not only FreeSWITCH, but all your software and your devices' firmware to the latest versions, as soon as they are released.

Specifically, pay attention to the new releases of phones' firmware; they close security bugs and add security features. When a new version of a software or firmware is released, the security bugs that are fixed become the "features" that attackers are looking for in systems that have not been updated.

Default configuration is a demo

The configuration installed when FreeSWITCH is built from source, or when the "Vanilla" config package is installed, is a mega-demo of a lot of features, a complex PBX with IVRs, conferences, registered phones, gateways, and so on. It is a demo, and a field to explore and to learn what can be done. You don't need it all, probably. Best practice would be to use only what you need and understand, and tailor it to your needs and environment. After some time practicing in your lab, start from a minimal configuration and build up from there.

Change passwords

In the standard "demo" installation, you have SIP users (for example, devices) named from "1000" to "1019" that can register (from the local LAN, not from the bad Internet outside) to FreeSWITCH with password "1234" defined in `conf/vars.xml` and then make and receive calls. If you don't change that password, you will experience a 20 second delay before connecting calls, and a flurry of red error messages on the fs_cli console and in the FS logs. Changing that password to something else will remove the nagging, but you can do more. Best practice would be to go to `conf/directory/default` and move all of its content away, then bring back the files you need one by one, and edit all the security information they contain, particularly:

```
<param name="password" value="$${default_password}"/>
<param name="vm-password" value="1001"/>
```

Use absolute values here instead of $${var} variables, and make them unique to each user, and not easily guessable.

Lock all that's not trusted

Running a VoIP server gives you many concerns: Service to your users must not be disrupted by malicious attackers, your (paid) connection to ITSPs must not be hijacked or otherwise exploited by third parties, and conversations of your legitimate users must remain private and confidential. Consider all that's not from your own LAN as hostile. This seemingly paranoid attitude will be your friend, and each time you'll hear about breaches into someone else's telephony system you'll pat yourself on the back.

- If you allow SIP devices to register to FreeSWITCH from outside your LAN, use a VPN or TLS Certificate. Nothing else. Not even 16 character passwords. They'll be almost in the clear. Beware: Allowing plain SIP registration from outside your LAN is a highway to toll fraud.

- Connect to your ITSP via VPN or TLS if possible, and in any case activate IP authentication (ITSP will accept traffic only from your FreeSWITCH server at your IP address).

- Set your firewall to open only the needed ports and to the needed addresses: Probably only your DIDs' provider(s) for incoming traffic (often the same company you use as ITSP for outbound traffic) and VPNs to your remote users.

Dropping root privileges (file permissions)

The more direct way to run FreeSWITCH is to run it as "root". Being root, the all-powerful user, the Overlord of the server, a program running as root has no limits whatsoever: No limits on how much memory it can allocate, which network port it can listen to and send from, how many files it can open, which priority and nice level it can escalate, which file and directories it can read and write.

While obviously very convenient for a casual test installation (no integration problems: FreeSWITCH simply owns the machine and all its resources), many users refrain from it.

To limit the reach and damage that a FreeSWITCH process can do after going awry because of a bug (or a malicious exploitation of a bug), you had better run FreeSWITCH as a user with the minimum possible privileges. A "system" kind of user is the most logical choice: No password, no way to login, no affiliation to groups but to "daemon".

This is how it is already implemented by ready-made packages distributed from FreeSWITCH core developers for Debian, CentOS, and other platforms.

Let's see how to do it when compiling FreeSWITCH from source. Start by creating the user:

```
# useradd --system --home-dir /usr/local/freeswitch -G daemon freeswitch
```

Then we need to give the new user the ownership of all files related to FreeSWITCH and set the right permissions (or our new user will not be able to access or execute the files):

```
# chown -R freeswitch:daemon /usr/local/freeswitch/
# chmod -R 770 /usr/local/freeswitch/
# chmod -R 750 /usr/local/freeswitch/bin/*
```

Instead of using some mechanism like "sudo", FreeSWITCH would be better started as root (or similarly privileged user) with -u and -g options. FS will switch to the desired user and group immediately after initialization:

```
# /usr/local/freeswitch/bin/freeswitch -u freeswitch -g daemon
```

Fail2ban on all services

Fail2ban is a tool designed to monitor systems' log files and to trigger actions in case it detects traces of something suspicious. It is widely considered as an intrusion prevention tool. Many log files from different programs can be monitored at once, meaning that you can monitor as many different services as you want (including FreeSWITCH, of course). Various kinds of reactions can be configured to be triggered.

The configuration of fail2ban relies on three different concepts: Filters, actions and jails. A "filter" is a set of regular expressions used to identify suspicious behaviors in the monitored log file. As log lines are generally specific to each service, you will probably have one filter per service you want to protect (but it is not a rule). Then you have the "action": They describe what to trigger in case a filter matches a line. It can be for instance:

- Block the attacker IP address in the iptable's firewall (most popular and useful)
- Send an alarm message or even an advanced e-mail complete with a whois lookup of the attacker IP address
- Modify the host routing table

As for filters, you can create your own actions even though the default set is already pretty useful. Finally, "jails" must be defined. A jail is a combination of a filter and an action, with instructions about what log files to watch for this combination. For instance, in a jail named ssh-iptables you can have the default filter sshd, with the default action iptables (which adds a rule to iptables to block the relevant IP address, in case of suspicious behavior) and the path to monitor /var/log/secure. The jail is very important because it also contains other parameters needed to completely harness the power of fail2ban:

- Number of occurrences before blocking (maxretry)
- The monitoring time window (findtime)
- The duration before unban (bantime)

This last parameter is particularly useful when a false positive is being blocked (that is, a customer badly configured, a user trying to access ssh with a wrong password, and so on).

FreeSWITCH jail

We are going to configure fail2ban to detect abnormal behavior related to our FreeSWITCH server. We assume fail2ban is successfully installed on the same host running the FreeSWITCH service.

The first step is to configure your FreeSWITCH server to add to its log the authentication failures. To do so, be sure your logfile reports lines at least at "WARNING" level (you can set this from fs_cli with: "fsctl loglevel 4"). Then you have to add to each of your SIP profiles the following line:

```
<param name="log-auth-failures" value="true"/>
```

Once this is done, we have to create a new fail2ban filter file (since version 0.8.12, fail2ban already includes a filter for FreeSWITCH. The latest version can be downloaded from: https://github.com/fail2ban/fail2ban/blob/master/config/filter.d/freeswitch.conf)

```
[Definition]
failregex = ^\.\d+ \[WARNING\] sofia_reg\.c:\d+ SIP auth
(failure|challenge) \((REGISTER|INVITE)\) on sofia profile \'[^']+\'
for \[.*\] from ip <HOST>$
^\.\d+ \[WARNING\] sofia_reg\.c:\d+ Can't find user \[\d+@\d+\.\d+\.\
d+\.\d+\] from <HOST>$
```

In the example above, the two regular expressions define the following rules:

* Identify the IP address of an attacker trying to authenticate a registration or a call without knowing the password (brute force)
* Identify the IP address of an attacker trying random users to setup calls

Additional regular expressions could be added, depending on your need. For a server using ACLs to authenticate SIP requests, you could also add this line:

```
\[WARNING\] sofia_reg.c:\d+ IP <HOST> Rejected by register acl
\"domains\"
```

When the filter is set up, the last step is to configure the jail by editing `jail.conf`, and adding:

```
[freeswitch]
enabled        = true
filter         = freeswitch
logpath        = /usr/local/freeswitch/log/freeswitch.log
maxretry       = 10
action         = iptables-allports[name=freeswitch, protocol=all]
```

Here `action` will add the IP address of the attacker in an iptables chain (named fail2ban-freeswitch) and drop everything from it whatever destination port or protocol.

Note that, if you want, you can block the IP address in iptables only for the service targeted by the attack. For FreeSWITCH, you could, for instance, use the action `iptables` (not `iptables-allports`) and add the parameter `port` with the value `5060,5080`.

Restart fail2ban to activate the configuration. You can check that everything is working as expected by either simulating an attack or simply waiting (you'll see how little time will pass before someone will probe your SIP ports).

Fail2ban also provides a `client` within its framework to interact with the server; you can use it for many monitoring purposes (for example, as a source for a Cacti graph).

SIP(S) and (S|Z)RTP

There are two completely separate flows to encrypt, they can even take different Internet paths to arrive at the same destination: SIP protocol transmits signaling, commands, and information about voice sessions, while RTP protocol transports the digitized audio, the voice proper.

SIPS (SIP Secure) uses certificates exactly in the same way as HTTPS do for HTTP: to encrypt SIP: It's about safeguarding signaling, like your registration passwords, and information about who you connect to. Born on the web as SSL, in our case it is most often called TLS (Transport Layer Security).

SIPS and TLS are NOT about encrypting voice. They protect only signaling: Digitized voice still travels clearly, transported by RTP, and can easily be eavesdropped with a network sniffer. For RTP (audio) encryption, look below at SRTP and ZRTP.

A completely secure and confidential solution would use TLS+SRTP or, better, TLS+ZRTP.

Encrypting SIP with TLS (SIPS)

TLS, as SSL, depends on certificates issued by a Certification Authority that guarantee the identity of the certificate bearer. You can buy a TLS certificate from the same CAs that sell Web HTTPS certificates. You can then use that same certificate with WebSockets, WebRTC and mod_verto too (and for the HTTPS website with the same name as your SIP registrar, for example, `https://pbx.freeswitch.org`).

Also, you can use free and valid certificates from `https://letsencrypt.org/`, (see the automatic script in FreeSWITCH Confluence about verto_communicator demo installation on Debian 8).

The tool you use to generate the various certificates involved is (aptly named) `gentls_cert`:

```
/usr/local/freeswitch/bin/gentls_cert command -cn pbx.freeswitch.org -alt
DNS:pbx.freeswitch.org -org freeswitch.org
```

(Instead of pbx.freeswitch.org and freeswitch.org, use the FQDN your clients will use as SIP registrar and SIP domain).You will use the same utility with the same arguments, but a different command: First of all, `setup` will create your CA. Then `create_server` will generate FreeSWITCH's agent certificate, and `create_client` will generate the (optional) client certificate. You will find them all in `/usr/local/freeswitch/conf/ssl/` (maybe you'll need to copy into clients the `cafile.pem` too, so that they have the entire chain up to the CA).

Then, edit `/usr/local/freeswitch/conf/vars.xml` and modify the following line so that it reads true:

```
<X-PRE-PROCESS cmd="set" data="internal_ssl_enable=true"/>
```

Restart FreeSWITCH and it's set. Then, configure the clients to use TLS and to connect to FreeSWITCH's port 5061. That's it. Your signaling is encrypted. (Beware: clients behind NATs or firewalls can have problems in receiving incoming calls. In that case, use VPNs instead of TLS).

Encrypting (S)RTP via SDES (key exchange in SDP)

SRTP in its oldest, simplest and most deployed implementation encrypts the (UDP) audio stream using a key that was exchanged via SIP(S), in the SDP body of the SIP packet.

This method, called SDES (SDP Security Descriptions), can be considered secure under two conditions:

- Encrypted SIPS (for example, TLS) was used for exchanging keys in signaling
- All the SIP(S) proxies between caller and callee are trusted

Because SIP(S) packets must be interpreted by proxies, the organizations that own or manage each single proxy between caller and callee know the key and can decrypt the audio. Also, someone can succeed in inserting him or herself into the proxy chain, and acting as a man-in-the-middle (mitm), pretending to be one such legitimate proxy, and then decrypt and/or tamper with the audio.

Many wrongly identify "SRTP" with "SRTP via SDES". SRTP is actually RTP encrypted via keys, and there are many different methods to exchange those keys.

Anyway, anyone that has no access to the key is unable to decrypt the audio, and there is a world of difference with plain, clear, unencrypted RTP, where audio can be listened to simply by sniffing the network.

To activate support for SDES SRTP, add the variable `sip_secure_media=true` to the call-origination string, to the dialplan extension, or to the session.

SDES offers can be spotted by a line like `a=crypto` in SDP body, and encryption status of the call can be checked via the variable `rtp_secure_audio_confirmed`.

Activate support for SRTP via SDES (or simply "SRTP", for some vendors) in clients, and audio will be encrypted.

Encrypting (S)RTP via ZRTP (key exchange in RTP)

ZRTP is a method for the end-to-end exchange of encryption keys. Caller and callee will directly exchange the keys that will be used to encrypt the audio stream, without any third-party intervention. No proxy is involved; no information is exchanged in SIP(S) or SDP: Key exchange is peer-to-peer via Diffie-Hellmann, in the RTP stream itself, in its initial phase.

ZRTP is compiled by default in FreeSWITCH. If clients support ZRTP, the session will be encrypted in the safest mode possible.

ZRTP is a young protocol, and is already implemented by some softphones (Blink, CSipSimple, iCall, Jitsi, Linphone, Phoner, SFLPhone, Twinkle, Zfone, and Zoiper has announced) but by almost no hardphone or ATA.

There are two ways to solve the lack of hardware devices implementing ZRTP. If you're using a softphone that does not support ZRTP, you can install on the client machine "Zfone", a software utility that will act as a "filter", encrypting and decrypting on the fly from and to ZRTP the plain RTP traffic for your softphone.

The other way is conceptually similar: You'll use FreeSWITCH as a filter. Arrive from your device (phone, ATA, softphone) to FreeSWITCH with plain RTP (perhaps through a VPN), and then FreeSWITCH will connect ZRTP to the callee. In this case you'll have an end-to-end encryption from FS to callee, without any proxy or third party being able to listen.

ZRTP is enabled globally in the default demo configuration, but you can enable and disable it (globally or per-call) via `ztp_secure_media=true`.

New frontiers of VoIP encryption (WebRTC, WebSockets, DTLS)

FreeSWITCH has been at the forefront of development and implementation of WebRTC and SIP over Secure WebSockets.

This is a script to obtain valid certificate from `https://letsencrypt.org/`; install it in a FreeSWITCH standard setup, and start using WebRTC DTLS encrypted calls:

```
https://freeswitch.org/confluence/display/FREESWITCH/
Debian+8+Jessie#Debian8Jessie-Scriptinstallfreeswitchdemowithverto_
communicator
```

Summary

In this chapter we touched on the most important features that determine the security of a production-grade FreeSWITCH installation. You had better assume that everything and everyone can be hostile and mischievous; implement all the known best practices in the industry, be up-to-date and aware of any threats and new software versions. Lock it all, via firewalls, VPNs, certificates, and encryption.

Better grumpy and safe than sad and sorry (quote, the grumpy cat. Meow!).

5
Audio File and Streaming Formats, Music on Hold, Recording Calls

Audio, audio, audio… If you're in telephony, you know what telephony is all about. End users' experience is determined by the quality of the sounds they are hearing, and, no matter how perfect the signaling and routing, their satisfaction will come from way down in the abstraction layers: their ears.

Creating and manipulating audio files and streams, for prompts, error messages, voicemails, call recordings, quality monitoring, and to entertain while waiting on the phone, is a sizeable part of any VoIP implementation.

FreeSWITCH gives us a lot of functions and primitives to deal with audio files and associate chores, and we'll see what the best practices are in this area, from how to combine audio fragments into meaningful phrases to how to stream live radio as music on hold.

In this chapter, we will cover:

- Audio in VoIP, traditional and HD
- FreeSWITCH audio formats, MP3, streaming
- **Music on Hold (MOH)**
- Recording and playing files, streams, and prompts
- Recording calls
- Tapping audio

Traditional telephony codecs constrain audio

There are so many ways to compress and digitize audio to be sent through the wire. A lot of codecs are available for use with FreeSWITCH, from ultra-wide band high definition (the quality of an audio CD) to the ultra-low bandwidth utilization, and all the variables involved can be confusing.

So, let's start with a bold simplifying assumption (we'll see complexity later): You only need to be aware of two codecs — G711 (which is available in two flavors: Ulaw and Alaw, also known as PCMU and PCMA) and G729.

G711 is the original, uncompressed format used since the beginning of time by telecom companies worldwide. It was designed to carry speech so that it only gets a very narrow audio band (300-3400 Hz), and to cut out the rest (humans can hear from 20 to 20,000 Hz; that's why music on hold sounds so bad on the phone). It samples that narrow speech band 8,000 times per second (8 khz sampling) in a logarithmic way (mimicking human hearing for different frequencies) producing 8 bit samples. 8 bit times 8,000 makes a stream of 64 kb/sec. Its two flavors (Ulaw, or µ-law, or pcmu, is used in the USA, and Alaw, or a-law or pcma, in the rest of the world) are only slightly different, and you would know if you mistook one for the other because it would sound understandable, but bad.

If your call is originated or terminated by PSTN, it will be converted to or from G711, so its quality cannot be better than that (mono, 8 bit, 8 khz, narrowband), only worse (there is no point in having an HD codec on one end and PSTN on the other end; you will just burn CPU cycles transcoding between the two codecs, and the quality will be lower than G711, because of the very process of transcoding).

G711, as the original PSTN format, can carry as audio (that is, inband) all traditional telephony contents, from DTMF digits to fax transmissions (also, a good success rate for faxing over SIP would require using T38 protocol on top of G711).

G711 is free from patents, and is supported by all software and devices out there. It is your safest bet when you're looking for compatibility and interoperability. Its usage does not load the CPU, because no compression is done. The drawback is that it takes 64 kb/s of bandwidth (two audio directions plus overhead will be roughly 200 kb/s). G711 support is mandatory on WebRTC, and choosing it instead of higher quality codecs lowers client-side processing power requirements considerably.

G729 is the other all-important codec: It is a patented, non-free, pay-for, audio codec that gives good quality/compression ratio for a payload similar to G711: Narrowband, mono, 8 bit, 8 khz. Its perceived quality (that is, **Mean Opinion Score** (**MOS**) what the end user experiences) is near G711, but it only uses 8 kb/sec bandwidth in each direction.

This commercial codec (*you need to buy licenses to use it* because of patents (feel free to check `https://freeswitch.org/` page for FreeSWITCH G729 licenses)), is very popular in legacy systems, commercial PBXs, interconnection with telecoms and ITSPs, and is almost always supported (maybe at additional cost) by hardware phones.

G729 cannot transport faxes or DTMFs, only speech (no fax at all, while DTMFs can be transmitted out of band via 2833 or INFO), and it requires the CPU to perform compression and decompression in real time.

```
root@vz139: /root                                    _ □ X
freeswitch@internal> show codecs
type,name,ikey
codec,ADPCM (IMA),mod_spandsp
codec,AMR,mod_amr
codec,B64 (STANDARD),mod_b64
codec,G.711 alaw,CORE_PCM_MODULE
codec,G.711 ulaw,CORE_PCM_MODULE
codec,G.722,mod_spandsp
codec,G.723.1 6.3k,mod_g723_1
codec,G.726 16k,mod_spandsp
codec,G.726 16k (AAL2),mod_spandsp
codec,G.726 24k,mod_spandsp
codec,G.726 24k (AAL2),mod_spandsp
codec,G.726 32k,mod_spandsp
codec,G.726 32k (AAL2),mod_spandsp
codec,G.726 40k,mod_spandsp
codec,G.726 40k (AAL2),mod_spandsp
codec,G.729,mod_g729
codec,GSM,mod_spandsp
codec,H.261 Video (passthru),mod_h26x
codec,H.263 Video (passthru),mod_h26x
codec,H.263+ Video (passthru),mod_h26x
codec,H.263++ Video (passthru),mod_h26x
codec,H.264 Video (passthru),mod_h26x
codec,LPC-10,mod_spandsp
codec,OPUS (STANDARD),mod_opus
codec,PROXY PASS-THROUGH,CORE_PCM_MODULE
codec,PROXY PASS-THROUGH,CORE_PCM_MODULE
codec,PROXY VIDEO PASS-THROUGH,CORE_PCM_MODULE
codec,RAW Signed Linear (16 bit),CORE_PCM_MODULE
codec,Speex,CORE_SPEEX_MODULE
codec,VP8 Video (passthru),mod_vp8
codec,red Video (passthru),mod_vp8
codec,ulpfec Video (passthru),mod_vp8

32 total.

freeswitch@internal>
```

Codecs available in FreeSWITCH default installation

HD audio frontiers are pushed by cellphones, right now

We've just seen that for regular, traditional telephony, we only need an audio source that is mono, narrowband, 8 bit, 8 khz. That is considered good quality, toll-grade quality.

It compares well with cellular phones' quality, which in the last decade has drastically lowered our expectations. Cellular phones' codecs did not sound very good; actually they were much worse than G711 or G729. But we're on the verge of a revolution in the sound quality of telecommunication.

First it was Skype, who introduced us all to 16 khz, wideband audio. Ever tried to listen to music via Skype? It sounds good. And speech too: You immediately hear and feel, you're not on PSTN (and neither on cellphone).

But there is much more to come: 4G and LTE cellular networks are starting to become available everywhere, with audio in ultra-wideband and **high definition (HD)**. The cellular network will once again change our expectations, but this time it will raise the bar. And WebRTC is almost always using HD codecs (mostly OPUS, at the moment), albeit support for G711 is still mandatory.

VoIP, and SIP-enabled devices, have been able to take up this challenge for a long while now. You can actually say that fast local networks available in offices and corporations allowed for the very development of HD audio itself, at first in SIP. And now high quality audio is ready to break out from the corporate LAN and begin to take over the majority of telecommunication.

```
 124 - AAL2-G726-16 && G726-16
 125 -
 126 -
 127 - BV32


<X-PRE-PROCESS cmd="set" data="global_codec_prefs=OPUS,G722,PCMU,PCMA,GSM"/>
<X-PRE-PROCESS cmd="set" data="outbound_codec_prefs=PCMU,PCMA,GSM"/>

     xmpp_client_profile and xmpp_server_profile
     xmpp_client_profile can be any string.
     xmpp_server_profile is appended to "dingaling_" to form the database name
     containing the "subscriptions" table.
                                              258,68        59%
```

You set the preference order for codecs in /usr/local/freeswitch/conf/vars.xml

FreeSWITCH audio, file, and stream formats

FreeSWITCH is able to interface automatically with a lot of codecs and file/stream formats, and it can translate between them. This means that a CD-like source at 48 khz, 16 bit, stereo and wideband will be decoded, downsampled, truncated, mixed, and then re-encoded to be sent in a G711 call.

Keeping with the general FreeSWITCH philosophy of *do not reinvent the wheel*, audio files and streams are read and written using open source libraries: FreeSWITCH has a specific API for audio formats; anyone can write a wrapper for a new sound format library and that format will be available everywhere in FS that a sound format is used (the same applies to codecs and to stream formats; just implement their FreeSWITCH's API).

This ensures the most efficient and timely support for new file formats and codecs (Brian West released FreeSWITCH's support for BroadVoice codec 40 minutes after it was open sourced).

Audio file formats

Most audio file formats are supported in standard installation by `mod_sndfile` (from `.au` to `.aiff`, `.gsm` to `.raw`) and the most popular of the formats is WAV.

There are various standard sets of prompts that can be automatically installed in FreeSWITCH. They're all in WAV format, 16 bit, mono, and they differ in the sampling frequencies: The whole sets are available in 8, 16, 32, 48 khz.

WAV sets of prompts provide the raw material that will be translated (encoded) by codecs. Waveforms will be read from the files by FreeSWITCH and then encoded. To save disk space and download time you will install only the sets with the sampling frequencies you're going to use. After compiling and installing FS, you should input:

```
make sounds-install && make moh-install
```

This will install the 8 khz set of prompts and on-hold music. That's the basic set, the most used one, the one that will be the base for all traditional telephony calls, both using G711, G729, and a lot of other 8 khz codecs. If you're not planning on using HD audio, that's the only set you'll need.

To install all the sets (8, 16, 32 and 48 khz) in one fell swoop, you should input:

```
make cd-sounds-install && make cd-moh-install
```

When you need to play a file, FreeSWITCH will automatically choose the one that is most convenient as a base for encoding. So, for Opus, Speex, Silk, and G722; FS will read the corresponding sampled set.

Anyway, encoding has a CPU cost, particularly for compressed codecs. To avoid any cost, `mod_native_file` comes to the rescue. This module, installed by default, will allow FreeSWITCH to read from files already encoded, such as those ready-made in G729, or Opus, or G722. This can be very useful where computational power is at a premium, like in embedded devices.

```
root@linode:~# /usr/local/freeswitch/bin/fs_encode
Usage: /usr/local/freeswitch/bin/fs_encode [options] input output

The output must end in the format, e.g., myfile.SPEEX
                 -c path                  Path to the FS configurations.
                 -k path                  Path to the FS log directory
                 -l module[,module]       Load additional modules (comma-separated
)
                 -m path                  Path to the modules.
                 -f format                fmtp to pass to the codec
                 -p ptime                 ptime to use while encoding
                 -r rate                  sampling rate
                 -b bitrate               codec bitrate (if supported)
                 -v                       verbose
root@linode:~#
```

You can use the program fs_encode to encode audio files in each one of the codecs supported by FreeSWITCH and its modules

MP3 and streaming

`Mod_shout` (not installed by default) allows FreeSWITCH to play local and remote MP3 files, and other streaming formats. To install, input the following:

```
cd /usr/src/freeswitch
make mod_shout-install
```

This will automatically download the needed `Lame` and `mpg123` libraries, build, and then install the module. Then, from `fs_cli`:

How to load mod_shout from fs_cli

To have `mod_shout` automatically loaded at FreeSWITCH startup, add it into `/usr/local/freeswitch/conf/autoload_config/modules.conf.xml`.

Once loaded in FS, `mod_shout` can be used to play and record local `mp3` files, and to interact with SHOUTcast and ICEcast servers (for example for listening to an Internet radio, as music on hold, or to broadcast a call or a conference via ICEcast).

Music on Hold

In FreeSWITCH, MOH has a distinct and unique meaning: One directory of files that will be broadcast in a loop as a stream to all listening sessions. For example, all calls connected to the same music on hold name will hear the same broadcast, like listening to the same radio.

MOH features are made available by mod_local_stream, and configured in local_stream.conf.xml.

```
<configuration name="local_stream.conf" description="stream files from local dir">
  <!-- fallback to default if requested moh class isn't found -->
  <directory name="default" path="$${sounds_dir}/music/8000">
    <param name="rate" value="8000"/>
    <param name="shuffle" value="true"/>
    <param name="channels" value="1"/>
    <param name="interval" value="20"/>
    <param name="timer-name" value="soft"/>
    <!-- list of short files to break in with every so often -->
    <!--<param name="chime-list" value="file1.wav,file2.wav"/>-->
    <!-- frequency of break-in (seconds)-->
    <!--<param name="chime-freq" value="30"/>-->
    <!-- limit to how many seconds the file will play -->
    <!--<param name="chime-max" value="500"/>-->
  </directory>
```

Files can be in whatever format is supported by FS modules, for example mod_sndfile, mod_shout, mod_file_native, and more. While it is possible to use local MP3s as local stream files, it would be advisable to preconvert them in WAV (so as not to waste CPU cycles in decoding that format). If you have built mod_shout you'll find mpg123 as /usr/src/freeswitch.git/libs/mpg123-1.13.2/src/mpg123.

```
cd /home/music/directory
for i in *.mp3; do mpg321 -w "`basename "$i" .mp3`".wav "$i"; done
```

Also, you can use remote MP3s, or streams supported by mod_shout as MOH. Refer to mod_shout confluence/wiki page for details and examples.

Playing and recording audio files and streams

Thanks to FreeSWITCH internal APIs, inspired by the Unix concept *all is a file*, you use the same primitive to play files and streams (assuming they're supported by some module).

From dialplan, to play a local file, a remote file, or a stream, input the following:

```
<action application="playback" data="sounds/soundfile.wav"/>
<action application="playback" data="http://example.com/ciao.mp3"/>
<action application="playback" data="shout://online.radiodifusion.
net:8024/" />
```

For listening to a MOH defined in `mod_local_stream` configuration, input the following:

```
<action application="playback" data="local_stream://default"/>
```

You can add an offset, in samples, at the end of the item definition, for example, for a 2 second offset from the beginning, in a 8 khz sampled file, input the following:

```
<action application="playback" data="/tmp/test.wav@@16000"/>
```

Also, you can define one or more DTMFs to be used as `terminator` keys to interrupt playback. The default is * (star). To disable `terminator` keys altogether, set the variable to `none`.

```
<action application="set" data="playback_terminators=none"/>
```

Recording and modifying prompts and audio files

You have two routes to custom prompts. You can have a commercial prompt company professionally record a set of prompts for you. Google for "FreeSWITCH Prompts" and you'll find various options for standard prompts, in English and in many other languages. Custom prompts, with the name of your company, or special messages, can be obtained for a reasonable cost, professionally recorded by corporate-sounding voices.

Or you can record prompts yourself, both from your voice or from a **Text to Speech (TTS)** software (from festival to smartphone's assistants).

To create an audio file from your voice, you call an extension that answers and then records your message. Put in dialplan, to record a file of max 20 seconds length, with 200 set as the energy level of silence, and 3 seconds of silence as terminator (as well as the default * key):

```
<extension name="Record File">
<condition field="destination_number" expression="^123456$">
<action application="playback" data="sounds/ivr-begin_recording.wav"/>
<action application="record" data="/tmp/${uuid}.wav 20 200 3"/>
</condition>
</extension>
```

Call 123456, record your prompt, press *, and you'll find a WAV file with the uuid of the call as a name (so, you can call many times without overwriting it) in `/tmp`.

You will definitely want to trim, clean, stretch, or otherwise modify this file. Enter Audacity! Audacity is a professional and open source tool for editing audio files.

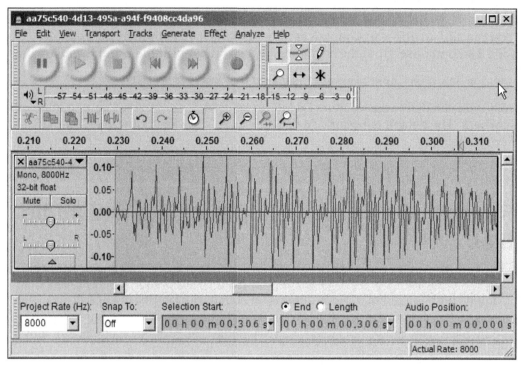

Editing an audio file with Audacity

It has tons of functions and features, but its basic usage is intuitive, while for advanced effects you'll find plenty of documentation and help from the community.

Recording calls

Call recording is different from message (prompt) recording. You want to record both the caller and the callee, that is, the entire conversation made by A-leg (caller) and B-leg (callee).

You may want to end up with two files (one file will contain the caller's audio, the other one the callee's speech), or one file that contains the two legs mixed together, or (and this is an elegant and practical solution) one stereo file that will contain the caller's audio on one channel (for example, the left channel), and the callee's on the other (right) channel.

Also, you may want this recording to happen automatically at each call, or to be activated by the end user (or administrator) pressing a special *feature key*.

Here the dialplan application you want to use is `record_session`. By default `record_session` will *do the right thing (TM)* and record a stereo file containing one leg per channel.

```
<action application="record_session" data="/tmp/${uuid}.wav"/>
```

To modify the default behavior of `record_session` you should setup variables. You can choose which direction (leg) to record (`RECORD_WRITE_ONLY`, `RECORD_READ_ONLY`), you can add metadata to the resulting file (`RECORD_TITLE`, `RECORD_COPYRIGHT`, `RECORD_SOFTWARE`, `RECORD_ARTIST`, `RECORD_COMMENT`, `RECORD_DATE`), you can record a mono file with the two legs mixed (`RECORD_STEREO=false`), and so on. (Refer to the confluence/wiki page of `record_session` for full documentation).

Calling `record_session` in dialplan will record each call, without user intervention and without the optional stop record key.

For full user control on recording start and stop, we need to use `bind_meta_app`, which will bind a keypress to the execution of an application. For starting/stopping session recording when the A-leg (caller) presses *2 (star-2), add the following extension to dialplan:

```
<extension name="Record_at_will">
<condition field="destination_number" expression="^(1212)$">
<action application="export" data="RECORD_STEREO=true"/>
<action application="export" data="RECORD_TOGGLE_ON_REPEAT=true"/>
<action application="bind_meta_app" data="2 a s record_session::/
tmp/${uuid}.wav"/>
<action application="bridge" data="user/$1@${domain_name}"/>
</condition>
</extension>
```

It will bind the key, set variables, and then originate and bridge the call to the user. Then the caller can control the recording by pressing the *2 key sequence (in a hardware phone you can program the REC button to send this to two DTMFs). See `bind_meta_app` documentation for full options.

Tapping audio

You may need to listen someone else's call. First of all be sure to be compliant with international laws and regulations and those of your country: Rumors that the Alphabet Soup is wiretapping the whole world will not shield you from a lawsuit or a criminal investigation. If you're positive you have the right to listen, FreeSWITCH has two dialplan applications to choose from: eavesdrop will allow you to listen to an arbitrary call (defined as an uuid argument to the app), while userspy will constantly eavesdrop on calls involving a specific user.

Using eavesdrop on a call (also known as call barging) requires knowing its uuid (you may use all as uuid, but you'll end up listening to all existing calls mixed together). One such technique is implemented in the standard dialplan. When a call is processed, its uuid is added to a spymap db table, indexed on extension. You can then dial a *prefix + extension*, and if there is a call involving that extension the uuid will be retrieved and fed to the eavesdrop application:

```
<extension name="global" continue="true">
<condition>
<action application="db" data="insert/spymap/${caller_id_
number}/${uuid}"/>
</condition>
</extension>


<extension name="eavesdrop">
<condition field="destination_number" expression="^88(.*)$|^\*0(.*)$">
<action application="answer"/>
<action application="eavesdrop" data="${db(select/spymap/$1$2)}"/> </
condition>
</extension>
```

You will dial *88 + extension* or **0 + extension* to listen to calls, and you may then talk to the caller, callee, or both (pressing *2, 1* or *3*), or just lurk there. Refer to *eavesdrop* documentation for full options and variables.

The userspy is a way to automate the eavesdropping on a particular user. You will need to compile mod_spy and load it into FreeSWITCH.

cd /usr/src/freeswitch

make mod_spy-install

Once loaded it adds the dialplan application userspy.

Loading newly compiled mod_spy in a running FreeSWITCH

You will then add to the dialplan an extension where the action is like:

```
<action application="userspy" data="1000@192.168.1.1
${hash(select/${domain_name}-spymap/1000)}"/>
```

The two parameters are user@domain to listen to future calls, and an optional uuid of an active call to immediately begin to barge in on. In between active calls, you'll be listening to MOH.

Summary

In this chapter we have browsed through various audio-related items and procedures of paramount importance in real life FreeSWITCH implementation. Audio is the Alpha and Omega of telephony, and by taking good care of it you will be the good guy in the VoIP world. FreeSWITCH gives you so many tools. We just scratched the surface here, and using FS positions your project at the forefront of telecommunication, ready to take on the challenge of HD audio. We demonstrated how to deal with audio files, transcoding formats, recording prompts and messages, and recording entire calls (both legs) to a stereo file. Lastly, we saw how to listen to, and interact with, someone else's call.

There is so much more to explore about Audio in FreeSWITCH, but we hope we gave you a glimpse, and the motivation to browse the official documentation.

6
PSTN and TDM

SIP dominates much of the telephony landscape in VoIP. The SIP protocol is also probably the most covered in FreeSWITCH books, documentation, and tutorials. Despite this apparent hegemony of the SIP protocol, there are a significant number of protocols that are used in the PSTN (public switched telephony network) and in other private and public telephony networks. Some of those protocols do not even run over IP, but use rudimentary analog audio signals to setup a call. (Yikes! This sounds almost as archaic as sending smoke signals!) One of the great powers of FreeSWITCH comes from its flexibility to interconnect different telephony protocols, from bleeding edge new media and signaling protocols such as WebRTC/Verto, to protocols as old as FXO/FXS and MFC-R2. In a sense, FreeSWITCH is a powerful translator that knows many different languages and is able to translate from one language to another quickly. These different languages are the protocols, and there are a great deal of both media and signaling protocols that FreeSWITCH understands and can translate to and from.

In general terms, signaling protocols supported by FreeSWITCH beyond SIP can be divided into two camps. The first camp is the "legacy", but there are still heavily prevalent protocols such as SS7, ISDN PRI/BRI (Q.931/Q.921), FXO/FXS, and GSM (2G). Although you may not come across them in some countries, other countries or areas within a country still rely heavily on them. For example, the SS7 suite of protocols are still pretty much the protocols running all the core telephony networks and it's an extremely reliable protocol, but most people do not come into contact with it because it's not heavily used for peripheral deployments. The second camp of signaling protocols belongs to "newer" IP telephony protocols such as H.323, Skinny (SCCP), and Jingle (Google Talk) (but they are still somewhat legacy when compared to the latest protocols like Verto and WebRTC).

The material in this chapter will focus on the legacy protocols used to interconnect with the PSTN.

In order to help you to fully appreciate how all these protocols fit together, I'd like to introduce briefly the FreeSWITCH concept of an "endpoint interface" or "endpoint driver". For FreeSWITCH to know about a signaling protocol, an endpoint driver must be loaded and configured by the FreeSWITCH process. Endpoint drivers allow FreeSWITCH to know how to receive and place calls in a particular protocol. In other words, an endpoint interface is a protocol plugin. This means each of the protocols that were previously mentioned (for example, SS7, H.323, FXO/FXS) must live within an endpoint driver that FreeSWITCH can configure and load. This leads us to FreeTDM and mod_freetdm (which was many years ago called mod_openzap), the Analog and TDM protocol plugin for FreeSWITCH.

OpenZap

Bear with me for a few paragraphs and you'll be wiser by understanding how the OSS telephony revolution started and how FreeTDM came into existence and was integrated in FreeSWITCH.

In the early days of the FreeSWITCH project, Anthony wrote the telephony library, "OpenZap" and the endpoint driver, mod_openzap to interconnect FreeSWITCH with analog and digital **time domain multiplexing** (**TDM**) networks, making use of telephony hardware from vendors such as Sangoma, Digium, and Pika Technologies. The OpenZap project was named after the older "Zapata Telephony"(ZapTel) project by Jim Dixon, who was probably the first person to come up with an open source driver to connect an ISDN telephony card and then a cheap voice modem to a BSD/Linux computer. ZapTel was a revolutionary project in many ways (hence the name "Zapata Telephony", after the Mexican revolutionary, Emiliano Zapata) and provided a critical boost to the open source telephony movement (which, arguably, really took off with the integration of ZapTel with the Asterisk PBX project).

The ZapTel project consisted of several Linux kernel drivers that exposed ioctl system calls to be able to control telephony hardware (both analog lines and ISDN digital lines such as T1 and E1 ports). The intelligence to make phone calls, however, was left to the application layer (hence the need for software, like Asterisk or FreeSWITCH). The OpenZap project that Anthony started was one level higher of abstraction, aiming to provide a generic and unified API (application programming interface) for both the telephony hardware and the signaling protocols for analog and TDM technologies. Anthony wrote the initial implementation and it worked pretty well. This way, with a single FreeSWITCH endpoint driver (mod_openzap, now called mod_freetdm), support for many analog and TDM protocols was implemented.

FreeTDM

Sangoma Technologies is a Canadian company that has always been sponsoring FreeSWITCH morally and financially. However, until 2009, the code contributions were sparse. In 2008, the ZapTel project was renamed to DAHDI due to some trademark issues. Around the same time, in 2009, Sangoma started heavily reworking some areas of OpenZap so it could better be used as an API outside of FreeSWITCH for other standalone applications. This rework changed the API completely and improved other core areas within OpenZap. The heavy changes along with the fact that the original ZapTel project was renamed led to the renaming of the OpenZap project. It was decided between Sangoma and the FreeSWITCH development team to rename OpenZap to FreeTDM.

The FreeTDM project is a software library. As a library it's independent from FreeSWITCH and can be used in projects outside FreeSWITCH's scope. The library provides a unified high level API for analog and TDM signaling and access to the input/output configuration and control of telephony hardware like Sangoma and Digium cards. FreeSWITCH then includes the mod_freetdm endpoint driver to interconnect with all protocols supported by FreeTDM.

FreeTDM, just like FreeSWITCH, follows a modular architecture to plug different signaling and I/O modules (more plugins!). For example, FreeTDM supports several different ISDN PRI/BRI stacks (each with different strengths and weaknesses). FreeTDM has been designed to work with telephony hardware from multiple vendors (and support for other vendors can be added by writing a plugin). The most well-known and used vendors are Sangoma, Xorcom, and Digium.

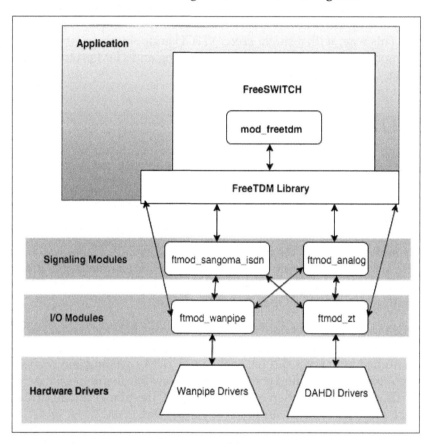

I/O modules

The input/output (IO) modules are responsible for controlling the telephony hardware. All FreeTDM modules are named with the prefix "ftmod" (as in FreeTDM module). The IO modules take care of reading and writing raw data bytes and executing low level control commands in the telephony hardware, but do nothing else; they are a kind of dumb module with not much, if any, knowledge of signaling protocols such as ISDN and SS7.

```
Wanpipe Module (ftmod_wanpipe)
```

This is the IO module that is used to talk to Sangoma telephony cards.

```
ZapTel / DAHDI Module (ftmod_zt)
```

This is the IO module to talk to Zaptel and DAHDI-compatible telephony cards, such as those distributed by Sangoma, Xorcom, and Digium.

 The Sangoma line of cards can work with both the native ftmod_wanpipe and with this DAHDI interface module.

Signaling modules

FreeTDM supports a wide range of analog and TDM protocols. Even for the same protocol (for example, PRI) there are several modules that implement it, each with different strengths and weaknesses. The following is a list of the most commonly used modules.

ISDN signaling modules

ISDN is a protocol still widely used over T1/E1, and BRI telephone lines. FreeTDM supports several ISDN stacks, most of them open source. This is the list of the modules you may come across and a brief description of their use case.

```
Sangoma ISDN Module (ftmod_sangoma_isdn)
```

This module offers telco-grade signaling support for both PRI and BRI signaling; however, it is only usable if you have Sangoma cards with the native Sangoma IO module (ftmod_wanpipe). The module is open source, but relies on a closed source binary library that can be downloaded for free from the Sangoma website (more details about this later in this chapter). This stack is fully supported by Sangoma.

```
LibPRI Modules (ftmod_libpri)
```

This module offers integration with the open source libpri library to provide support for PRI and BRI signaling. This module offers community-based support. In order to get BRI support enabled you have to install a recent libpri version (it's best to install the latest available from the Asterisk downloads website: http://www.asterisk.org/downloads/libpri).

Analog modules

Analog modules offer integration with FXO/FXS and E&M lines. We will have a look at some of them here.

```
Analog Module (ftmod_analog)
```

This module offers generic FXS/FXO connectivity (these are the kind of landlines most people have at home in North and South America). These are strictly analog lines and use voltage changes to signal the start (and sometimes the end) of a call in addition to audio signals for notifications such as "ringing"or "disconnected".

```
Analog E&M Module (ftmod_analog_em)
```

This module currently only works with hardware that supports the DAHDI I/O module (ftmod_zt), and this includes Sangoma and Digium cards. Although this module is called "analog", in reality it currently works with E1/T1 digital lines using CASE&M signaling. In theory it should work with real analog E&M lines, if you find a piece of hardware that can do analog E&M signaling that is compatible with the ZapTel/DAHDI programming interface.

MFC-R2

The MFC-R2 protocol is still significantly used in countries like Mexico, Brazil, and some South American countries. This protocol runs on E1 lines and it's used for the same purposes PRI is used in North America. This is an older protocol though and offers more basic functionality.

```
OpenR2 Module (ftmod_r2)
```

This is the only module in FreeTDM currently implementing the MFC-R2 protocol. It requires the open source OpenR2 library (libopenr2.org) to be installed.

SS7

SS7 is really a suite of protocols, not a single protocol. In the scope of call control, the ISUP protocol is the one responsible for setting up and tearing down calls in an SS7 network.

```
SangomaSS7 (ftmod_sangoma_ss7)
```

The SangomaSS7 module is open source, but requires a closed source proprietary SS7 library licensed by Sangoma to be installed on the system. Although included with FreeTDM, Sangoma does not officially support standalone SS7 implementations and refers users to purchase the SangomaNSG (NetBorderSS7 Gateway) product, which uses FreeSWITCH as a base.

Cellular GSM / CDMA (ftmod_gsm)

You can connect to wireless networks using the ftmod_gsm module (which also supports some CDMA hardware). You will need the libwat (wireless AT) library and a supported hardware device like the SangomaW400 PCIe card.

FreeTDM installation

FreeTDM and its integration FreeSWITCH module, mod_freetdm, can be installed from several sources. The recommendation is to install it along with FreeSWITCH using the Linux distribution package installers.

Having said that, some FreeTDM modules may not be included in the packaged versions (for example, ftmod_r2) or you may be using an OS for which FreeSWITCH does not distribute binaries (for example, Arch Linux). In order to compile from sources you need to have previously installed the required dependencies. During build time the FreeTDM "configure" script will detect which libraries are available in your system and build only the modules that have their dependencies satisfied. The following is a list of dependencies you need to have installed on any of the listed modules. The FreeTDM core does not really depend on any libraries (any that are not shipped and built-in with it); it's only some of the signaling and IO modules that have dependencies on a number of libraries or kernel drivers.

Naturally, you will need a C and C++ compiler to build most of the FreeTDM software and its dependencies. Please refer to your Linux distribution instructions to install gcc, the recommended compiler to use. You will also need the "autotools" utilities. In Debian you can do:

```
# apt-get install build-essential
```

Wanpipe drivers

You want to install the Sangoma Wanpipe driver suite and libraries whenever you have a Sangoma card that you will use with FreeSWITCH. Even if you plan on using the DAHDI IO module (ftmod_zt) with your Sangoma card instead of the native ftmod_wanpipe, you still need the Sangoma Wanpipe suite installed.

 It's also worth noting that if you are on Windows, your only option at this point is Sangoma cards and Wanpipe, as none of the other IO drivers are supported under Windows.

You can download the latest Wanpipe from the Sangoma wiki: `http://wiki.sangoma.com/Wanpipe-Driver`

You will need to install the kernel headers for your Linux distribution and the "flex" package. In Debian you can do:

```
# apt-get install linux-headers-$(uname -r)
# apt-get install flex
```

Installing the Wanpipe drivers for FreeTDM is quite easy:

```
# wget ftp://ftp.sangoma.com/linux/current_wanpipe/wanpipe-current.tgz
# tar -xvzf wanpipe-current.tgz && cd wanpipe-*
# make freetdm && make install
```

DAHDI drivers

The DAHDI drivers (previously called ZapTel), can be used with any telephony hardware compatible with their interface. This includes devices from Sangoma, Xorcom, and Digium. If you have any such hardware you'll want to install the DAHDI drivers first. If you have Sangoma you can opt out from using DAHDI and use just the native ftmod_wanpipe module. There is one case, however, where you may want to use Sangoma with the DAHDI interface. That is when you want to use E&M signaling. The DAHDI drivers implement some E&M logic in the kernel that has not been implemented yet in the Wanpipe module and therefore you're better off using the DAHDI interface in that particular case.

 You can download the latest DAHDI version from the Asterisk project website: `http://www.asterisk.org/downloads/dahdi`

Note that FreeTDM always compiles the DAHDI module ftmod_zt even if you don't have the DAHDI drivers installed because FreeTDM includes its copy of the DAHDI C headers.

It's recommended that you install libnewt headers to be able to use the dahdi_tool utility to check for DAHDI span status.

```
# apt-get install libnewt-dev
```

You can then proceed to download and install the DAHDI drivers. Use the following commands:

```
# wget http://downloads.asterisk.org/pub/telephony/dahdi-linux-complete/
dahdi-linux-complete-current.tar.gz
# tar -xvzf dahdi-linux-complete-current.tar.gz
# cd dahdi-linux-complete-*
# make && make install
```

LibPRI

If you plan on using the ISDN module ftmod_libpri, you'll need the latest libpri version. You will find it in the Asterisk project website: http://www.asterisk.org/downloads/libpri

```
# wget http://downloads.asterisk.org/pub/telephony/libpri/libpri-1.4-
current.tar.gz
# tar -xvzf libpri-1.4-current.tar.gz
# cd libpri*
# make && make install
```

Sangoma ISDN stack

If you plan on using ISDN PRI or BRI with a Sangoma card you can also use libpri, but it's recommended you use the Sangoma ISDN stack instead as it's supported by Sangoma. You can download Sangoma's ISDN stack from here: http://wiki.sangoma.com/FreeTDM-Sangoma-ISDN-Library-Installation

Assuming you're on a 64-bit platform:

```
# wget ftp://ftp.sangoma.com/linux/libsng_isdn/libsng_isdn-current.
x86_64.tgz
# tar -xvzf libsng_isdn-current.x86_64.tgz
# cd libsng_isdn*
# make install
```

OpenR2

If you need MFC-R2 signaling support (ftmod_r2), then you'll need to install the openr2 stack: https://libopenr2.org/

You need to have cmake installed to build it.

```
# apt-get install cmake
# wget https://github.com/moises-silva/openr2/archive/master.zip
# unzip master.zip && cd openr2-master
# mkdir -p build && cd build
# cmake .. && make && make install
```

LibWAT

Using ftmod_gsm for GSM or CDMA signaling requires installing libwat. The wireless AT library is available from Sangoma's FTP. You need to have cmake installed to build it.

```
# apt-get install cmake
# wget ftp://ftp.sangoma.com/linux/libwat/libwat-2.1-current.tgz
# tar -xvzf libwat*
# cd libwat*
# cd build/ && cmake ../ && make install
```

Analog modules

The analog modules do not depend on any libraries beyond FreeTDM itself and at least one IO module.

Once you've installed all of your dependencies you can proceed to compile and install FreeTDM itself. Assuming you already have a copy of the FreeSWITCH git repository, you can do the following (assuming you installed freeswitch in /usr/local/freeswitch):

```
# cd libs/freetdm/
# ./configure -prefix=/usr/local/freeswitch
```

At the end of the execution of the configure script, you will see which FreeTDM modules will be built. That list is built depending on the dependencies that are installed and were detected by the configure script and by any command line options provided to the configure script. The libpri module is an exception and requires explicit specification even if the libpri library is installed. If you need the libpri module you must specify it explicitly.

```
# ./configure -prefix=/usr/local/freeswitch -with-libpri
```

Once the configure script finishes you can see the module summary as shown in the following screenshot:

```
============================ FreeTDM configuration ============================

+ Modules

  Signalling:
          ftmod_analog........................ yes
          ftmod_analog_em..................... yes
          ftmod_isdn.......................... no
          ftmod_libpri........................ yes
          ftmod_sangoma_isdn.................. yes
          ftmod_sangoma_ss7................... no
          ftmod_r2............................ yes
          ftmod_gsm........................... yes
          ftmod_pritap........................ no
  I/O:
          ftmod_zt............................ yes
          ftmod_wanpipe....................... yes
          ftmod_misdn......................... no

================================================================================

root@debian freetdm (v1.6)
```

Now you can type `make && make install` to compile and install the modules.

After compilation you can now install the mod_freetdmFreeSWITCH module.

```
# cd mod_freetdm/ && make install
```

At this point you're now ready to configure FreeTDM.

Configuring FreeTDM

Any system configuration is typically best built from the bottom up. This means starting with configuring the lower layers and moving your way up as you go. In order to interface with FreeTDM from FreeSWITCH you must configure several different components:

- Hardware devices (for example, Wanpipe or DAHDI configuration)
- The FreeTDM library
- The FreeSWITCH mod_freetdm endpoint configuration

Wanpipe

If you are using Wanpipe cards the first thing you want to do is configure your `/etc/wanpipeX.conf` devices. There are several ways of creating the configuration but the easiest one is to use the wancfg_fs script installed with Wanpipe. Just follow the interactive prompts.

You can then start each device with `wanrouter start`. This starts all devices and populates `/dev/wanpipe/` with a device for each channel (for example, for a T1 it will create `/dev/wanpipe1_if1` to `/dev/wanpipe1_if24`). A span and channel number physically identifies each device. This is important to keep in mind, as it will determine how each device is referenced in the FreeTDM configuration file later on.

For one T1ISDN configuration this is what `wanpipe1.conf` should look like:

```
[devices]
wanpipe1 = WAN_AFT_TE1, Comment

[interfaces]
w1g1 = wanpipe1, , TDM_VOICE_API, Comment

[wanpipe1]
CARD_TYPE            = AFT
S514CPU              = A
CommPort             = PRI
AUTO_PCISLOT         = NO
PCISLOT              = 0
PCIBUS               = 9
FE_MEDIA             = T1
FE_LCODE             = B8ZS
FE_FRAME             = ESF
FE_LINE              = 1
TE_CLOCK             = MASTER
TE_REF_CLOCK         = 0
TE_SIG_MODE          = CCS
TE_HIGHIMPEDANCE         = NO
TE_RX_SLEVEL         = 180
HW_RJ45_PORT_MAP = DEFAULT
LBO                  = 0DB
FE_TXTRISTATE        = NO
MTU                  = 1500
UDPPORT              = 9000
TTL                  = 255
IGNORE_FRONT_END         = NO
TDMV_SPAN                = 1
TDMV_DCHAN               = 24
TE_AIS_MAINTENANCE = NO
TDMV_HW_DTMF             = YES
TDMV_HW_FAX_DETECT       = YES
HWEC_OPERATION_MODE      = OCT_NORMAL
HWEC_DTMF_REMOVAL        = NO
HWEC_NOISE_REDUCTION     = NO
HWEC_ACUSTIC_ECHO        = NO
HWEC_NLP_DISABLE         = NO
HWEC_TX_AUTO_GAIN        = 0
HWEC_RX_AUTO_GAIN        = 0
HWEC_TX_GAIN             = 0
HWEC_RX_GAIN             = 0


[w1g1]
ACTIVE_CH            = ALL
TDMV_HWEC            = YES
MTU                  = 80
```

DAHDI

The DAHDI interface configuration is needed if you are using native DAHDI hardware devices (for example, from Digium or Xorcom), or if you want to use your Sangoma device in DAHDI mode. You have to configure the devices in `/etc/dahdi/system.conf`. Please refer to the sample configuration file installed at `/etc/dahdi/system.conf.sample` which comes with extensive documentation comments on how to configure different type of devices.

For one T1 ISDN configuration this is what `system.conf` should look like:

```
#Sangoma A104 port 1 [slot:0 bus:9 span:1] <wanpipe1>
span=1,1,0,esf,b8zs
bchan=1-23
hardhdlc=24
```

FreeTDM library configuration

The `freetdm.conf` file follows an INI-like format. Here you'll declare your Wanpipe or DAHDI devices (or any other hardware devices that are supported by FreeTDM).

The syntax rules for the files are:

- You can specify an optional [general] section for global configurations
- Span definitions are declared with [span <IO module type><span name>]
- Any channel declaration must be inside a span section
- The channel declaration must appear below the parameters it intends to use within that span
- Any lines starting with ";" or "#" will be ignored and treated as comments
- The ";" can be used for comments anywhere in the file (even inline comments)
- Both "=" and "=>" can be used to separate a parameter from its value

The first section in the file is for global definitions not related to a particular device. This section is not mandatory and can be completely omitted and defaults will be used for those settings. The defaults are safe and you only need to configure other values for advanced use cases. Refer to the sample configuration file in `conf/freetdm.conf.sample` for more information on other parameters. We will use some of those parameters in the *Debugging* section later in this chapter. The following sections in the file are span declarations with their parameters and channels specifications.

This is a pseudo-configuration to illustrate the general file format:

```
[general]
global_parameter => value

# Span comment here
[span<io module>< span name>]
; Inline comment here
parameter1 =>value1 ; Comment at the end of the line
parameter2 =>value2
<signaling>-channel =><channel device format>
```

For every [span] section above, you must specify the IO module that will control that span and the span name. These are some examples:

```
[spanwanpipetrunk1]
```

The span declaration above specifies a new span named `trunk1` (you can pick any name, no spaces allowed) that will be controlled by the "wanpipe" IO FreeTDM module.

```
[spanzttrunk2]
```

The span declaration above specifies a new span named `trunk2` that will be controlled by the "zt" IO FreeTDM module (for example, DAHDI devices).

Inside a span declaration the following are common valid parameters:

- `trunk_type`: This sets the trunk type for this span (for example, E1, T1, FXO, and FXS).
- `group`: This is just a group name that can be used later on to refer to multiple trunks as a group.
- `txgain` and `rxgain`: Audio gain for transmission and reception. Any float value is acceptable. Be aware that very big values can clip your audio. It's safe to omit this parameter; just no gain will be applied. Typical values range from -5.0 to 5.0.

In addition to these parameters, you must declare the channel devices for that span. The channel declaration format depends on the IO module type controlling that channel. The valid channel types are:

- b-channel: These are audio channels for ISDN and most non-analog trunks
- d-channel: These are data channels for ISDN and other non-analog trunks

- fxo-channel: These specify one or more analog FXO channels
- fxs-channel: These specify one or more analog FXS channels
- em-channel: These specify E&M signaling channels

This is what the span declaration for a WanpipeT1PRI looks like:

```
[spanwanpipetrunk1]
trunk_type =>T1
b-channel => 1:1-23
d-channel => 1:24
```

The channel declaration follows the format `<span>:<channel range>`. In this case it declares that trunk1 uses audio channels 1 to 23 from span 1 and that the data channel (HDLC for Q.931 PRI signaling) is on channel 24 of that same span (also called port in other documentation).

For a DAHDIT1 device, the declaration changes slightly:

```
[spanzttrunk1]
trunk_type =>T1
b-channel => 1-23
d-channel => 24
```

The first change is the IO type in the span is "zt" instead of "wanpipe". The second change is in the channel declaration. Because DAHDI uses an ever-increasing channel count, there is no need to specify the span number in the channel declaration. The second span for DAHDI would start at channel 25.

As you can see, most parameters are optional, the only mandatory parameters are the `trunk_type` and you must include the channel definitions for that type of span (for example, `d-channel`, `b-channel`). You can then start adding other parameters to adjust to your environment, such as the tx and rx gains. For example, if you feel the volume on your line is too low, you can increase the `rxgain` parameter:

```
[spanwanpipetrunk1]
trunk_type =>T1
rxgain =>3.5
b-channel => 1:1-23
d-channel => 1:24
```

Note that the `rxgain` parameter must be before the b-channel declaration otherwise it won't take effect in the voice channels. Because the gain parameter only applies to voice channels (b-channel, fxo-channel, and so on), it will be ignored for the d-channel declaration automatically.

FreeTDM configuration is as simple as that. Note we have not yet defined anything related to higher-level call control signaling such as PRI configuration settings. Call control signaling configuration is left to the application layer, in our case, that will be done by FreeSWITCH.

FreeSWITCH configuration

The mod_freetdm configuration is done in a FreeSWITCH configuration XML file located at `$prefix/conf/autload_configs/freetdm.conf.xml`. This file defines what devices FreeSWITCH will use from the set of FreeTDM configured devices and what signaling stacks will be set up for those devices. Most of the time those device definitions will match one to one the definitions in `freetdm.conf` (the number of devices defined in `freetdm.conf` will correspond to the number of devices defined in `freetdm.conf.xml`). However, you can have some devices defined in `freetdm.conf` but not in use in `freetdm.conf.xml`, but not the other way around.

The `freetdm.conf.xml` file is composed of a global `<settings>` XML section followed by multiple span definitions. The span definitions are declared inside an XML section for each signaling type. For example, analog spans are enclosed in a section called `<analog_spans>` and Sangoma PRI spans are enclosed in the `<sangoma_pri_span>` section. Please refer to the sample configuration file in the FreeSWITCH source directory at `libs/fretedm/conf/freetdm.conf.xml` for documentation in all the span types and their respective XML sections. Here we'll cover the basic Sangoma PRI configuration.

Inside each section, you can declare individual spans, like this:

```
<sangoma_pri_spans>
<span name="trunk1">
</span>
</sangoma_pri_spans>
```

Note the "name" attribute for the first `<span>` element. That name must match one of the span names you used in the `freetdm.conf` file. This is how you associate a particular physical device declared in `freetdm.conf` with the signaling configuration you're creating in `freetdm.conf.xml`.

All span signaling types accept the same `<span name="">` format. What follows inside the `<span>` definition is a series of `<param name= "p1" value= "val1" />` elements for each parameter. The parameter names depend on the signaling being configured (in this case the valid parameters will be those defined for the Sangoma PRI signaling module). Before we dig into the signaling-specific parameters, there are a few parameters that are common to all signaling stacks.

```
<param name="dialplan" value="XML" />
<param name="context" value="default" />
```

You may have seen those two parameters already in SIP profile configurations (sofia profiles). They determine where incoming calls will be routed to. All other parameters inside a `<span>` definition are specific to the signaling module you're configuring, and most of them are pushed down directly to the FreeTDM library to configure the signaling stack. Here is an example of a T1 PRI with a Sangoma ISDN stack:

```
<sangoma_pri_spans>
<span name="trunk1">
<param name="signalling" value="cpe" />
<param name="switchtype" value="national" />
<param name="dialplan" value="XML" />
<param name="context" value="default" />
</span>
</sangoma_pri_spans>
```

You can keep adding more <span> definitions as needed. There are a lot more parameters that can be configured for the Sangoma ISDN stack, but those four are the only ones that are mandatory. You can refer to the Sangoma ISDN stack documentation for more information on other available parameters. The sample configuration file shipped with FreeTDM also contains all of them with a brief explanation of what each parameter does.

At this point you're ready to load the mod_freetdm module. However, you may want to add mod_freetdm to `$prefix/conf/autoload_configs/modules.conf. xml` in order to have it loaded automatically when you restart FreeSWITCH. Having said that, you may want to load it manually while you get everything working at first. Loading it manually gives you the benefit of quickly seeing any errors during load time.

Operation

First you must load the mod_freetdm module. You can do this using the `load` command in fs_cli (the FreeSWITCH command line).

```
fs_cli> load mod_freetdm
```

You should see all spans getting started, with messages similar to this (note you may not see some if you do not enable FreeSWITCH debugging):

```
2016-01-31 16:31:58.576814 [INFO] ftdm_io.c:5523 Auto-loaded I/O module 'wanpipe'
2016-01-31 16:31:58.576814 [DEBUG] ftdm_io.c:5197 created span 1 (trunk1) of type wanpipe
2016-01-31 16:31:58.576814 [DEBUG] ftdm_io.c:5215 span 1 [trunk_type]=[T1]
2016-01-31 16:31:58.576814 [DEBUG] ftdm_io.c:5220 setting trunk type to 'T1'
2016-01-31 16:31:58.576814 [DEBUG] ftdm_io.c:5215 span 1 [b-channel]=[1:1-23]
2016-01-31 16:31:58.576814 [INFO] ftmod_wanpipe.c:423 [s1c1][1:1] Configured wanpipe device FD: 57, DTMF: hardware, HWEC: available, HWEC_IDLE: enabled
2016-01-31 16:31:58.576814 [INFO] ftmod_wanpipe.c:423 [s1c2][1:2] Configured wanpipe device FD: 68, DTMF: hardware, HWEC: available, HWEC_IDLE: enabled
2016-01-31 16:31:58.576814 [INFO] ftmod_wanpipe.c:423 [s1c3][1:3] Configured wanpipe device FD: 71, DTMF: hardware, HWEC: available, HWEC_IDLE: enabled
2016-01-31 16:31:58.576814 [INFO] ftmod_wanpipe.c:423 [s1c4][1:4] Configured wanpipe device FD: 74, DTMF: hardware, HWEC: available, HWEC_IDLE: enabled
2016-01-31 16:31:58.576814 [INFO] ftmod_wanpipe.c:423 [s1c5][1:5] Configured wanpipe device FD: 77, DTMF: hardware, HWEC: available, HWEC_IDLE: enabled
2016-01-31 16:31:58.576814 [INFO] ftmod_wanpipe.c:423 [s1c6][1:6] Configured wanpipe device FD: 80, DTMF: hardware, HWEC: available, HWEC_IDLE: enabled
2016-01-31 16:31:58.576814 [INFO] ftmod_wanpipe.c:423 [s1c7][1:7] Configured wanpipe device FD: 83, DTMF: hardware, HWEC: available, HWEC_IDLE: enabled
2016-01-31 16:31:58.576814 [INFO] ftmod_wanpipe.c:423 [s1c8][1:8] Configured wanpipe device FD: 86, DTMF: hardware, HWEC: available, HWEC_IDLE: enabled
2016-01-31 16:31:58.576814 [INFO] ftmod_wanpipe.c:423 [s1c9][1:9] Configured wanpipe device FD: 89, DTMF: hardware, HWEC: available, HWEC_IDLE: enabled
2016-01-31 16:31:58.576814 [INFO] ftmod_wanpipe.c:423 [s1c10][1:10] Configured wanpipe device FD: 92, DTMF: hardware, HWEC: available, HWEC_IDLE: enabled
2016-01-31 16:31:58.576814 [INFO] ftmod_wanpipe.c:423 [s1c11][1:11] Configured wanpipe device FD: 95, DTMF: hardware, HWEC: available, HWEC_IDLE: enabled
2016-01-31 16:31:58.576814 [INFO] ftmod_wanpipe.c:423 [s1c12][1:12] Configured wanpipe device FD: 98, DTMF: hardware, HWEC: available, HWEC_IDLE: enabled
2016-01-31 16:31:58.576814 [INFO] ftmod_wanpipe.c:423 [s1c13][1:13] Configured wanpipe device FD: 101, DTMF: hardware, HWEC: available, HWEC_IDLE: enabled
2016-01-31 16:31:58.576814 [INFO] ftmod_wanpipe.c:423 [s1c14][1:14] Configured wanpipe device FD: 104, DTMF: hardware, HWEC: available, HWEC_IDLE: enabled
2016-01-31 16:31:58.576814 [INFO] ftmod_wanpipe.c:423 [s1c15][1:15] Configured wanpipe device FD: 107, DTMF: hardware, HWEC: available, HWEC_IDLE: enabled
2016-01-31 16:31:58.576814 [INFO] ftmod_wanpipe.c:423 [s1c16][1:16] Configured wanpipe device FD: 110, DTMF: hardware, HWEC: available, HWEC_IDLE: enabled
2016-01-31 16:31:58.576814 [INFO] ftmod_wanpipe.c:423 [s1c17][1:17] Configured wanpipe device FD: 113, DTMF: hardware, HWEC: available, HWEC_IDLE: enabled
2016-01-31 16:31:58.576814 [INFO] ftmod_wanpipe.c:423 [s1c18][1:18] Configured wanpipe device FD: 116, DTMF: hardware, HWEC: available, HWEC_IDLE: enabled
2016-01-31 16:31:58.576814 [INFO] ftmod_wanpipe.c:423 [s1c19][1:19] Configured wanpipe device FD: 119, DTMF: hardware, HWEC: available, HWEC_IDLE: enabled
2016-01-31 16:31:58.576814 [INFO] ftmod_wanpipe.c:423 [s1c20][1:20] Configured wanpipe device FD: 122, DTMF: hardware, HWEC: available, HWEC_IDLE: enabled
2016-01-31 16:31:58.576814 [INFO] ftmod_wanpipe.c:423 [s1c21][1:21] Configured wanpipe device FD: 125, DTMF: hardware, HWEC: available, HWEC_IDLE: enabled
2016-01-31 16:31:58.576814 [INFO] ftmod_wanpipe.c:423 [s1c22][1:22] Configured wanpipe device FD: 128, DTMF: hardware, HWEC: available, HWEC_IDLE: enabled
2016-01-31 16:31:58.576814 [INFO] ftmod_wanpipe.c:423 [s1c23][1:23] Configured wanpipe device FD: 131, DTMF: hardware, HWEC: available, HWEC_IDLE: enabled
```

From the FreeSWITCH command line (fs_cli) you can type `ftdm` to display the help.

```
freeswitch@internal> ftdm
USAGE:
--------------------------------------------------------------------
ftdm list
ftdm start <span_id|span_name>
ftdm stop <span_id|span_name>
ftdm reset <span_id|span_name> [<chan_id>]
ftdm alarms <span_id> <chan_id>
ftdm dump <span_id|span_name> [<chan_id>]
ftdm sigstatus get|set <span_id|span_name> [<chan_id>] [<sigstatus>]
ftdm trace <path> <span_id|span_name> [<chan_id>]
ftdm notrace <span_id|span_name> [<chan_id>]
ftdm gains <rxgain> <txgain> <span_id|span_name> [<chan_id>]
ftdm dtmf on|off <span_id|span_name> [<chan_id>]
ftdm queuesize <rxsize> <txsize> <span_id|span_name> [<chan_id>]
ftdm iostats enable|disable|flush|print <span_id|span_name> <chan_id>
ftdm ioread <span_id|span_name> <chan_id> [num_times] [interval]
ftdm cas read|write <span_id|span_name> [<chan_id>] [<write_bits>]
ftdm core state [!]<state_name>
ftdm core flag [!]<flag-int-value|flag-name> [<span_id|span_name>] [<chan_id>]
ftdm core spanflag [!]<flag-int-value|flag-name> [<span_id|span_name>]
ftdm core calls
--------------------------------------------------------------------
```

If instead of the preceding output you see something like `-ERR ftdm Command not found!`, then it means your mod_freetdm module was not loaded.

You can then use the `ftdm list` command to check the status of each span:

```
freeswitch@internal> ftdm list
+OK
span: 1 (trunk1)
type: Sangoma (ISDN)
physical_status: ok
signaling_status: UP
chan_count: 24
dialplan: XML
context: default
dial_regex:
fail_dial_regex:
hold_music:
analog_options: none
+OK
span: 2 (trunk2)
type: Sangoma (ISDN)
physical_status: ok
signaling_status: UP
chan_count: 24
dialplan: XML
context: default
dial_regex:
fail_dial_regex:
hold_music:
analog_options: none
```

A few important fields to look at are:

- `physical_status`: This tells you if the physical layer is OK or alarmed
- `signaling_status`: This tells you if the signaling is up
- `context`: This tells you where the calls will be routed to when coming into this span

In the example above, there are two spans, and both have signaling status down, but the physical status is up, so we know the problem is in the signaling configuration.

Each type of signaling has a set of commands not shown in the `ftdm help` output. You can type `ftdm <signaling_module>` to see the help of that particular signaling type as shown in the following screenshot:

```
freeswitch@internal> ftdm sangoma_isdn
Invalid arguments ☐
Usage:
        ftdm sangoma_isdn trace <q921|q931> <span name>
        ftdm sangoma_isdn l1_stats <span name>
        ftdm sangoma_isdn show_spans [<span name>]
```

The Sangoma ISDN stack commands can show you much more detailed information about the signaling status. For example, to see very detailed layer 1 signaling status on trunk1 you can use `ftdm sangoma_isdn l1_stats trunk1`.

Your output will be as shown in the following screenshot:

```
freeswitch@internal> ftdm sangoma_isdn l1_stats trunk1


    Span:trunk1


    Performance Counters

RX Packets:      0      TX Packets:      0      Events:0
RX Bytes:        0      TX Bytes:        0

TX Queue:        0/0    RX Queue:        0/0    Events Queue:    0/0


    Errors

RX Errors:       0      TX Errors:       0
RX Dropped:      0      TX Dropped:      0      Events Dropped: 0


    RX Errors Details

CRC:             0      Frame:           0      Overruns:       0
Fifo:            0      Aborts:          0      Missed:         0
Length:          0


    TX Errors Details

Aborted:         0      Fifo:            0      Carrier:        0
Command executed OK
```

Outbound calls

Once you have your FreeTDM spans up and running you can start to originate or receive calls. Routing calls from the SIP network to the PSTN network is a common use case for FreeTDM (FreeSWITCH then becomes a PSTN gateway). You should be already familiar with the "bridge" FreeSWITCH application that is used to bridge channels. You can use this same application to bridge to FreeTDM channels. The bridging syntax is as follows:

```
<action application="bridge" data="freetdm/<span number/name|group
name>/<channel number|huntingselector>[/destination number]" />
```

With the exception of FXS analog spans, pretty much all types of spans require you to provide the destination number to dial. Here is an example of how to dial using our configured `trunk1` span.

```
<actionapplication="bridge" data="freetdm/trunk1/1/${destination_
number}" />
```

The action above will use channel 1 of trunk1 to dial to the number specified by the `destination_number` channel variable. In most circumstances however you don't want to specify a specific channel number, but rather let the system select the first available channel using a hunting strategy. Let's pick the first available channel in trunk1 starting from the bottom up.

```
<action application="bridge" data="freetdm/trunk1/a/${destination_
number}" />
```

We replaced the channel number 1 for the letter `a` (available) to indicate we want any available channel starting from the first channel defined in the span and working our way up until one available channel is found. You could use upper case `A` to start your search for an available channel from top to bottom.

There are other hunting strategies, each identified by a letter:

- `a`: Start hunting from the bottom
- `A`: Start hunting from the top
- `r`: Round robin from the bottom
- `R`: Round robin from the top

You can use also span groups to hunt for an available channel across spans. This is useful when you have many spans and you want a group of them for outbound dialing, failing over in case one of the spans goes into an alarmed state (the hunting strategy skips alarmed spans as unavailable).

First, you must configure a group in `freetdm.conf` for every span.

```
[spanwanpipetrunk1]
group => outbound
b-channel => 1:1-23
d-channel => 1:24

[spanwanpipetrunk1]
group => outbound
b-channel => 2:1-23
d-channel => 2:24
```

Now you can use the outbound group to select any channel either on trunk1 or trunk2 spans.

```
<action application="bridge" data="freetdm/outbound/a/${destination_
number}" />
```

We replace the span name for a group name. This means that span names and group names share the same name space when dialing. It's recommended to avoid picking the same names for your groups and spans.

When making a call you can also override some parameters (depending on the signaling stack). For ISDN, for example, you can set a few variables in the channel to override protocol values. For example:

```
<action application="export" data="freetdm_outbound_ton=reserved" />
<action application="bridge" data="freetdm/outbound/a/${destination_
number}" />
```

The preceding `export` action will set the outbound type of number for this particular call.

Inbound calls

For inbound calls you can follow the usual FreeSWITCH routing and send them an IVR, Conference, the SIP network, FreeTDM spans, or any other supported endpoint.

It's worth noting that you will also see many inbound channel variables prefixed with `freetdm_` that you can use for routing, billing, or any other purpose you see fit. The following screenshot is an example of the list of variables you will see (some of them will depend on the signaling type and on whether the values were provided by the other end of the call).

```
variable_channel_name: FreeTDM/2%3A1/9198
variable_freetdm_span_name: trunk2
variable_freetdm_span_number: 2
variable_freetdm_chan_number: 1
variable_freetdm_bearer_capability: 0
variable_freetdm_bearer_layer1: 2
variable_freetdm_calling_party_category: unknown
variable_screening_ind: user-provided-not-screened
variable_presentation_ind: presentation-allowed
```

Debugging

Things always go wrong. With so many moving parts and different complex protocols and configurations it's expected mistakes will be made at some point. You may provide invalid configuration, the software may have a bug, the remote equipment may be misbehaving, and so on. You need to be prepared to deal with all those problems. Debugging a problem is often a matter of working your way up, verifying that each hardware or software layer is working as expected, until you find the layer that is not doing its job. The first layer to check is the physical layer. For T1/E1 lines, verify there are no alarms and the port is in the Connected status (for Sangoma cards) or OK for DAHDI (use the DAHDI tool application).

Checking the physical layer

Run the following command:

```
# wanpipemon -i w1g1 -c Ta
```

This command will check physical alarms on span number 1 (you can just increase the first number for span 2, for example, w2g1).

```
# wanpipemon -i w2g1 -c Ta

***** w2g1: T1 Rx Alarms (Framer) *****

ALOS:    OFF      | LOS:  OFF
RED:     OFF      | AIS:  OFF
LOF:     OFF      | RAI:  OFF

***** w2g1: T1 Rx Alarms (LIU) *****

Short Circuit:  OFF
Open Circuit:   OFF
Loss of Signal: OFF

***** w2g1: T1 Tx Alarms *****

AIS:     OFF      | YEL:  OFF


***** w2g1: T1 Performance Monitoring Counters *****

Line Code Violation     : 0
Bit Errors (CRC6/Ft/Fs) : 0
Out of Frame Errors     : 0
Sync Errors             : 0


Rx Level        : > -2.5db
```

This very detailed output shows alarms in the framer (the hardware responsible for splitting T1/E1 frames) and the LIU (the line interface unit-the hardware responsible for receiving the analog signals from the wire).

 You can find more detailed information in Sangoma documentation: http://wiki.sangoma.com/Wanpipemon-T1-E1-physical-Line-alarms

If you are using DAHDI hardware, you cannot get that detailed view, but you can still see traditional alarms (red, yellow, blue, and so on) using the "dahdi_tool" command.

Enabling ISDN tracing

If your physical layer doesn't show any errors, the next step is to try to troubleshoot the signaling protocol layer. If you are using ISDN this means Q.921 and Q.931 debugging.

To verify your Q.921 layer is working you can enable Sangoma Q.921 tracing with `ftdm sangoma_isdn trace q921 trunk1` (note the trunk name at the end, you need to adjust this to your own trunk name):

```
freeswitch@internal> ftdm sangoma_isdn trace q921 trunk1
Command executed OK

2016-01-31 18:24:16.210098 [INFO] ftmod_sangoma_isdn_stack_cntrl.c:261 trunk1:Enabling q921 trace
freeswitch@internal> freeswitch@internal>
freeswitch@internal>
2016-01-31 18:24:22.810098 [DEBUG] ftmod_sangoma_isdn_trace.c:117 [SNGISDN Q921] trunk1 FRAME OUTGOING:
  format: Supervisory
  sapi: 000  c/r: 1  ea: 0
   tei: 000         ea: 1
  n(r): 001  p/f: 1
   cmd: RR - receive ready
  [ 02 01 01 03 ]

2016-01-31 18:24:22.810098 [DEBUG] ftmod_sangoma_isdn_trace.c:117 [SNGISDN Q921] trunk1 FRAME INCOMING:
  format: Supervisory
  sapi: 000  c/r: 0  ea: 0
   tei: 000         ea: 1
  n(r): 001  p/f: 1
   cmd: RR - receive ready
  [ 00 01 01 03 ]

2016-01-31 18:24:22.810098 [DEBUG] ftmod_sangoma_isdn_trace.c:117 [SNGISDN Q921] trunk1 FRAME OUTGOING:
  format: Supervisory
  sapi: 000  c/r: 0  ea: 0
   tei: 000         ea: 1
  n(r): 001  p/f: 1
   cmd: RR - receive ready
  [ 00 01 01 03 ]

2016-01-31 18:24:22.810098 [DEBUG] ftmod_sangoma_isdn_trace.c:117 [SNGISDN Q921] trunk1 FRAME INCOMING:
  format: Supervisory
  sapi: 000  c/r: 1  ea: 0
   tei: 000         ea: 1
  n(r): 001  p/f: 1
   cmd: RR - receive ready
  [ 02 01 01 03 ]
```

You should be seeing those "Receive Ready" frames coming and going. If you don't see them coming (FRAME INCOMING) then the other end has a problem. Those frames are sent/received every 10 seconds approximately. When your signaling status is not "Up" in the output of `ftdm list` it's usually because of physical alarms or a problem in the ISDN configuration that prevents Q.921 from bringing the link up (for example, both sides configured as net or cpe).

For call problems (for example, your link is up but calls fail) you want to enable Q.931 tracing using `ftdm sangoma_isdn trace q931 trunk1`. Then place a call. If no calls are being placed you won't see anything. Q.931 takes care of sending and receiving calls.

You will see all Q.931 messages. This is a SETUP message used to prepare an outbound call as shown in the following screenshot:

```
2016-01-31 18:33:29.850099 [INFO] ftmod_sangoma_isdn_stack_out.c:62 [s1c1][1:1] Outgoing call: Called No:[9198] Calling No:[]
2016-01-31 18:33:29.850099 [INFO] ftmod_sangoma_isdn_stack_out.c:79 [s1c1][1:1] Sending SETUP (suId:1 suInstId:3 spInstId:0 dchan:1 ces:0)
2016-01-31 18:33:29.850099 [DEBUG] ftmod_sangoma_isdn.c:923 [s1c1][1:1] Completed state change from DOWN to DIALING in 0 ms
2016-01-31 18:33:29.850099 [DEBUG] mod_freetdm.c:2705 got clear channel sig [DIALING]
2016-01-31 18:33:29.850099 [DEBUG] switch_core_state_machine.c:473 (FreeTDM/1:1/9198) Running State Change CS_INIT
2016-01-31 18:33:29.850099 [DEBUG] ftmod_sangoma_isdn_trace.c:224 [SNGISDN Q931] trunk1 FRAME OUTGOING:
  Prot Disc:Q.931/I.451 (0x08)
  Call Ref:0002 (Originating side)
  Type:SETUP (0x5)
  Bearer Capability:Coding:ITU-T(0) TransferCap:Speech(0) TransferRate:64 Kbit/s(16) L1Prot:G.711 u-Law(2)
  Channel Id:No:1 Type:B-chans(3)  Exclusive/Implicit
  Called Party Number:9198(1:4) plan:isdn(1) type:national(2)
  [ 08 02 00 02 05 04 03 80 90 a2 18 03 a9 83 81 70 05 a1 39 31 39 38 ]
```

The response coming back from the other end is shown in the following screenshot:

```
2016-01-31 18:33:29.870112 [DEBUG] ftmod_sangoma_isdn_trace.c:224 [SNGISDN Q931] trunk1 FRAME INCOMING:
  Prot Disc:Q.931/I.451 (0x08)
  Call Ref:0002 (Destination side)
  Type:PROCEED (0x2)
  Channel Id:No:1 Type:B-chans(3)  Exclusive/Implicit
  [ 08 02 80 02 02 18 03 a9 83 81 ]

2016-01-31 18:33:29.870112 [INFO] ftmod_sangoma_isdn_stack_rcv.c:194 [s1c1][1:1] Received PROCEED (suId:1 suInstId:3 spInstId:3 ces:0)
2016-01-31 18:33:29.870112 [DEBUG] ftmod_sangoma_isdn_stack_hndl.c:391 [s1c1][1:1] Processing PROCEED (suId:1 suInstId:3 spInstId:3 ces:0)
2016-01-31 18:33:29.870112 [DEBUG] ftmod_sangoma_isdn_stack_hndl.c:425 [s1c1][1:1] Early media not available
2016-01-31 18:33:29.870112 [DEBUG] ftmod_sangoma_isdn_stack_hndl.c:436 [s1c1][1:1] Changed state from DIALING to PROCEED
```

These messages should allow you to determine what the problem is or at least share them with your service provider.

Audio tracing

Another useful debugging feature is tracing the raw audio at the FreeTDM layer. With this type of tracing you can determine if bad audio comes right from the physical layer or is something that FreeSWITCH is somehow introducing. Whenever you have a no audio situation this command might prove useful. Try typing `ftdm trace` as shown in the following screenshot:

```
freeswitch@internal> ftdm trace
-ERR Usage: ftdm trace <path> <span_id|span_name> [<chan_id>]

freeswitch@internal>
```

The command takes a `<path>` argument, a `<span id or name>`, and optionally a channel ID. The path argument is a directory that will be used to store the recordings. If no channel is specified then all channels in the span will be recorded. For each channel, two recording files will be saved, one for incoming audio, the other for outgoing audio as shown in the following screenshot:

```
freeswitch@internal> ftdm trace /tmp/recordings/span trunk1 1
+OK trace enabled with prefix path /tmp/recordings/span

2016-01-31 23:58:41.761831 [DEBUG] ftdm_io.c:3142 [s1c1][1:1] Tracing input to [/tmp/recordings/span-in-s1c1]
2016-01-31 23:58:41.761831 [DEBUG] ftdm_io.c:3158 Tracing channel 1:1 output to [/tmp/recordings/span-out-s1c1]
```

The audio tracing is permanent until explicitly disabled, so if you place multiple calls all the audio is stored in the same files. You can stop the trace with `ftdm notrace` as shown in the following screenshot:

```
freeswitch@internal> ftdm notrace trunk1 1
+OK trace disabled
```

Once disabled, you can open the files in audacity (`http://www.audacityteam.org/`). Because this is unformatted raw audio taken from the line, you have to import the files using the format of your channel. If you are using a T1 line, the format is ulaw at 8kHz sampling rate. If you are using an E1 line, then the format is alaw at 8kHz sampling rate.

> More information about configuring and debugging FreeTDM in FreeSWITCH can be found in the confluence wiki:
> `https://freeswitch.org/confluence/display/FREESWITCH/FreeTDM`

Summary

In this chapter we saw all that's related to interfacing FreeSWITCH directly to PSTN, both for originating and for terminating calls.

First of all we made a tribute to one of Jim Dixon's great contributions to Open Source - Open Hardware Telecommunication, the Zapata Telephony project.

We found out how to configure the FreeTDM library and module for FreeSWITCH usage, how to interact with DAHDI drivers, and how to install Sangoma libraries (Sangoma being a major corporate sponsor of FreeTDM).

We covered all of the many different current and legacy protocols for PRI, FXO/FXS, trunking, and so on.

We then delved into practical usage in the FreeSWITCH operation, both dialplan and debugging troubleshooting levels.

That's really all you may possibly want to know about PSTN and TDM.

7
WebRTC and Mod_Verto

WebRTC is all the rage these days. And with a cause! Maybe you end up buying this book just to know how you can release your existing services to hundreds of millions of browsers out there, or maybe you want to start coding the next killer app from scratch.

Anyway, you're on the right path; read on. You'll find both the needed theory and real world implementation examples.

In this chapter we will cover:

- What WebRTC is and how it works
- Encryption and NAT traversing (STUN, TURN, etc)
- Signaling and media
- Interconnection with PSTN and SIP networks
- FreeSWITCH as a WebRTC server, gateway, and application server
- SIP signaling clients with JavaScript (SIP.js)
- Verto signaling clients with JavaScript (mod_verto, verto.js)

WebRTC

Finally something new! How refreshing it is to be learning and experimenting again, especially if you're an old hand! After at least ten years of linear evolution, here we are with a quantum leap, the black swan that truly disrupts the communication sector.

Browsers are already out there, waitin'

With an installed base of hundreds of millions, and soon to be in the billions ballpark, browsers (both on PCs and on smart phones) are now complete communication terminals, audio/video endpoints that do not need any additional software, plugins, hardware, or whatever. Browsers now incorporate, per default and in a standard way, all the software needed to interact with loudspeakers, microphones, headsets, cameras, screens, etc.

Browsers are the new endpoints, the CPEs, the phones. They have an API, they're updated automatically, and are compatible with your system. You don't have to procure, configure, support, or upgrade them. They're ready for your new service; they just work, and are waiting for your business.

Audio and Video Communication in the browser

Web Real-Time Communication is coming

There are two completely separated flows in communication: Signaling and media. Signaling is a flow of information that defines who is calling whom, taking what paths, and which technology is used to transmit which content. Media is the actual digitized content of the communication, for example, audio, video, screen-sharing, etc.

Media and signaling often take completely unrelated paths to go from caller to callee, for example, their IP packets traverse different gateways and routers. Also, the two flows are managed by separate software (or by different parts of the same application) using different protocols.

WebRTC defines how a browser accesses its own media capture, how it sends and receives media from a peer through the network and how it renders the media stream that it receives. It represents this using the same **Session Description Protocol (SDP)** as SIP does.

So, WebRTC is all about media, and doesn't prescribe a signaling system. This is a design decision, embedded in the standard definition. Popular signaling systems include SIP, XMPP, and proprietary or custom protocols. Also, WebRTC is all about encryption. All WebRTC media streams are mandatorily encrypted.

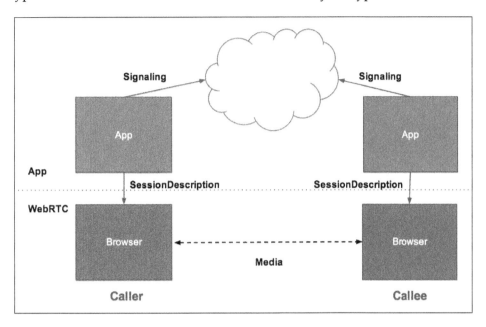

Chrome, Firefox, and Opera (together they account for more than 70 percent of the browsers in use) already implement the standard; Edge is announcing the first steps in supporting WebRTC basic features, while only Safari is still holding its cards (Skype and FaceTime on WebRTC with proprietary signaling? Wink wink).

Under the hood

More or less, WebRTC works like this:

1. Browser connects to a web server and loads a webpage with some JavaScript in it.

2. JavaScript in the webpage takes control of the browser's media interfaces (microphone, camera, speakers, and so on), resulting in an API media object.

3. The WebRTC Api Media object will contain the capabilities of all devices and codecs available, for example, definition, sample rate, and so on, and it will permit the user to choose their own capabilities preferences (for example, use QVGA video to minimize CPU and bandwidth).

4. Webpage will interface with the browser's user, getting some input for signing in the webserver's communication service (if any).

5. JavaScript will use whatever signaling method (SIP, XMPP, proprietary, custom) over encrypted secure websocket (wss://) for signing in the communication service, finding peers, originating and receiving calls.

6. Once signed up in the service, a call can be made and received. Signaling will give the protocol address of the peer (for example, sip:gmaruzz@ opentelecom.it).

These points are represented in the following image:

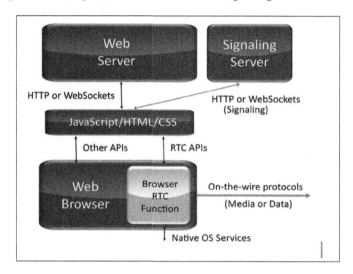

7. Now is the moment to find out actual IP addresses. JavaScript will generate a WebRTC API object for finding its own IP addresses, transports and ports (ICE candidates) to be offered to peer for exchanging media (JavaScript WebRTC API will use ICE, STUN, TURN, and will send to peer its own local LAN address, its own public IP address, and maybe the IP address of a TURN server it can use).

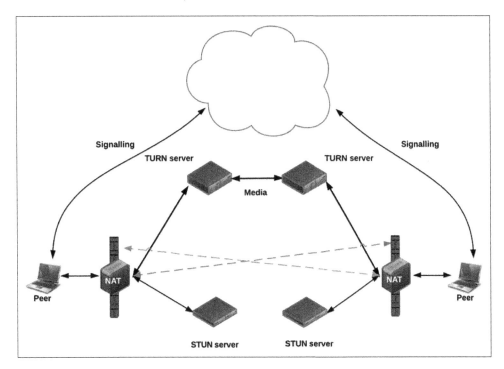

8. Then, WebRTC Net API will exchange ICE candidates with the peer, until they both find the most "rational" triplets of IP address, port and transport (udp, dtls, and so on), for each stream (for example, audio, video, screen share, and so on).

9. Once they get the best addresses, the signaling will establish the call.

These points are represented in the following image:

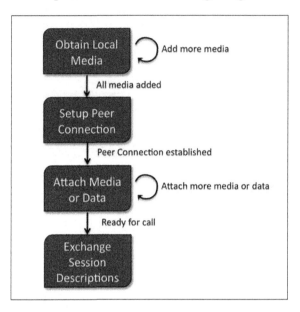

10. Once signaling communication with the peer is established, media capabilities are exchanged in SDP format (exactly as in SIP), and the two peers agree on media formats (sample rates, codecs, and so on).

11. When media formats are agreed, JavaScript WebRTC Transport API will use secure (encrypted) websockets (wss://) as transport for media and data.

12. JavaScript WebRTC Media API will be used to render the media streams received (for example, render video, play sound, capture microphone, and so on).

13. Additionally or in alternative to media, peers can establish one or more data channels, through which they bidirectionally exchange raw or structured data (file transfers, augmented reality, stock tickers, and so on).

14. At hangup, signaling will tear down the call, and JavaScript WebRTC Media API will be used to shut down streams and renderings.

These points are represented in the following image:

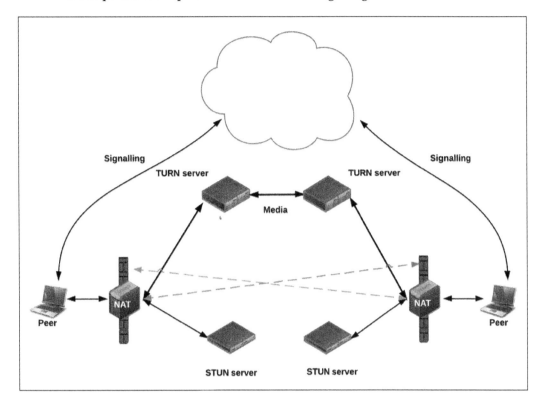

This is a high level, but complete, view of how a WebRTC system works:

Encryption – security

Please note that in normal operation everything is encrypted, uses real PKI certificates from real Certification Authorities, actual DNS names, SSL, TLS, HTTPS, WSS, DTLS-SRTP. This is how it is supposed to work. In WebRTC, security is not an afterthought: It is mandatory.

To make signaling work without encryption (for example, for debugging signaling protocols) is not so easy, but it is possible. Browsers will often raise security exceptions, and will ask for permission each time they access a camera or microphone. Some hiccups will happen, but it is doable. Signaling is not part of WebRTC standard, as you know.

On the contrary, it is not possible to have the media or data streams leave the browser in the clear, without encryption.

The use of plain RTP to transmit media is explicitly forbidden by the standard. Media is transmitted by SRTP (Secure RTP), where encryption keys are pre-exchanged via DTLS (Datagram Transport Layer Security, a version of TLS for Datagrams), basically a secure version of UDP.

Beyond peer to peer – WebRTC to communication networks and services

WebRTC is a technique for browsers to send media to each other via Internet, peer to peer, perhaps with the help of a relay server (TURN), if they can't reach each other directly.

That's it.

No directories, no means to find another person, and also no way to "call" that person if we know "where" to call her.

No way to transfer calls, to react to a busy user or to a user that does not pickup, and so on.

Let's say WebRTC is a half-built phone: It has the handset, complete with working microphone and speaker, from which it comes out, the wiring left loose. You can cross join that wiring with the wiring of another half-built phone, and they can talk to each other.

Then, if you want to talk to another device, you must find it and then join the wires anew.

No dial pad, no Telecom Central Office, no interconnection between Local Carriers, and with International Carriers. No PBX. No way to call your grandma, and no possibilities to navigate the IVR at Federal Express' Customer Care.

We need to integrate the media capabilities and the ubiquity of WebRTC with the world of telecommunication services that constitute the planet's nervous system.

Enter the "WebRTC Gateway" and the "WebRTC Application Server"; in our case both are embodied by FreeSWITCH

WebRTC gateways and application servers

The problem to be solved is: We can implement some kind of signaling plane, even implement a complete SIP signaling stack in JavaScript (there are some very good ones in open source, we'll see later), but then both at the network and at the media plane, WebRTC is only "kind of" compatible with the existing telecommunication world; it uses techniques and concepts that are "similar", and protocols that are mostly an "evolution " of those implemented in usual Voice over IP.

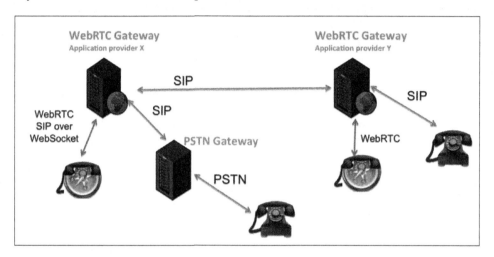

At the network plane, WebRTC uses the ICE protocol to traverse NAT via STUN and TURN servers. ICE has been developed as Internet standard to be the ultimate tool to solve all NAT problems, but has not yet been implemented in either telco infrastructure, nor in most VoIP clients. Also, ICE candidates (the various different addresses the browser thinks they would be reachable at) need to be passed in SDP and negotiated between peers, in the same way codecs are negotiated. Being able to pass through corporate firewalls (UDP blocked, TCP open only on ports 80 and 443, and perhaps through protocol-aware proxies) is an absolute necessity for serious WebRTC deployment.

At media plane, WebRTC specific codecs (V8 for video and Opus for audio) are incompatible with the telco world, with audio G711 as the only common denominator.

Worse yet, all media are encrypted as SRTP with DTLS key exchange, and that's unheard of in today's telco infrastructure.

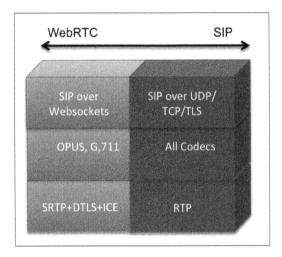

So, we need to create the signaling plane, and then convert the network transport, convert the codecs, manage the ICE candidates selection in SDP, and allow access to the wealth of ready-made services (PSTN calls, IVRs, PBXs, conference rooms, etc), and then complement the legacy services with special features and new interconnected services enabled by the unique capabilities of WebRTC endpoints.

Yeah, that's a job for FreeSWITCH.

Which architecture? Legacy on the Web, or Web on the Telco?

Real-time communication via the Web: From the building blocks we just saw, we can implement it in many ways.

We have one degree of freedom: Signaling. I mean, media will be anyway agreed upon via SDP, transmitted via websockets as SRTP packets, and encrypted via DTLS key exchange.

We still have the task of choosing how we find the peer to exchange media with. So, this is an exercise in directory, location, registration, routing, presence, status, etc. You get the idea.

So, at the end of the day you need to come out with a JavaScript library to implement your signaling on the browsers, commanding their underlying mechanisms (Comet, Websockets, WebRTC Data Channel) to find your beloved communication peer.

Actually it boils down to different possibilities:

- SIP
- XMPP (eg: jabber)
- In-house signaling implementation
- VERTO (open source)

SIP and XMPP make today's world spin around. SIP is mostly known for carrying the majority of telephone and VoIP signaling traffic. The biggest implementations of instant messaging and chatting are based on XMPP. And there is more: Those two signaling protocols are often used together, although each one of them has extensions that provide the other one's functionality.

Both SIP and XMPP have been designed to be expandable and modular, and SIP particularly is an abstract protocol, for the management of "sessions" (where a "session" can be whatever has a beginning and an end in time, as a voice or video call, a screen share, a whiteboard, a collaboration platform, a payment, a message, and so on).

Both have robust JavaScript implementations available (for SIP check SIP.js, JsSIP, SIPML, while for XMPP check Strophe, stanza.io, jingle.js).

If your company has considerable investments and/or expertise in those protocols, then it makes sense to expand their usage on the web too.

If you're running Skype, or similar services, you may find it an attractive option to maintain your proprietary, closed-signaling protocol and implement it in JavaScript, so you can expand your service reach to browsers and exploit those common transport and media technologies.

VERTO is our open source signaling proposal, designed from the ground up to be familiar to Web application developers, and allowing for a high degree of integration between FreeSWITCH-provided services and browsers. It is implemented on the FreeSWITCH side by a module (mod_verto) that talks JSON with the JavaScript library (verto.js) on the browser side.

FreeSWITCH accommodates them ALL

FreeSWITCH implements all of WebRTC low-level protocols, codecs, and requirements. It's got encryption, SRTP, DTLS, RTP, websocket and secure websocket transports (`ws://` and `wss://`). Having got it all, it is able to serve SIP endpoints over WebRTC via mod_sofia (they'll be just other SIP phones, exactly like the rest of soft and hard SIP phones), and it interacts with XMPP via mod_jingle.

Crucially, FreeSWITCH has been designed since its inception to be able to manage and message high-definition media, both audio and video. Support for OPUS audio codec (8 up to 48 khz, enough for actual audio-cd quality) started years ago as a pioneering feature, and has evolved over the years to be so robust and self-healing as to sustain a loss of more than 40% (yep, as in FORTY PERCENT) packets and maintain understandability. WebRTC's V8 video codec is routinely carrying our mixed video conferences in FullHD (as in 1920x1080 pixel), and we're looking forward to investing in fiber and in some facial cream to look good in 4K.

That's why FreeSWITCH can be the pivot of your next big WebRTC project: its architecture was designed from the start to be a multimedia powerhouse.

There is lot of experience out there using FreeSWITCH in expanding the reach of existing SIP services having the browsers acting as SIP phones via JavaScript libraries, without modifying in any way the service logic and implementation. You just add SIP extensions that happen to be browsers.

We covered SIP based services in other parts of this book (and you can find an implementation example using browsers and SIP.js in the 1.6 Cookbook), so for the remainder of this chapter we'll write about VERTO, a FreeSWITCH proposal especially dedicated to Web development.

What is Verto (module and jslib)?

Verto is a FreeSWITCH module (mod_verto) that allows for JSON interaction with FreeSWITCH, via secure websockets (wss). All the power and complexity of FreeSWITCH can be harnessed via Verto: Session management, call control, text messaging, and user data exchange and synchronization. Take a note for yourself: "User data exchange and synchronization". We'll be back to this later.

Verto is like **Event Socket Layer** (**ESL**) on steroids: Anything you can do in ESL (subscribe, send and receive messages in FS core message pumps/queues) you can do in Verto, but Verto is actually much more and can do much more. Verto is also made for high-level control of WebRTC!

Verto has an accompanying JavaScript library, verto.js. Using verto.js a web developer can videoconference and enable a website and/or add a collaboration platform to a CRM system in few lines of a code that he understands, in a logic that's familiar to web developers, without forcing references to foreign knowledge domains like SIP.

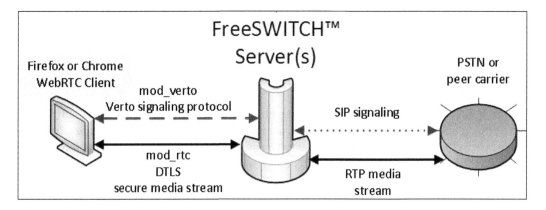

Also, Verto allows for the simplest way to extend your existing SIP services to WebRTC browsers.

The added benefit of "user data exchange and synchronization" (see, I'm back to it) is not to be taken lightly: You can create data structures (for example, in JSON) and have them synchronized on the server and all clients, with each modification made by the client or server to be automatically, immediately and transparently reflected on all other clients.

Imagine a dynamic list of conference participants, or a chat, or a stock ticker, or a multiuser ping pong game, and so on.

Configure mod_verto

Mod_verto is installed by default by standard FreeSWITCH implementation. Let's have a look at its configuration file, verto.conf.xml.

The most important parameter here, and the only one I had to modify from the stock configuration file, is ext-rtp-ip. If your server is behind a NAT (that is, it sits on a private network and exchanges packets with the public Internet via some sort of port forwarding by a router or firewall), you must set this parameter to the public IP address the clients are reaching for.

Other very important parameters are the codec strings. Those two parameters determine the absolute string that will be used in SDP media negotiation. The list in the string will represent all the media formats to be proposed and accepted. WebRTC has mandatory (so, assured) support for vp8 video codec, while mandatory audio codecs are opus and pcmu/pcma (eg, g711). Pcmu and pcma are much less CPU hungry than opus. So, if you are willing to settle for less quality (g711 is "old PSTN" audio quality), you can use "pcmu,pcma,vp8" as your strings, and have both clients and server use far less CPU power for audio processing.

```
admin@ip-172-31-13-216: ~                              – + ×
admin@ip-172-31-13-216: ~ 80x36
<configuration name="verto.conf" description="HTML5 Verto Endpoint">

  <settings>
    <param name="debug" value="9"/>
  </settings>

  <profiles>
    <profile name="default-v4">
      <param name="bind-local" value="$${local_ip_v4}:8081"/>
      <param name="bind-local" value="$${local_ip_v4}:8082" secure="true"/>
      <param name="force-register-domain" value="$${domain}"/>
      <param name="secure-combined" value="$${certs_dir}/wss.pem"/>
      <param name="secure-chain" value="$${certs_dir}/wss.pem"/>
      <param name="userauth" value="true"/>
      <!-- setting this to true will allow anyone to register even with no accou
nt so use with care -->
      <param name="blind-reg" value="false"/>
      <param name="mcast-ip" value="224.1.1.1"/>
      <param name="mcast-port" value="1337"/>
      <param name="rtp-ip" value="$${local_ip_v4}"/>
      <!-- <param name="ext-rtp-ip" value=""/> -->
      <param name="ext-rtp-ip" value="52.28.144.113"/>
      <param name="local-network" value="localnet.auto"/>
      <param name="outbound-codec-string" value="opus,vp8"/>
      <param name="inbound-codec-string" value="opus,vp8"/>

      <param name="apply-candidate-acl" value="localnet.auto"/>
      <param name="apply-candidate-acl" value="wan_v4.auto"/>
      <param name="apply-candidate-acl" value="rfc1918.auto"/>
      <param name="apply-candidate-acl" value="any_v4.auto"/>
      <param name="timer-name" value="soft"/>

    </profile>

    <profile name="default-v6">
                                                          1,1            Top
```

This can make a real difference and very much sense in certain setups, for example, if you must cope with low-power devices. Also, if you route/bridge calls to/from PSTN, they will have no use for opus high definition audio; much better to directly offer the original g711 stream than decode/recode it in opus.

Test with Communicator

Once configured, you want to test your mod_verto install. What better moment than now to get to know the awesomeness of Verto Communicator, a JavaScript videoconference and collaboration advanced client, developed by Italo Rossi, Jonatas Oliveira and Stefan Yohansson from Brazil, Joao Mesquita from Argentina, and our core devs Ken Rice and Brian West from Tennessee and Oklahoma?

If it's not already done, copy the Verto Communicator distribution directory (`/usr/src/freeswitch.git/html5/verto/verto_communicator/dist/`) into a directory served by your web server in SSL (be sure you got all the SSL certificates right).

To see it in all its splendor, be sure to call from two different clients, one as simple participant, the other as moderator (see the next chapter on Videocalls and Conferencing), and you'll be presented with controls to manage the conference layout, for giving floors, for screen sharing, for creating banners with name and title for each participant, for real-time chatting, and much more. It is simply astonishing what can be done with JavaScript and mod_verto.

Build Your Own Verto App

Now for something completely different: The simplest possible demo of a working Verto client, complete with audio and video call, and real-time chat.

Code for this example is extremely readable, short, and allows for studying exactly how it works. The JavaScript debug console of your browser is your friend. It uses the bootstrap framework to have nice looking buttons and fonts.

`Index.html` actually contains very little: Apart from CSS and interface compatibility for each browser, it just sets up the values that will be passed to JavaScript for establishing the Verto call. Then it contains a "video" HTML tag with an ID that will be used by JavaScript as input-output for WebRTC, and two text areas that will be the input and the output of our chat. Then it includes JavaScript libraries, and our JavaScript application code, high.js.

High.js (our application JavaScript code) is where all the action is. At page load it does the show/hide of all page elements that will then be manipulated.

```html
<body>
 <div id="conference">
  <input type="hidden" id="hostname" value="self2.gmaruzz.org"/>
  <input type="hidden" id="wsURL" value="wss://self2.gmaruzz.org:8082"/>
  <input type="hidden" id="login" value="1017"/>
  <input type="hidden" id="passwd" value="12345"/>
  <input type="hidden" id="cidnumber" value="WebRTC"/>
  <div class="form-signin">
   <h2 class="form-signin-heading">WebRTC Rooms</h2>

   <div id="content" class="form-signin-content">
    <input type=number id="ext" min=3000 max=3999 step=1 class="form-control"
        placeholder="Conference Room's Number ? (eg: 3000)" required autofocus>
    <button class="btn btn-lg btn-primary btn-success" data-inline="true"
        id="extbtn">Choose Room</button>
    <input type="text" id="cidname" class="form-control"
        placeholder="insert here your NAME (eg: Giovanni Maruzzelli)" required autofocus>
    <button class="btn btn-lg btn-primary btn-success" data-inline="true"
        id="callbtn">Call Conference</button>
    <button class="btn btn-lg btn-primary btn-danger" data-inline="true"
        id="backbtn">Back</button>
   </div>
   <div id="video1" align="center" class="embed-responsive embed-responsive-4by3">
    <video id="webcam" autoplay="autoplay" class="embed-responsive-item"> </video>
   </div>
   <button class="btn btn-lg btn-primary btn-danger" data-inline="true"
        id="hupbtn">Hangup</button>
   <br id="br"/>
   <textarea id="chatwin" class="form-control" rows="5" readonly></textarea>
   <br id="br"/>
   <textarea id="chatmsg" class="form-control" rows="1"
        placeholder="type here your chat msg" autofocus></textarea>
   <button class="btn btn-primary btn-success" data-inline="true"
        id="chatsend">Send Msg</button>
  </div>
  <div align="center" class="inner">
   <p>2015<br/>OpenTelecom.IT</p>
  </div>
 </div>
 <script type="text/javascript" src="js/jquery.min.js"></script>
 <script type="text/javascript" src="js/jquery.json-2.4.min.js"></script>
 <script type="text/javascript" src="js/verto-min.js"></script>
 <script type="text/javascript" src="high.js"></script>
</body>
</html>
```

```
admin@ip-172-31-13-216: ~          —  +  ×

function init() {
 cur_call = null;

 verto = new $.verto({
  login: $("#login").val() + "@" + $("#hostName").val(),
  passwd: $("#passwd").val(),
  socketUrl: $("#wsURL").val(),
  tag: "webcam",
  iceServers: true
 },callbacks);

 $("#ext").keyup(function (event) {
  if (event.keyCode == 13 && !event.shiftKey) {
   $( "#extbtn" ).trigger( "click" );
  }
 });

 $("#cidname").keyup(function (event) {
  if (event.keyCode == 13 && !event.shiftKey) {
   $( "#callbtn" ).trigger( "click" );
  }
 });

 $(document).keypress(function(event) {
  var key = String.fromCharCode(event.keyCode || event.charCode);
  var i = parseInt(key);

  if (key === "#" || key === "*" || key === "0" || (i > 0 && i <= 9)) {
   cur_call.dtmf(key);
  }
 });

 setupChat();
}

$(window).load(function() {
 cur_call = null;
 $("#conference").show();
 $("#backbtn").hide();
 $("#cidname").hide();
 $("#callbtn").hide();
 $("#hupbtn").hide();
 $("#chatwin").hide();
 $("#chatmsg").hide();
 $("#chatsend").hide();
 $("#webcam").hide();
 $("#video1").hide();
 init();
});
                                                    222,1        99%
```

Current call is NULL, and last step at page load is to call the `init` function.

The `init()` will create a new Verto object, using values hardcoded in the HTML file for login, password, server, etc. As last argument, it assigns to the Verto object the callbacks we'll see later. Then set up the management of "enter" into textareas (eg, they're treated like clicks on "forward" button) and the passing to the future "current call" of keypress that represents DTMFs (su user can interact with IVRs). Last Init instruction is a call to the `setupchat()` function (we're still at initial page load time).

The `setupchat()` clears the chat textareas, then creates the `chatsend` function, that will call the `message` Verto JavaScript method of the current call object with arguments as the chat ID (we'll see later where the ID comes from) and the input typed by the user.

```
admin@ip-172-31-13-216: ~                    - + X
function setupChat()
$("#chatwin").html("");

$("#chatsend").click(function() {
  if (!cur_call && chatting_with) {
    return;
  }
  cur_call.message({to: chatting_with,
    body: $("#chatmsg").val(),
    from_msg_name: cur_call.params.caller_id_name,
    from_msg_number: cur_call.params.caller_id_number
  });
  $("#chatmsg").val("");
});

$("#chatmsg").keyup(function (event) {
  if (event.keyCode == 13 && !event.shiftKey) {
    $( "#chatsend" ).trigger( "click" );
  }
});

                                      220,1           79%
```

Then a series of functions define the behavior of buttons, for example, the "Call Conference" button when clicked (if the `textarea #cidname` has been filled with the caller name) will call the `docall()` function.

The `docall()` function does nothing during a call, else it creates a call Verto object using the Newcall Verto method, the arguments gathered until now, and a lot of hardcoded defaults (for example: use mono audio, use video, use default microphone/webcam).

```
function docall() {
 if (cur_call) {
  return;
 }
 cur_call = verto.newCall({
  destination_number: $("#ext").val(),
  caller_id_name: $("#cidname").val(),
  caller_id_number: $("#cidnumber").val(),
  useVideo: true,
  useStereo: false,
  useCamera: $("#usecamera").find(":selected").val(),
  useMic: $("#usemic").find(":selected").val()
 });
}

$("#callbtn").click(function() {
 if($("#cidname").val() ){
  docall();
 }
});
```

If the Verto call created by `docall()` is successfully connected to our Verto server, it will then begin to be managed by the callbacks associated with the Verto object (remember when we created the Verto object?).

Callbacks are of three types: onMessage, onEvent, and onDialogState.

- OnMessage callbacks are activated when FreeSWITCH sends a message to the Verto client: in our case we choose to react to the "info" message (that will contain what to display as chat output) and to the "pvtEvent" message (where we look for data describing conference joining and leaving)

- OnEvent callback foes nothing, we just show it was called.

- OnDialogState signals the establishment and tearing down of the call.

```
admin@ip-172-31-13-216: ~                    − + ×
```

```javascript
var callbacks = {
 onMessage: function(verto, dialog, msg, data) {
  console.error("msg ", msg);
  console.error("data ", data);
  switch (msg) {
   case $.verto.enum.message.pvtEvent:
    if (data.pvtData) {
     console.error("data.pvtData ", data.pvtData);
     switch (data.pvtData.action) {
      case "conference-liveArray-join":
       chatting_with = data.pvtData.chatID;
       break;
      case "conference-liveArray-part":
       cur_call = null;
       break;
     }
    }
    break;
   case $.verto.enum.message.info:
    var body = data.body;
    var from = data.from_msg_name || data.from;
    if (body.slice(-1) !== "\n") {
     body += "\n";
    }
    $('#chatwin')
     .append(from + ': ')
     .append(body)
     $('#chatwin').animate({"scrollTop": $('#chatwin')[0].scrollHeight}, "fast");
    break;
   default:
    break;
  }
 },
 onEvent: function(v, e) {
  console.error("GOT EVENT", e);
 },
 onDialogState: function(d) {
  if (!cur_call) {
   cur_call = d;
  }
  switch (d.state) {
   case $.verto.enum.state.hangup:
    cur_call = null;
    console.error("HANGUP");
    break;
   case $.verto.enum.state.active:
    console.error("ACTIVE");
    break;
   default:
    break;
  }
 },
};
                                          51,4              3%
```

And that's all, folks! If the call is correctly established (connect to server, server verifies login auth, server and client agree on media types), then the "video" tag will be substituted for a live stream, the chat textareas will react in realtime to inputs, our client is able to fully participate in an audio-video conference with real-time text chatting and dtmf keyboard management (for example, "press 0 to mute/unmute yourself").

And now, go and test by yourself, debug, add features, hack already, for Pete's sake!

Summary

In this chapter we delved into WebRTC design, what infrastructure it requires, and what is similar and what is different from known VoIP.

We understood that WebRTC is only about media, and leave the signaling to the implementor.

Also, we get the specifics of WebRTC, its way of traversing NAT, its omnipresent encryption, and its peer to peer nature.

We witnessed going beyond peer to peer, connecting with the telecommunication world of services that need gateways for transport, protocol, and media translations.

FreeSWITCH is the perfect fit, as a WebRTC server, WebRTC gateway, and also as an application server.

And then we saw how to implement Verto, a signaling born on WebRTC, a JSON web protocol designed to exploit the additional features of WebRTC and of FreeSWITCH, like real time data structure synchronization, session rehydration, event systems, and so on.

8
Audio and Video Conferencing

Let's start with two concepts here: audio conferencing is huge and video conferencing is HUGE. Actually, conferencing (audio and/or video) is one of the drivers of our industry, and sure, it's a big part of what businesses look for in a telecommunications system.

FreeSWITCH has always been the best platform for conferencing, starting many years ago as a hugely scalable audio conferencing bridge to becoming, with version 1.6, a multimedia powerhouse serving PSTN, SIP, and WebRTC users.

In this chapter, we will cover:

- Conference concepts
- Audio conferencing
- Profiles, DTMF commands interaction, PINs, and so on
- Managing audio conferences
- Video conferencing
- Video conference layouts
- Screen sharing
- Managing video conferences
- Conference performances
- Conference concepts

Conferencing is about taking stuff from different sources, doing something with that stuff, and distributing the result to different recipients. That process must allow for real-time change of all factors: which sources send you stuff, what kind of stuff you get, what to do with it, which recipients you distribute it to, and so on. Wow.

Also, it needs simple ways for participants to interact with it (for example, enter an access PIN code, increase and decrease the volume, mute/unmute themselves, and so on) and for moderator(s) to manage the conversation (for example, give the floor to a presenter, switch the microphone to another presenter, mute/unmute all or one participant, broadcast music and messages, record the conversation, originate an outbound call that gives the recipient the option to join the conference, and so on).

Conferencing used to be about switching, mixing, and regulating the volumes of the audio streams. Those operations on audio end up being simple math applied to a series of unrelated bytes (on top of standard transcoding). **High Definition (HD)** audio increases CPU load on transcoding, but the inner workings are still the same:

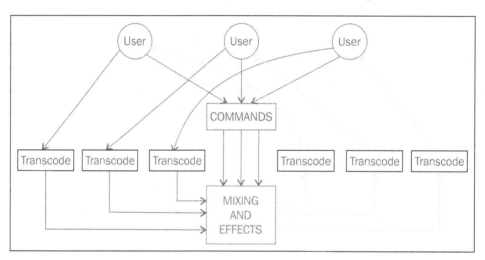

Video added an entire new world of processing: video streams are not a series of unrelated values; they're organized by frames (for example, a description of what is to be shown on the screen). You do not join two video wires to obtain the superimposition of the two images, and you do not lower their electrical signals to do fading.

Video processing is very complex and computationally demanding. You can imagine what it means CPU-wise to have a picture in a picture, multiple attendants' live faces on the bottom row, each one with a name caption, and the background shared between the presenter's face and its shared screen.

Conferencing is arguably the most inherently complex service you can offer to your users and one of the most value-added ones.

FreeSWITCH has it all and with sane default configurations. That's the perfect platform for deploying your service.

Conference basics

Let's start simply. Add this snippet to dialplan:

```
admin@ip-172-31-3-216: ~                                    _ □ ✕

<!--
start a dynamic conference with the settings of the "default"
conference profile in conference.conf.xml
-->
<extension name="conferences">
  <condition field="destination_number" expression="^(31\d{2})$">
    <action application="answer"/>
    <action application="conference" data="$1-${domain_name}@default"/>
  </condition>
</extension>
<extension name="conferences-moderator">
  <condition field="destination_number" expression="^(31\d{2})1$">
    <action application="answer"/>
    <action application="conference" data="$1-${domain_name}@default++flags{mode
rator}"/>
  </condition>
</extension>

                                                    17,0-1           All
```

After a comment, we create an extension that answers incoming calls to 3100-3199 (inclusive), then connect the caller to the conference named [destination_number]-[domain_name]. If the conference does not exist yet, it will be started using settings from profile "default". (For example, if you call extension 3110 on a server where the domain is 172.31.3.216, the conference name will be "3110-172.31.3.216". If the FreeSWITCH domain was set to biloxi.com, the conference name would be "3110-biloxi.com".)

The second extension is identical to the first one, but will answer calls to 31001-31011-31021... up to 31991 (for example, they're all ending with "1"), and the caller will be connected to a conference named in the same way as the first example (taking into account only the first four numbers in "expression"), and will be given a "moderator" role.

So, calling 3188 will connect you as a participant to the conference room named "3188-biloxi.com", while calling 31881 will connect you as a moderator to the same conference.

As participant, with stock configuration files you'll be able to mute/unmute yourself by pressing *0* on the keypad, leave the conference by pressing #, isolate yourself (for example, deaf mute) by pressing *, up-down your listening volume by pressing *6* and *4*, and so on.

As a moderator, without special conference configuration you gain only the badge (quote: Al Capone, The Untouchables), that is, you're not different from a normal participant. You actually have all the power over the conference (meaning that you can kick people out, give the floor, mute, play messages, end the conference, and so on), but you have no means to exercise it. We'll see it better later, in the "managing" sections. Now, suffice to say a conference can be configured to play music on hold to all participants until the moderator arrives, making them wait for him. Also, a conference can be configured to have a different set of DTMF commands for the moderator (the command set can be tailored to let him exercise his power).

Conference.conf.xml (profiles, DTMF interaction, and so on)

All the magic in the previous example comes from the many settings loaded automatically by conferences.

You cannot define the individual conference rooms in `conference.conf.xml`. In that file, you define named groups of settings. Then, from dialplan, you send a call to an individual conference room, and you specify which settings group will apply. If the conference room does not exist, it will be created on the fly, as shown in the following screenshot:

```
admin@ip-172-31-3-216: ~                    _ □ x
configuration name="conference.conf" description="Conference configuration">

  <profiles>
    <profile name="default">
      <param name="member-flags" value="waste"/>
      <param name="conference-flags" value="livearray-sync"/>
      [... other configs here ...]
    </profile>
    <profile name="arbitrary">
      <param name="member-flags" value="wastemute"/>
      <param name="conference-flags" value="livearray-sync"/>
      <param name="caller-controls" value="arbitrary-controls"/>
      <param name="moderator-controls" value="moderator-arbitrary-controls"/>
      [... other configs here ...]
    </profile>
    <profile name="another">
      <param name="caller-controls" value="moderator-arbitrary-controls"/>
    </profile>
  </profiles>

  <caller-controls>
    <group name="default">
      <control action="vol talk up" digits="3"/>
      <control action="vol talk dn" digits="6"/>
      [... other controls here ...]
    </group>
    <group name="arbitrary-controls">
      <control action="vol talk up" digits="33"/>
      <control action="vol talk dn" digits="66"/>
      [... other controls here ...]
    </group>
    <group name="moderator-arbitrary-controls">
      <control action="vol talk up" digits="33"/>
      <control action="vol talk dn" digits="66"/>
      <control action="execute_application" digits="00" data="playback /tmp/bell
_ring2.wav"/>
      <control action="execute_application" digits="55"   data="set api_result=$
{conference(${conference_name} tmute non_moderator)}"/>
      [... other controls here ...]
    </group>
  </caller-controls>

</configuration>
                                                    1,1            Top
```

Configuration sections logic

The profiles section contains each specifically named profile. As we saw before, when you start (or join) a conference you can optionally add @profilename after the conference name. If you don't, the conference will get its settings from the "default" profile. So, you had better create at least that "default" profile.

Inside profiles you can specify dozens of disparate conference features, behaviors, and quirks. FreeSWITCH provides sane values to all parameters you don't explicitly set.

The caller-controls section contains each specifically named group of DTMF controls.

In each profile you can define a `caller-controls` parameter. If you don't, that profile will be assigned the caller-controls group "default" (again, create it). Or, you can assign the magic caller-controls group "none", and participants will be assigned no DTMF controls.

Each profile can also contain a `moderator-controls` parameter. Moderators of conferences started with that profile will be assigned that named group of controls. If not specified, moderators will get the same controls group as normal participants.

Pay attention: `moderator-controls` are not additional commands on top of `caller-controls`. If you set `moderator-controls`, they need to be specified in full, they will be the only DTMF controls moderators will get (if you don't set moderator-controls at all, moderators will get caller-controls, like all other participants).

Profile

There are actually many parameters you can set inside a profile.

Parameters of type `flags` will be overridden by the ones passed as arguments in dial strings and channel variables. All other parameters (that is, not flags) are usually set once, when the conference starts, and apply to the whole of the conference and to all participants.

- **Conference-flags**: A pipe- ("|") delimited list of conference modifiers that apply to the whole of a single conference. You can make members keep music on hold until a moderator arrives (`wait-mod`), have the conference emit a real-time JSON describing what happens, like a presence, and IM system (`livearray-json-status`), so you can have interactive graphic interfaces telling you who is talking now, or choose not to use an energy threshold to determine which incoming audio stream must be mixed in and instead go straight to mixing all incoming streams, whatever their energy (`audio-always`).

- **Member-flags**: A pipe- ("|") delimited list of participant modifiers. Can define that callers will enter the conference with their microphone muted (`mute`); to be heard, they'll have to unmute themselves, or be unmuted by the moderator. Another useful flag is `mute-detect`, which will play a message to the user that is detected to be talking while being muted (so he knows no one can hear).

- **Caller-controls**: The name of the group of commands defined in the section caller-controls that will be assigned to all participants.

- **Moderator-controls**: The name of the group defined in the section `caller-controls` that will be assigned to moderators.

- **Sounds**: A good number of parameters deal with sounds that give an acoustic feedback when something has happened, or a command has been executed (for example, "volume is now minus 1", or "you are the only person in this conference"). You can define none, some, or all of them. If the value of a "sound parameter" is not defined, nothing will be played, nothing special will happen, and things will continue as normal (for example, you press 4, your listening volume is actually lowered, but no announcement of the new volume level is read to you). You can define sounds as relative or absolute file paths. Relative file paths would be prepended by the `sound_prefix` channel variable of the first call (the one that starts the conference). You can override that by setting "sound-prefix" parameter in profile, as shown in the following screenshot:

- Others:
    - ° `auto-record`: To have conferences automatically recorded in an audio file, you can set the file path (for example, `/tmp/myconf.wav`) or use variable substitution to have a unique filename for each conference (for example, `/tmp/${conference_name}_${strftime(%Y-%m-%d-%H-%M-%S)}.wav`).
    - ° `channels`: How many audio channels, "1" for mono, "2" for stereo.
    - ° `energy-level`: Defines the threshold volume the incoming audio stream must have to be mixed in (so, it avoids mixing in streams where there is only background noise. The participant will have to speak louder to be mixed in).
    - ° `pin` and `moderator_pin`: If specified, will be requested to participants and moderators to be allowed in (both are immutable for the whole conference duration, which cannot be modified after conference starts).
    - ° `ivr-dtmf-timeout`: Maximum time between two digits in DTMF controls; allows the participant keypad presses like "1" and "11" to execute different commands.

Caller-Controls group

A group defined inside the `caller-controls` section contains a named set of DTMFs-to-actions mappings. For example, what happens if you press on your keypad.

Those groups are just lists, and can be used to define participants' and/or moderators' mapping, inside the `profiles` section, as shown in the following screenshot:

```
admin@ip-172-31-3-216: ~                                    _ □ ✕
<caller-controls>
  <group name="test1">
    <control action="mute" digits="0"/>
    <control action="deaf mute" digits="*"/>
    <control action="energy up" digits="9"/>
    <control action="energy equ" digits="8"/>
    <control action="energy dn" digits="7"/>
    <control action="vol talk up" digits="3"/>
    <control action="vol talk zero" digits="2"/>
    <control action="vol talk dn" digits="1"/>
    <control action="vol listen up" digits="6"/>
    <control action="vol listen zero" digits="5"/>
    <control action="vol listen dn" digits="4"/>
    <control action="hangup" digits="#"/>
    <control action="hangup" digits="11"/>
    <control action="deaf mute" digits="22"/>
  </group>
  <group name="test2">
    <control action="execute_application" digits="00"  data="playback /tmp/be
ll_ring2.wav"/>
    <control action="execute_application" digits="55"  data="set api_result=$
{conference(${conference_name} tmute non_moderator)}"/>
  </group>
</caller-controls>
                                                  316,6            99%
```

Most control actions are self-descriptive, like "vol talk up", and similarly, "energy" actions are for moving and resetting the audio volume threshold that is taken as a sign of activity, to activate mixing.

"execute_application" is way more flexible! It allows for the usage of any dialplan tool (for example, playback, execute_extension, log, lua, socket. Check them all!). On top of that, we can use one of those "applications" (provided by mod_dptools) to execute API commands in response to keypad presses. In our example, we use the set dptools application to create a variable (api_result) that we don't use, but its assignment is the perfect excuse for executing a FreeSWITCH API call on the right side, complete with arguments. This way you can command the full power of fs_cli in your phone keypad. In our example, if we press "55" on the keypad, we obtain the same result as in typing "conference 3110-172.31.3.216 tmute non-moderator" into fs_cli: all non-moderator participants in our conference will be muted. If we press "55" again, they'll be unmuted.

Conference invocation, dialplan, channel variables

"conference" is a dialplan application provided by mod_dptools. Canonical invocation is shown in the following screenshot:

```
admin@ip-172-31-3-216: ~
<action application="conference" data="[bridge:]confname[@profile][+[pin][+flags
{mute|deaf|...}]][:dialstring]">
:
```

As shown in the preceding screenshot, the parts in square brackets are optional, but their order MUST be respected, so if you want a non-bridging conference with no participants' pin, using a default profile and "mute" flag, the invocation will be as shown in the following screenshot (note the "++"):

```
admin@ip-172-31-3-216: ~
<action application="conference" data="confname++flags{mute}">
:
```

While in the same conference, bridging the caller with internal extension 1000 would be as shown in the following screenshot:

```
admin@ip-172-31-3-216: ~
<action application="conference" data="bridge:confname++flags{mute}:user/1000@${
domain_name}">
:
```

Outbound conference

An "outbound conference" is similar to a bridging conference, but instead of having the dialstring(s) part of its own invocation, an outbound conference will originate all of the call legs that were set by the "conference_set_auto_outcall" dialplan application. Also, before invoking the outbound conference, you can set other specific channel variables that give you full control of how the origination will take place, which caller_id will be used, which no answer timeout, what file will be played to the recipient, and so on. Check out the online documentation for all of the "conference_auto_outcall_*" channel variables.

Moderating and managing conferences – API

A conference is managed by its own moderators, and by FreeSWITCH server admin(s), via moderator_controls and API calls.

API calls are much more powerful than moderator controls; actually, anything that can be done in/by FreeSWITCH, can be done via API calls.

There are so many ways to invoke FreeSWITCH APIs: from fs_cli prompt, from command line (again, via fs_cli), via Event Socket (ESL), via HTTP, and via moderator_controls.

As our dear Michael Collins explained many years ago in the mailing list, yes you can build a conference management system that will work completely via the phone keypad: as we saw before in the caller-controls section, we're able to access the full power of FreeSWITCH API. It is just uncomfortable, particularly if you need to select one particular participant among many as the target of a command.

Conference API calls have the generic format: conference confname command [arg1 arg2...argN].

A couple of API calls from fs_cli are as shown in the following screenshot:

```
freeswitch@internal> conference 3000-172.31.3.216 list
23;sofia/internal/1010@52.28.144.113;5db59538-530d-4af4-8b47-735c4303a11e;1010;1
010;hear|speak|talking|floor|vid-floor;0;0;0;100

freeswitch@internal> conference 3000-172.31.3.216 mute 23
OK mute 23

freeswitch@internal>
```

The same API calls, but from Linux command line, as shown in the following screenshot:

```
root@ip-172-31-3-216:~# fs_cli -x "conference 3000-172.31.3.216 list"
23;sofia/internal/1010@52.28.144.113;5db59538-530d-4af4-8b47-735c4303a11e;1010;1
010;hear|floor|vid-floor;0;0;0;100

root@ip-172-31-3-216:~# fs_cli -x "conference 3000-172.31.3.216 mute 23"
OK mute 23

root@ip-172-31-3-216:~#
```

Using the same API calls from Verto Communicator (I'm connected as a moderator):

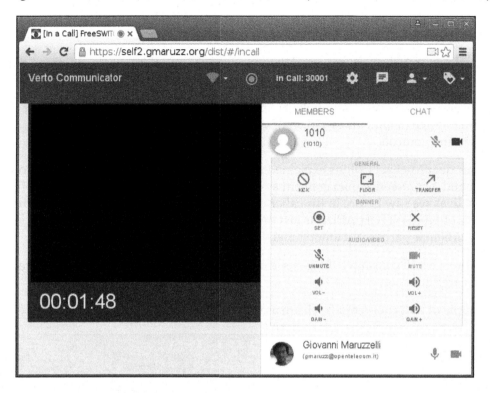

The most useful conference API commands:

- `tmute` (toggle mute/unmute)
- `play` (play an audio file)
- `record` (record conference to an audio file or stream)
- `energy` (volume threshold to be mixed in)
- `floor` (toggle floor status)
- `hup and kick` (kick a user out of the conference
- `hup` (do it without playing the kick audio file)
- `list` (list participants)
- `volume_in` and `volume_out` (adjust audio level of streams coming from and going to participants).

Check all conference API commands invocations and arguments in the online documentation, or by typing `conference help` in fs_cli.

Video conference

"There's only two ways of doing things. The right way and FreeSWITCH's way. And they're both the same." (adapted quote, John Turturro, Mac, 1992)

In a breakthrough at ClueCon 2015 in Chicago Illinois, FreeSWITCH's creator Anthony Minessale II announced support for video transcoding, mixing, manipulation, and **Multipoint Control Unit** (**MCU**) functionality.

FreeSWITCH now has the most advanced and mature video conferencing features:

- Multiple video codecs support and transcoding
- Multiple video layouts
- Screen splits
- Picture in picture
- Screen sharing
- Video superimposing (captions, logos, and so on)
- Video mixing
- Video effects and real-time manipulation

Video conference configuration

Video conferences in FreeSWITCH are just normal conferences with "something more".

They're defined and invoked exactly the same way as an audio-only conference as far as `conference.conf.xml` and dialplan. Actually, an audio-only conference is a video conference where no participants happen to request or send a video stream. Also, if participants are video capable, and call into the normal audio conferences we described in the previous section, they will be in a `passthrough` mode video conference.

So, you need to thoroughly read all of the previous sections about audio conference configuration, because here you'll find only the additional, video-related, configs.

The big difference is between three different kinds of video conference (`parameter video-mode`, defined in `conference-flags` or inside `profile`, see preceding section):

- passthrough
- transcode
- mux

Setting `video-mode` to `passthrough` (that's default if you don't set it at all) will direct FreeSWITCH to act in a video-follow-audio way: the input video stream is automatically chosen by FS based on who is talking at the moment, and is re-sent as-is (no transcoding nor any manipulation) to all those participants that are able to accept it.

Setting `video-mode` to `mux` allows FreeSWITCH to do all kind of video processing, transcoding, and effects: you can have different clients seeing each other using different codecs, can have picture-in-pictures, can have many clients present concurrently in different areas of the screen, logos superimposed to a presenter overlapping attendees, and so on.

Setting `video-mode` to `transcode` allows for clients with different codecs to see each other, and smooth switch from one to another; other features are the same as `passthrough`.

Mux profile settings

Almost all video-related profile settings apply only when conference is in mux video-mode, for obvious reasons (other modes will not process video; they pass it along and transcode).

Most important of the lot are:

- `video-canvas-size`: Defines, in pixels, the size of the canvas on which the video will be "painted" after all processing (scaling, mixing, and so on), for example, `1920x1080`.

- `video-fps`: Defines how many frames per second will be painted, for example, `15`.

- `video-codec-bandwidth`: Defines the max value for the resulting video stream and will internally modify codec parameters to match. Can be expressed in kb, mb (kilobit and megabit per second), in KB and MB (kilobytes and megabytes per second), or the magic word "auto". For example, `1MB`.

- `video-layout-name`: Defines the name of the layout or of the group of layouts we want to impose on the canvas, from the file `conference_layouts.conf.xml` (see below). By the way, if you set this parameter to anything, the conference will be `automatically in video-mode=mux`. If you set it to an individual layout name, the value will be (not surprisingly) the name of the layout you want. The other option is to set it to `group:groupname` (note the mandatory prefix `group:`, complete with colon). For example, `mylayoutname` or `group:mygroupname`.

Video conference screen layouts

When a conference has been defined as `video-mode mux`, it can aggregate, mix, transform, inject, superimpose, and apply to input streams, all the useful video effects that enhance the attendees' experience and sponsors' branding.

Screen layouts define how the resulting output video stream will be composed: the canvas is divided into one or more regions (boxes), and each region (box) will convey content from one of the input streams. Not all input streams are required to be on screen at once (you can show only the presenter and five attendees, or all attendees and no presenter, or two animations and a music video).

Screen layouts can be associated with criteria to assign video-floor (for example, which input stream is displayed), and each layout defines in which of its regions (boxes) the video-floor blessed stream will be displayed.

Layouts are abstract representations, directly proportional to the canvas size, and adapt to both 4:3 and 16:9 form factors.

Layouts have a conventional dimension of 360x360, and all coordinates are relative to those conventional lengths.

Layout regions (or boxes) are defined by the xml tag "image" that can have many attributes. The most important are:

- x and y: The box-origin, the upper left corner of the box, relative to the upper left corner of the layout. If the box originates from the canvas's upper-left corner, x=0 and y=0, the upper-left corner of the box is exactly at the center of the canvas, x=180 and y=180. If the box's origin is at half the upper canvas border, x=0 and y=180.

- `scale`: Canvas being assumed to be equal to 360, how much the box is relative to canvas; for example, if the box takes all the canvas, scale is 360. If the box takes half the canvas, the box is 180.

- `hscale`: Horizontal scale, transformation of one dimension on the box stream.

- `zoom`: Act on the box stream, that can have a different aspect ratios than the box (those differences are normally filled by side bands).

- `floor`: If set to `"true"`, the box will dynamically show the video floor owner (for example, will switch to who is getting video focus).

- reservation-id: A tagname that specifies who will be in this box. That tagname is assigned to a conference participant with a vid-res-id API command:

```
admin@ip-172-31-2-148: ~                              _ ☐ ✕
<configuration name="conference_layouts.conf" description="Audio Conference">
  <layout-settings>
    <layouts>
      <layout name="1x1">
        <image x="0" y="0" scale="360" floor="true"/>
      </layout>
      <layout name="1x2" auto-3d-position="true">
        <image x="90" y="0" scale="180"/>
        <image x="90" y="180" scale="180"/>
      </layout>
      <layout name="2x1" auto-3d-position="true">
        <image x="0" y="90" scale="180"/>
        <image x="180" y="90" scale="180"/>
      </layout>

      <layout name="2x1-zoom" auto-3d-position="true">
        <image x="0" y="0" scale="180" hscale="360" zoom="true"/>
        <image x="180" y="0" scale="180" hscale="360" zoom="true"/>
      </layout>
      <layout name="3x1-zoom" auto-3d-position="true">
        <image x="0" y="0" scale="120" hscale="360" zoom="true"/>
        <image x="120" y="0" scale="120" hscale="360" zoom="true"/>
        <image x="240" y="0" scale="120" hscale="360" zoom="true"/>
                                                      16,1          Top
[ ip-172-31-2-148 ][  0$ shell0  1$ bash  2$ bash  3$ bash  4-$ bash  (5*$bash)
```

A simple example is shown in the screenshot taken from FreeSWITCH Confluence conference documentation page:

2x1 layout, with captions:

The following screenshot shows a canvas of 640x480 pixels, using the 2x1-zoom, with me and my screen shared while I'm writing this. You can see that through video manipulation, we succeeded in filling the entire canvas, with no black sidebands:

The next screenshot shows the same thing, but with a canvas of 1024x768 pixels (that is, higher resolution):

Same again, at 1920x1080, full screen:

And a screenshot from a YouTube broadcast of our weekly conference call, 720 pixels, with a desktop share, attendees' live streams, avatars, captions, and logos (yes, you can stream to YouTube directly from a FreeSWITCH video conference):

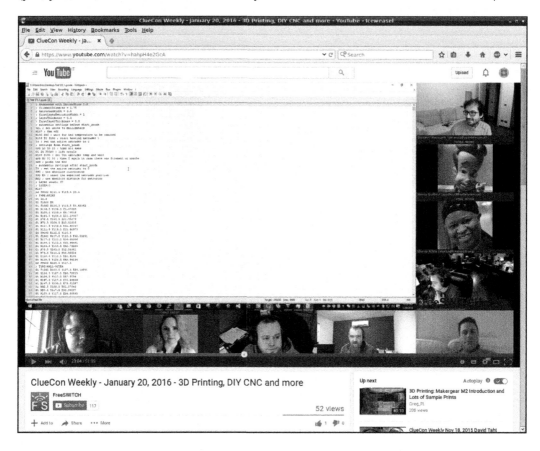

Screen sharing

Screen sharing is of paramount importance in video conferences. It allows for playing presentation' slides, sifting through documents, showing pictures, websites, and so on.

Screen sharing is possible because in a video stream with desktop (or window), live content is sent as input to the server and is then distributed to attendees. Many SIP softphones are able to originate that screen share stream. The problem is those streams are often proprietary (working only with their own specific server), non-compatible (working only with a specific server protocol), they're for payable add-ons, and so on.

Because it is so important for business communication, it is also an open avenue for vendor lock-in.

WebRTC has changed it all. Browsers are able to originate streams of the entire desktop or a specific application window, in addition to the stream they can generate from the webcam. Verto Communicator takes that stream and builds a second, parallel call to FreeSWITCH (the original one being the call of the person that wants to screen share, for example, me), and that screen-sharing video stream then becomes a legitimate conference attendee, an input as any other, that can be mixed in.

Screen sharing dialplan extension

Verto Communicator generates the additional call to the same extension as the original call, with a "-screen" suffix. You need to add that extension to dialplan for the screen-sharing stream to reach the conference. If the original call was to extension `3000`, the additional screen-sharing call will be to `3000-screen`.

Actions defined inside the two extensions need to point to the same conference name for the screen to be visible in the same conference the caller is in. It can be hardcoded (for example, `myconferencename`), or can be calculated dynamically to yield the same result:

Please note that in the second case, the match is done on, for example, `3000-screen`, but the capture is done only on the first four digits that compose the extension's destination number. In both cases we later use $1, the variable that contains the captured substring, to build the conference name to connect to.

Managing video conferences

Video related management commands follow the same format we saw before, in the "Moderating and Managing Conferences, API" section.

Most useful video conference API commands:

- `tvmute` (toggle video mute/unmute)
- `play` (play a video file)
- `record` (record conference to a video file)
- `vid-banner` (put a caption on participants' video)
- `vid-logo-img` (put an image on participants' video)
- `vid-res-id` (assign the `reservation-id` to a participant, who will be displayed in a specific box - see previous layouts section), put an image on participants' video).

Check all conference API commands invocations and arguments in the online documentation or by typing `conference help` in fs_cli.

Most of those commands can be given dynamically from the moderator interface of Verto Communicator. In the following picture, we see a conference with two participants (from my desktop and my laptop), one screen-sharing (the window with the ncmpcpp clock), and a video clip (Big Buck Bunny, Blender Foundation):

In this picture, one participant was given the "presenter" reservation-id, then layout presenter-overlap-small-top-right was applied to the conference, and the presenter became a small picture-in-picture while the same video clip of Big Buck Bunny (Blender Foundation, Creative Commons Attribution License, from YouTube, `https://www.youtube.com/watch?v=YE7VzlLtp-4`) continues to play, as shown in the following screenshot:

Conference performances

You can have video mixing or you can have little CPU load. You can't have them both.

And when I'm talking about CPU load I really mean it. For MCU style conferences, get a machine with the most cores and CPUs you can afford. That's the rule of the game. Ask Industrial Light and Magic about video effects and CPU cycles.

That said, let's see how to be Magicians On the Cheap (TM).

You can achieve very good results without sacrificing much, if you don't need fancy effects:

- pcmu or pcma (for example, g711) audio, one channel (mono), 8khz (support is mandatory in WebRTC and ubiquitous in SIP)
- video-mode passthrough
- (be sure no layout is mentioned in conference profile, if one is mentioned, the conference is automatically started in mux video-mode)

With those settings, you'll have an incredibly low CPU load: you're actually just switching between different video inputs, choosing one, and retransmitting it as-is to all participants. As for audio, you get input streams that are not compressed, almost a direct representation of a PSTN-sounding audio. Mixing them is a matter of summing their bytes.

You cannot put captions on video, you cannot inject video clips (or at least not using the play API), and you cannot have picture-in-pictures or multiple participants sharing the screen at the same time. Also, you do not have High Definition, CD quality audio (anyway, are your presenters using studio grade microphones?).

But you can have High Definition video (you're not mixing streams, just passing them along), screen sharing, and switch back and forth between one or more presenters, and one or more screen shares. You can have the presenter's voice talking over screen share.

Also, you can "inject" a video clip in the conference by playing it in a desktop window, and sharing that window.

You define `video-mode` as `passthrough` inside the conference profile in `conference.conf.xml`, while audio codecs must be defined in both `vars.xml` and `verto.conf.xml`.

If you only have lemons, you can make delicious lemonade!

Summary

In this chapter, we first had an overview of how audio and video conferencing works, then we saw how FreeSWITCH can be configured as a conferencing server.

We defined our conferences' profiles as setting groups that can be assigned to conferences when they start. In the same configuration file that contains the conferences' profiles we define caller-controls sections. Caller-controls are groups of DTMF-command mappings that are assigned to a conference inside profiles, and define how participants and moderators can interact using the dialpad.

We saw how to create a dialplan extension pointing to a conference, setting its channel variables. Also, we learned how to add participants having the conference to originate outbound calls to prospective attendees.

Management of conferences, who has the floor, who is kicked out, muting and unmuting participants, and the like, is best done with API calls. We saw how to use API via command line and via graphical interfaces, the best one being Verto Communicator.

We then introduced video conferencing, with its own additional settings.

Video-mode can be `passthrough` or `mux`, with `mux` being the all-powerful mode. We saw how to implement video mixing and effects in mux mode, such as multiple people being on the screen concurrently, logos and captions superimpositions, and how to set the screen layout by defining regions in which video streams are displayed.

We then delved into screen-sharing techniques, and management APIs specific to video conferences.

We closed the chapter with some hints on how to provide high quality video conferences on a shoestring.

9
Faxing and T38

Faxing is here to stay. Let's admit it: however much we VoIP practitioners hate fax, however much frustration we feel, most of us must deal with fax transmission. Fax is a way to transmit images via voice circuits that were not designed to work on packet networks, and is inherently difficult to implement reliably over VoIP.

T38 is a standard that mediates between SIP and fax to achieve a reliable transmission, trying to overcoming network induced problems. FreeSWITCH implements world-class T38 (and T30, traditional fax) support, and is widely used to serve from occasional to very high traffic fax communication.

In this chapter, we will cover:

- How traditional fax works on PSTN
- How fax works on VoIP
- How to configure and operate FreeSWITCH for faxing
- Tips, tricks, and caveats to achieve workflow integration, max success rate, and fax Nirvana

What is Fax on PSTN?

Fax is scanning an image at one end of the communication, and sending the result to the other end, where it will be transformed back into an image.

However impossible it might seem, faxing was invented and patented before voice telephony. The first commercial faxing service was introduced in 1865 between Paris and Lyon. The first desktop fax machine for end users was introduced in 1948, while the 80s saw mass market distribution of compact fax machines very similar and completely compatible with today's models.

Every office still has a fax machine, or a fax server. Modern faxing is governed by the **International Telecommunication Union (ITU)** standard T30, which is ubiquitous, very reliable (that is, 99% or better completion rates between fax machines connected to PSTN), and is required by law for many legal document transmissions in many countries.

How it works

On a standard PSTN-transmitting fax machine, an image is scanned, the result is converted into TIFF digital image format (multipage), and the resulting data is sent via a *voice* call to a receiving fax machine, where it will be stored (in memory or as a file) and/or immediately printed.

The emphasis here is on *voice*: TIFF data is transmitted via a *voice* call through PSTN (a call between the two modems inside the fax machines, the sending and the receiving ones):

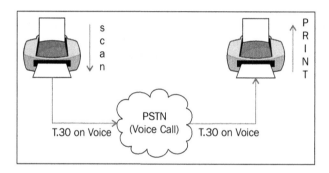

A voice call on PSTN (actually, on PSTN any call is a *voice* call) has some specific features: it is a direct electric circuit, established end to end from caller to recipient, completely synchronous, where analog electrical signals are sent on two wires (contemporary PSTN techniques are able to perfectly simulate that original technology). Born to transmit speech (for example, electrical signals like those that go from the microphone to the loudspeakers in a **public address**, or **PA**, system) PSTN has later been used by modems to transmit digital data (for example, information codified in binary format). Initially using two audio tones (called mark and space) to represent 1 and 0, modems have then evolved to adopt very complex audio and electrical techniques for transmitting data at higher speed.

Modem transmitting techniques (used by fax machines) rely on specific electric characteristics of the PSTN circuit, particularly continuity (zero loss, zero jitter, and synchronicity). The T30 protocol (the fax transmission protocol spoken by fax machines) uses underlying modem protocols (for example, V17 for 14400 baud/sec data transmission) as transport.

What is Fax over IP?

Fax over IP (FoIP) is *not* the scanning of an image and transmission of the results to a remote end via the Internet. That would be e-mailing (the resulting TIFF file), or FTPing it, or sending the file via HTTP PUT. Or whatever. No, that would be very easy; the Internet was born for it, but that is not faxing.

Fax over IP is actually to interact via the Internet with a remote, *regular* (T30, PSTN) fax machine. The problem is, to exactly reproduce the characteristics of a PSTN electrical circuit via a packet network is almost impossible. Packets get delayed, they arrive out-of-order (for example, the third packet arrives after the fifth), they get lost (for example, the fourth and seventh packets do not arrive at all), delays are not constant as a transmission proceeds (for example, jitter), and so on. All of this is not a problem for file transfer protocols like HTTP, and is a minor nuisance for voice transmission (both software correction and the human ear are very adaptable), but it will doom any T30 fax machine to fail.

The closest simulation of PSTN characteristics in a VoIP network can be obtained by using G711 (ulaw or alaw, also known as PCMU or PCMA) codec over a network without packet loss and jitter, for example, a well-managed LAN. That's because G711 is a *raw* codec, uncompressed and unmassaged, that almost faithfully reproduces the audio speech frequencies used by PSTN. And a good LAN would not lose packets or let them arrive out-of-order, thus respecting the very strict timing requirements of T30 fax protocol, as enshrined in fax machines' chipsets.

So, you can have a good (but not stellar) fax completion rate if you let two fax machines interact inside your LAN via G711 VoIP voice calls. Using G711, you may even have some success faxing via the Internet (depending on network quality, traffic conditions, remote end connection, phase of the moon, and so on).

What about if you want to reliably send and receive faxes *for real* (to/from someone else's fax machine)? You can't do that via *pure* T30 fax protocol over a voice call.

Two additional protocols were devised to help faxing via VoIP networks and the Internet: T37 and T38. T37 is a store and forward protocol, in some way similar to e-mail, that's perfect for IP networks. Unfortunately, the allure of faxing is its *synchronicity*, that is, you want the paper to get printed on the other end while you are sending the fax, and that would be missed in T37. In store-and-forward, a server would accept the entire fax from the scanner (or from a local fax machine via T30), and send it as a file to a remote server, which would then transmit it via T30 to its local receiving fax machine. Enough about T37; nobody is using it.

Enter T38

T38 is your bread and butter in Fax over IP, and is the only solution that actually works. Forget about anything else. It is not as 100% reliable as faxing over PSTN, but when well implemented can come close. Let's look at it:

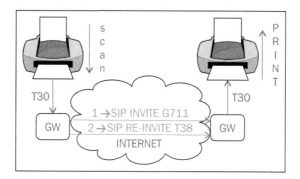

An end-to-end *traditional* fax transmission via VoIP and T38 would comprise:

1. Document is scanned to a TIFF fax format by fax machine.

2. Fax machine transmits via voice call and T30 protocol to the gateway.

3. As soon as it receives the first tones from the fax machine (before getting any actual data), the gateway originates (for example, INVITE) a G711 SIP voice VoIP call to the remote end.

4. As soon as the SIP call is established (before any actual data exchange) Gateway tries to upgrade the SIP call from G711 to T38 (for example, RE-INVITE the remote end using a different SDP).

5. If the remote end supports T38 (because it is a T38 gateway or, more rarely, because it is a smart network fax machine) they agree to a data exchange with much more relaxed timing and constraints, with some buffering and redundancy, and other facilities to overcome WAN fax transmission problems.

6. If the remote end does not support T38 (for example, it is a plain dumb fax machine), the call goes on as T30 on G711, hoping for the best.

7. If T38 was agreed, before any data is exchanged, the remote gateway would establish a T30 voice call with the receiving end fax machine.

8. When the call chain is established (originating fax machine <=> originating gateway <=> terminating gateway <=> receiving fax machine), the originating gateway will signal to the originating fax machine that transmission can start, and the stream of data would flow in real time from the caller fax machine, through gateways, to the recipient fax machine.

9. The document is printed by the terminating fax machine while it is being transmitted by the originating fax machine.

T38 acts as an error correcting, packet reordering, buffering filter, that connects the originating and terminating T30 fax streams.

T38 most often does not use the media transports used by voice calls (RTP), but a protocol unique to itself, UDPTL (if you're interested, both T30, T38, and UDPTL can be interpreted and visualized by the Wireshark open source packet analyzer).

T38 terminals and gateways

There is an important difference between a T38 terminal and a T38 gateway. A terminal would not connect to T30, for example, is free from the very strict timing and constraints of real-time fax machine interfacing, and so is a much simpler piece of software. *Smart* network fax machines could be T38 terminals. T38 fax servers can be a terminal when transmitting or receiving to/from another T38 terminal (a smart network fax machine, or another fax server).

When conversion to/from PSTN fax machines (T30) is involved, that's a job for T38 gateways, with all real-time related features.

Fax and FreeSWITCH

Receiving and sending a fax in FreeSWITCH is excruciatingly simple, consisting of two applications:

- `rxfax` (/path/where/to/write/TIFF)
- `txfax` (/path/where/to/read/TIFF)

That's it. Isn't that a beauty? Thanks to the world-class work of Steve Underwood, the recognized Godfather of Digital Signal Processing, `SpanDSP` library is integrated into FreeSWITCH and, amid many other goodies, provides complete T30 and T38 fax communication support.

 FreeSWITCH sends and receives TIFF files. You must do all the necessary conversions (to/from PDF, and so on).

All the finer details of fax communication are determined by a `mod_spandsp` configuration file (overridable runtime for each application invocation) and by information contained in the TIFF file itself (for example, resolution, size, color or b/w, and so on). Again, `mod_spandsp` configuration (overridable) determines if and how a T38 call upgrade will be attempted, and T38 terminal or gateway behavior to/from T30 and TDM (PSTN).

The mod_spandsp configuration

`mod_spandsp` is compiled by default and is part of the basic packages selection when installing from repositories; we can go straight to configuration. In the `conf/autoload_configs` directory we find `spandsp.conf.xml`. Relevant fax items are shown in the following screenshot:

```
<fax-settings>
    <param name="use-ecm"              value="true"/>
    <param name="verbose"             value="false"/>
    <param name="disable-v17"          value="false"/>
    <param name="ident"               value="SpanDSP Fax Ident"/>
    <param name="header"              value="SpanDSP Fax Header"/>

    <param name="spool-dir"            value="$${temp_dir}"/>
    <param name="file-prefix"          value="faxrx"/>
    <!-- how many packets to process before sending the re-invite on tx/rx -->
    <!-- <param name="t38-rx-reinvite-packet-count" value="50"/> -->
    <!-- <param name="t38-tx-reinvite-packet-count" value="100"/> -->
</fax-settings>
                                                       27,0-1          25%
```

Most of them you will probably override with dialplan or script commands, but let's start with some sane defaults:

- `use-ecm`: Best set this to false; some fax machines and oh-so-many T38 implementations do not work well with Error Correction Mode.

- `verbose`: During development, best set this to true. It will print an astonishing amount of information in debug log; you'll be able to follow the flow of protocol handshaking, the details of exchanged capabilities, and so on. Then, you disable it in production.

- `disable-v17`: Leave this set to false; if v17 (for example, 14,400 kbps) negotiation fails, it will fall back to 9,600 kbps. It is possible that in your specific case (for a multitude of factors), you will have a much higher rate of success if you disable v17 (set disable-v17 to true), and go directly with 9600, without negotiation.

- **ident**: This should be set to the telephone number you want to appear on the remote page header. To disable, put it to `_undef_` (note the underscores).

- **header**: This should be set to the text you want to appear on the remote page header. For example, `MyCompany`, `www.mycompany.com`. To disable, put it to `_undef_` (note the underscores).

- **spool-dir**: The filesystem directory where you want your incoming (received) fax files to be written into. For example, `/usr/local/freeswitch/received-faxes`.

- **file-prefix**: This one concurs to form a filename when the filename is not given as an argument.

- **rx-tx**: Leave the values of `rx-tx` re-invite packets to their default, that is, do not set them.

mod_spandsp usage

We saw it before: receiving and sending a fax are simple operations in FreeSWITCH. Let's see them in the proper context, with errors and results checking and so on.

To receive faxes (from dialplan):

```
<extension name="fax_receive">
<condition field="destination_number" expression="^9978$">
<action application="answer" />
<action application="playback" data="silence_stream://2000"/>
<action application="set" data="fax_enable_t38_request=true"/>
<action application="set" data="fax_enable_t38=true"/>
<action application="rxfax" data="/tmp/FAX-${uuid}.tif"/>
<action application="hangup"/>
</condition>
</extension>
```

1. We create an extension that will be reached by dialing 9978.

2. Answer the incoming call.

3. Play two seconds of silence (to allow for media to establish, remote fax to begin sending tones, and communication to stabilize).

4. Set the two variables that will allow for T38 (for example, we will answer positively to a T38 re-invite initiated by the remote party, and we will also actively re-invite to T38. If the remote party supports T38, we're sure we use it).

5. Start the `rxfax` application, with, as argument, a path composed including a variable (in this case the UUID of the incoming call).

6. After `rxfax` completion (successful or not), we hang up.

 If we had passed an empty argument to `rxfax` (`<action application="rxfax" data=""/>`), the default argument would kick in. The received filename and path would have been constructed from variables in `spandsp` configuration: `spool-dir/file-prefix-progressivenumber-timestamp.tif`.

For detecting incoming faxes (from dialplan):

```
<extension name="2010_with_fax_detect">
  <condition field="destination_number" expression="^(2010)$">
    <action application="answer"/>
    <action application="set" data="transfer_ringback=${us-ring}"/>
    <action application="spandsp_start_fax_detect" data="transfer '9198 XML default' 6"/>
    <action application="bridge" data="user/$1@${domain_name}"/>
  </condition>
</extension>
```

Let's use the same extension (for example, the same DID) for fax and voice calls. We want to automatically check if the incoming call is a fax transmission. If it's a fax, receive it. If it's not, connect the voice call to the user:

1. When a call is incoming to extension 2010.

2. Answer it.

3. Set a ringtone.

4. Start fax detection. Listen for a maximum of six seconds. If it's a fax, transfer the call to extension 9198 of XML dialplan (in default dialplan, 9198 is rxfax extension).

5. If the call was not transferred to 9198 (fax was not detected) bridge it (that is, transfer it) to registered user 1010 (while sending the ringtone to the caller).

For sending faxes (from a Lua script):

```
-- Send Fax
session:set_variable('absolute_codec_string', 'PCMU,PCMA')
session:set_variable('ignore_early_media', 'true')

session:set_variable('fax_ident',    my_number_string)
session:set_variable('fax_header',   my_companyname_string)
session:set_variable('fax_verbose', 'false')
session:set_variable('fax_enable_t38', 'true')
session:set_variable('fax_enable_t38_request', 'true')
session:set_variable('fax_use_ecm', 'false')

session:execute('txfax', fax_tiff_filename)
```

The first two lines are of most importance:

- We set the codecs in a non-negotiable way to G711 (ulaw or alaw, also known as PCMU and PCMA), the only codecs that can support fax transmission, and also the only codecs from which we can re-invite to T38

- To avoid possible problems with tone misinterpretation at call start, we set `ignore_early_media`; `txfax` will only start after the remote party has answered the call (for example, not while ringing or whatever) and audio will only be analyzed after that

- Then we set all fax-related variables

- Eventually, we send the fax tiff file

For checking results:

As we know, faxing on VoIP is tricky, and has nowhere near the reliability that faxing over PSTN offers. Yes, you can reach a very high success rate, but will probably never reach 100%, if nothing else, because the remote fax machine is out of paper, or was switched off mid-transmission.

After both sending and receiving faxes, FreeSWITCH fills a lot of channel variables. You use those variables to understand what happened, and in case of sending, to decide if and how to retry (for example, changing speed, ecm, or T38 variables). Variables you may want to check (see Confluence documentation for less useful vars):

- `fax_success` gives 0 on error, 1 on success
- `fax_result_text` gives info on what error has happened
- `fax_document_total_pages` gives how many pages were supposed to be transferred
- `fax_document_transferred_pages` gives how many pages were actually transferred
- `fax_transfer_rate` gives after negotiation, which speed was used for transmission
- `fax_ecm_used` gives after negotiation, if ecm was actually used
- `fax_image_resolution`
- `fax_image_size`

Debugging faxes

When first testing your installation, or when something is fishy with a transmission that does not want to go through, you want to debug the various negotiations and the transmission itself.

As we saw before, there are many negotiations potentially involved:

- SIP negotiation of the initial G711 call (initial INVITE)
- SIP negotiation of T38 (RE-INVITE)
- T30 negotiation (happens both in pure G711 T30 transmission and for T38 transmission)
- T38 negotiation

WireShark will be able to analyze it all at protocol level, on the wire, and display it nicely for you. But, for the sake of really understanding what's going on, you want to see things as seen from FreeSWITCH's vantage point. For example, you want to see dialplan, scripts, applications, protocols, codecs, and so on, interact dynamically in real time during your fax communication. When testing a new installation, you debug on the same machine. In a busy production system, you may want to debug on another machine with the same settings as the production machine:

```
freeswitch@internal> sofia global siptrace on
+OK Global siptrace on
freeswitch@internal> fsctl loglevel 7
+OK log level: DEBUG [7]

freeswitch@internal> console loglevel 7
+OK log level 7 [7]
+OK console log level set to DEBUG

freeswitch@internal> {ignore_early_media=true,absolute_codec_string='PCMU,PCMA',
fax_enable_t38=true,fax_verbose=true,fax_use_ecm=false,fax_enable_t38_request=tr
ue}sofia/gateway/default/1231231234 &txfax('test_fax.tif')
```

From `fs_cli`:

- Enable SIP packets visualization: `sofia global siptrace on`
- Enable debug output: `fsctl loglevel 7`
- Enable debug output: `console loglevel 7`
- Enable `fax_verbose=true` as channel variable, in the bridge/originate string, or in `spandsp.conf.xml`

You will then see it all, much more information than you would have thought is possible, and if you're not able to spot the problem yourself, copy and paste from the terminal to a pastebin, and reach out for help at FreeSWITCH community support or a professional.

How to maximize reliability of fax traffic

To transmit a fax after a previous failure, you retry by changing parameters. It seems a trivial solution, but is just the best practice, and the only path to a higher completion rate.

Fax transmission depends on oh-so-many external items, such as the model of the remote fax machine, software implementation of intermediate gateways, network delay, jitter, packet loss, local PSTN termination systems, and so on. Each item interacts with all others to influence fax transmission (fax being a transmission protocol that was not designed for packet networks).

So, you try to send a fax, and if you fail, you try again in a different way, trying to devise the progression that would maximize success rate with the minimum of attempts. This is a possible list (you must check the permutations that work best in your own situation):

- `originate_fax_enable_t38=true, originate_fax_enable_t38_request=true, originate_fax_use_ecm=false, originate_fax_disable_v17=false`

- `originate_fax_enable_t38=true, originate_fax_enable_t38_request=true, originate_fax_use_ecm=false, originate_fax_disable_v17=true`

- `originate_fax_enable_t38=true, originate_fax_enable_t38_request=false, originate_fax_use_ecm=false, originate_fax_disable_v17=true`

All attempts disable `ecm` and answer to T38 re-invites. The first attempt transmits at v17 speed (14,400 bauds) and actively re-invites T38. The second attempt is the same, but at lower speed (9,600). The third attempt is the same as second, but does not actively re-invite T38.

PDF to fax and fax to PDF

FreeSWITCH only deals with correctly formatted TIFF files; anything else will not work. No PDFs, nor JPGs, not even TIFF files slightly wrongly built.

A TIFF file contains in itself all information needed by `mod_spandsp`, such as resolution, paper size, how many pages it is composed of, and so on.

The best way is to start from a PDF file (easily exported or printed by any desktop program) and use the open source GhostScript software to convert it into a suitable (perhaps multipage) TIFF file.

So, install GhostScript (available on all platforms, it can be scripted on headless servers and does not need a desktop) and follow the examples listed at `http://www.soft-switch.org/spandsp_faq/ar01s14.html`, a page written by the very Steve Underwood.

As reported on the webpage, high volume PDF to TIFF conversion can be heavy on CPU. For a trafficked server it is better to do conversions on another machine.

PDF to TIFF, for the most standard format, would be as follows:

```
gs -q -sDEVICE=tiffg3 -r204x98 -dBATCH -dPDFFitPage -dNOPAUSE \
-sOutputFile=out.tif in.pdf
```

TIFF to PDF conversion is provided by the aptly named `tiff2pdf` utility made available on all platforms by `libtiff` open source library.

You can explore all its possible options with `tiff2pdf -h`, while to convert a TIFF produced by FreeSWITCH's `rxfax` into a PDF file with A4 page size and `Received Fax` title:

```
tiff2pdf -o out.pdf -p A4 -t "Received Fax" -F in.tif
```

Fax to mail

Once a fax has been successfully received, and perhaps converted to PDF, you may want to send it via e-mail. In doing so, you must pay attention to some small details, such as if the PDF or TIFF file is attached to the outgoing mail following all standards, and if it's correctly visualized by all mail clients on all platforms.

As an example, *Heirloom mailx* (`http://heirloom.sourceforge.net/mailx.html`) works well when used like this:

```
echo -e "This is the mail text" | mailx -s "this is mail subject"\ -S
from="sender@mycompany.com" -a "fax.pdf" \

-c "cc@yourcompany.com" -b "bcc@yourcompany.com" \ "receiver@yourcompany.
com"
```

HylaFax and FreeSWITCH

Since time immemorial, faxes on Unix systems have meant HylaFax. HylaFax interacts with local TTYs (for example, serial AT modems) for sending and receiving faxes on PSTN. Over the years, this has grown into an ecosystem of software applications, both on server and client sides, for managing enterprise size fax management and service providing.

You can find HylaFax at `http://www.hylafax.org/content/Main_Page`. HylaFax+, a derivative slightly more skewed toward VoIP, is at `http://hylafax.sourceforge.net/`.

HylaFax was designed to interact with modems, and modems do not work with VoIP. But companies were invested in HylaFax, had an internal workflow based on it, and were unwilling to switch over to other untested and unintegrated transmission methods.

How to reap the advantages and cost reduction of VoIP, and still operate through HylaFax? Yeah, simulating modems. `mod_spandsp` can provide softmodems for HylaFax to use. See the section modem-settings in `spandsp.conf.xml`:

But the latest and greatest in FreeSWITCH-HylaFax setup bypasses entirely the simulation of modems entirely, and interfaces HylaFax directly with FreeSWITCH, via Event Socket interface.

GOfax.IP is written in GO, supports both T30 and T38, and has been lauded by FreeSWITCH community. Check it out at `https://github.com/gonicus/gofaxip`.

ITSPs and Real World Fax Support

T38 is your best bet for fax communication through VoIP networks. But, not every VoIP connection has been created equal, nor are all VoIP providers one and the same. Completion rate can be poor, or interoperability wobbly.

You must make careful enquiries about T38 support when shopping for an ITSP or VoIP provider. Ask around, learn which are the proven operators in your region, and do your your research.

It is not unusual for a medium company to use an ITSP specifically for faxes, while using another one for voice traffic. This setup can also double as failover; for example, if one ITSP is down, you will redirect all traffic to the other one.

Summary

In this chapter, we first had an overview of how fax works in both traditional PSTN and VoIP. Then we described a T38 protocol, which makes faxing available on packet networks.

We delved into FreeSWITCH `mod_spandsp`, the module in charge of faxing (and other Digital Signal Processing features). We've seen how to configure the module, and how to receive, detect, and send faxes.

We then looked at the most common fax-related processing, like conversion from and to PDF, and mail attachment. We closed the chapter with hints on how to integrate FreeSWITCH's fax capabilities with workflows and ITSPs.

10
Advanced IVR with Lua

And now for something completely different!

In both of our cookbook and FreeSWITCH book you can find different examples and snippets of basic and intermediate Lua FreeSWITCH scripting. I will not repeat that.

What follows in this chapter is a moderately complex IVR application that makes use of different Lua FreeSWITCH techniques: logging, nesting, multiple files, setting and getting channel variables, accounting, asynchronous execution, web access, database access, error handling, post-hangup execution, functions, and so on.

Because this is not a basic snippet, and because it must strike a balance between comprehensibility and number of pages, I ask you to be patient and to bear with me while I describe the various steps.

I promise you will find reusable techniques, common patterns, and perhaps some inspiration.

Installing IVR

The complete application is made up of various files:

- `welcome.lua`: This is the main script
- `utils.lua`: This contains the utility functions provided to all other scripts
- `LuaRunWeb.lua`: This script is spawned by a function in `welcome.lua` for non-blocking web access
- `LuaRunMoh.lua`: This script is spawned by `welcome.lua` for non-blocking audio playback to the caller.
- `welcome.xml`: This is the dialplan entry

Because we will often reference different parts of the scripts you really must download the code from `www.packtpub.com`.

Then, copy all LUA files into the script directory of FreeSWITCH (default: `/usr/local/freeswitch/scripts/`), and put the XML file into the `default` subdirectory of FreeSWITCH dialplan (`/usr/local/freeswitch/conf/dialplan/default/`).

You will then load `mod_flite` into FreeSWITCH, because this script needs **Text To Speech** (**TTS**). If you have compiled from sources, go to `/usr/src/freeswitch.git` and type (pay attention to dash-underscore differences):

```
makemod_flite-install
```

Then you can `load mod_flite` from `fs_cli`, or add `mod_flite` to `/usr/local/freeswitch/conf/autoload_configs/modules.conf.xml` and restart FreeSWITCH.

Also, you need to load `mod_curl`, which is already compiled by default, and remember to add it to `modules.conf.xml`.

That's all you need to get started.

Structure of welcome.lua

The `welcome.lua` nucleus was originally written as a TTS menu demo by *Meftah Tayeb*, a blind Algerian tech enthusiast, who by sheer willpower and strength became a very active FreeSWITCH community member, and then a respected engineer for Algeria Telecom, and now is continuing his career in a private business.

We'll read it in detail in next section, but let's start with an outline of how its different sections fit together:

- **line 1**: Use `include`, and all its functions and variables

- **line 3 to 21**: A function that will be called later

- **line 23**: Here we check if we are answering the call or we are after hangup

- **line 25 to 51**: This block will be executed as `api_hangup_hook`, after call hangup

- **line 53 to 268**: This block is executed when the call comes in

- **line 54 to 78**: Set and get some session (for example, channel) variables

- **line 80**: Incoming call is answered

- **line 83**: First voice menu

  - **line 87 to 166**: Processing DTMFs pressed in the `first` voice menu

- **line 170**: Second voice menu
  - ○ **line 174 to 185**: processing DTMFs pressed in the `second` voice menu
- **line 189**: Third voice menu
  - ○ **line 193 to 207**: Processing DTMFs pressed in the `third` voice menu
- **line 211**: Fourth voice menu
  - ○ **line 215 to 261**: Processing DTMFs pressed the in `fourth` voice menu
- **line 265 to 268**: Some logging before hangup

Incoming call processing

At line 23 in the code we checked if the `env` array exists or is `nil`.

If `env` exists, the script is being executed as API `hangup_hook`, the call has been already hung up, there is no session (the call does not exist anymore), but all channel variables have been saved into `env`. We'll look into it in the next section.

If `env` does not exist then we know the script is called in `normal` mode, for example, there is an incoming call and a dialplan extension (in our case `2910`, in `welcome.xml`) is calling the script:

```
-- we are in the call, not in the API hangup hook
session:setInputCallback("input_callback", "ciao")
session:setHangupHook("myHangupHook")

session:setVariable("tts_engine", "flite")
session:setVariable("tts_voice", "rms")

session:set_tts_params("flite", "rms")

local call_uuid = session:getVariable("call_uuid")
local sip_P_Asserted_Identity = session:getVariable("sip_P-Asserted-Identity")
local caller_id = session:getVariable("effective_caller_id_number")
local this_call_caller_id = nil
if(not(sip_P_Asserted_Identity == nil)) then
  this_call_caller_id = sip_P_Asserted_Identity
else
  this_call_caller_id = caller_id
end
local log_filename = "/tmp/welcome"..call_uuid..".log"
local logfile = assert(io.open(log_filename, "a"))
stamp("***BEGIN***",whichline(),logfile,call_uuid,this_call_caller_id)

session:setVariable("this_call_log_filename", log_filename )
session:setVariable("this_call_caller_id", this_call_caller_id )
-- execute this file again, this time as api_hangup_hook, see before
session:setVariable("api_hangup_hook", "lua welcome.lua" )

session:answer()
```

Before answering

We are at **line 54** right now. The code in the preceding screenshot begins by setting an input callback function. That would be a function that process DTMFs entered by the caller when there is no other DTMF processor in execution (for example, when we are directly playing an audio file, and not while we're `playAndGetDigits` a menu, see the following (voice menu processing).

Then we set a `hangup` hook function. Note that this is very different from `api_hangup_hook` (we'll see that in the *After hangup* section, later). A `hangup` hook function is executed when there is a hangup on the call before the call/channel is destroyed and ceases to exist. A `hangup` hook function is indeed executed during the very same script run that set it, and has access to all session methods, channel variables, and more.

We'll see the content of the two functions we just set up, and how/what they do, later.

`session:setVariable` is the standard way to set a channel variable. In this case we set two channel variables (`tts_engine` and `tts_voice`) that affect the behavior of the module `mod_flite`. Very often you can affect the behavior of module-provided features by setting the appropriate channel variable(s) that override the module's configuration file content.

Also, we set `session:set_tts_params("flite", "rms")`, which will affect which TTS engine (`flite`) and voice (`rms`, voice by Richard Marshall Stallman, the GNU founder) the `session:speak()` function will use later.

Then we create some local variables (scope limited variables, as opposed to normally global variables). They get their value assigned from `session:getVariable`, the standard way to access the value of a channel variable.

One of the quirk in Lua is that if you use a `NIL` (or `nil`) value in a string concatenation (the `..` operator), you get a fatal error, and the script aborts. And if you `session:getVariable` a non-existing channel or session variable, you will get a `NIL` value. So you must always check and manage cases where a variable could contain `NIL`.

`assert(io.open(log_filename, "a"))` is a typical Lua construct for dealing with the operating system (the filesystem, in this case). It tries to create a `filehandle` (by opening or creating a file) to which it subsequently appends content. If it fails to create the `filehandle` (the directory does not exist, the directory is not writable, or the file exists but is not writable by the script), the script aborts. If it succeeds, we assign the `filehandle` to a local variable that will later be used as a target for writing (appending).

stamp() is a logging function we included from utils.lua file; we'll see it later, and we give it the filehandle to write to via a logfile local variable.

Then we create and assign a value to a couple of channel variables. We will need those channel variables when the script is re-executed as api_hangup_hook.

With session:setVariable("api_hangup_hook", "luawelcome.lua") we designate what FreeSWITCH API will do after the call hangup. The value we assign to api_hangup_hookchannel variable is exactly what we would type in the console or fs_cli command line. In this case we use the lua command to execute the welcome.lua script in the default FreeSWITCH scripts' directory. In this particular case the script file to be executed after hangup and call/session/channels/variables are destroyed is the same one we are reading right now. There's more on API hangup hook later in the chapter.

Eventually, on the last line in the previous screenshot, we session:answer() the call, and (hopefully) establish the audio bidirectional communication:

```
stamp("ANSWERED",whichline(),logfile,call_uuid,this_call_caller_id)

::FIRST_MENU::
stamp("FIRST_MENU",whichline(),logfile,call_uuid,this_call_caller_id)
while (session:ready() == true) do
  local digits = session:playAndGetDigits(1, 1, 3, 3000, "#", "say:Welcome to the Vo
Ip World! This is Blind Users Programming Community. Powered by Freeswitch, the free u
ltimate PBX. Thanks to Tony! Please select an action. To go to a nested menu, press 1.
 To call Freeswitch I V R, press 2. To hear classical music at very low volume, press
3. For originating an outgoing call to FreeSWITCH conference, and bridge the two legs,
 press 4. Press 5 to break out from while ready loop and exit the call. 6 will tell yo
u the exact time from web. Press 7 to interrogate the internal filesystem database. Fo
r remote database, press 8. Press 9 for a back ground asynchronous web query.","say:Yo
u have not pressed a key between 1 and 9!","[1-9]", digits, 3000, "operator")
    if (digits == "1") then
      stamp("FIRST_MENU: 1",whichline(),logfile,call_uuid,this_call_caller_id)
      goto SECOND_MENU
    end
    if (digits == "2") then
      stamp("FIRST_MENU: 2",whichline(),logfile,call_uuid,this_call_caller_id)
      session:execute("transfer","5000")
    end
    if (digits == "3") then
      stamp("FIRST_MENU: 3",whichline(),logfile,call_uuid,this_call_caller_id)
      session:streamFile("/usr/local/freeswitch/sounds/music/8000/suite-espanola-op-47
-leyenda.wav")
    end
```

First voice menu

Code in the preceding screenshot begins at **line 81**. In the first line, we `stamp()` we have answered in the `logfile` (we'll see later how the `stamp()` function works and what it does).

Then we see a line with `::FIRST_MENU::`. That's the Lua way to create a `label`, a marked position in code that we can jump to using a `goto` statement. Yes, I know there is a lot of bad press for `goto`, at least since the BASIC era. I would probably agree with it, if I had read it. But in the case of Lua IVRs, it is a nice way to separate voice menus without adding too much complexity. Sure, you can do it by transferring from a script with one voice menu to a different extension that calls a different script (or the same script with different arguments) leading to a different voice menu. Or you can nest loops into loops. You know, there is more than one way in programming.

We then `stamp()` that we've just arrived after the label, and are about to enter the first voice menu.

`while (session:ready() == true) do` (followed by `end` at the end of the code you want to conditionally execute) is a nice way to bail out of a loop when a call is hung up. You must always check the call was not hung up before doing anything that takes time to execute, or wait for user's input. If you wait for the user to press *1* when the call is already hung up, you'll wait a lot. For a similar reason, you'll want to check for hangup before doing a time-consuming call to a database, or web server, or a lengthy I/O.

In our case, we use `while (session:ready() == true) do` as a guard for not entering the first voice menu (even when coming from other voice menus via `goto`) in case the call is not up, and to create an infinite `while` loop that terminates only when the caller hangs up or is transferred away.

`session:playAndGetDigits()` is the workhorse function of voice menus. It's got it all, and the kitchen sink. You'll want to consult its official documentation in Confluence I'll try here to convey the feeling.

The caller input in the case of success will be stored in the local digits script variable.

Its arguments are `min_digits`, `max_digits`, `max_attempts`, `timeout`, `terminators`, `prompt_audio_file`, `input_error_audio_file`, `digit_regex`, `variable_name`, `digit_timeout`, and `transfer_on_failure`.

If you want a fixed number of digits, give `min_digits` the same value as `max_digits`. If they're not the same, the caller must input one of the DTMFs in the `terminators` string to let FreeSWITCH understand that they're done before having entered all of `max_digits` (or wait for `timeout`). `max_replays` is how many times `prompt_ audio_file` will be replayed because of non allowed digits or timeouts. `timeout` is 3 seconds (3000 milliseconds). If you want to manage input errors yourself in a different way than playing `input_error_audio_file` and coming back playing `prompt_ audio_file` (for example, maybe you want to read additional instructions, or go to a different menu, or transfer to an extension), then set `max_replays` to 1. `digit_regex` is a regular expression that defines which ones are the acceptable DTMFs. The last three arguments are `optional`, and define the channel variable name that will be created and assigned a string value made of gathered valid DTMFs, the inter-digit timeout when more than one DTMF is expected (3456), and to which extension the call will be transferred if there are more than `max_replays` errors.

In our case, we want just one DTMF, we try three times to get the correct input, the only terminator char is # (but we don't use it, we have min and max digits at the same value, 1), we use the TTS construct `say:text` to synthesize audio from text instead of providing the names of `prompt_audio_file` and `input_error_audio_ file`, we accept numbers from 1 to 9 as valid input, we create (and set) a channel variable named `digits`, and we explicitly set the inter-digit timeout (not used) to 3 seconds. That would in any case be its default value (it defaults to the timeout value). The last argument is the operator named `extension` we defined in our dialplan, to which the call will be transferred in case of final failure to gather input. If we omitted this last optional argument, the `while (session:ready() == true) do` would re-enter the `session:playAndGetDigits` line again and again, restarting anew after reaching the `max_replays (3)` number of tries. The only way out would be to hang up.

If input has not been gathered by `session:playAndGetDigits`, after `max_replays` the local script variable digits will be empty (not in our case, because we transfer to the operator in case of final failure) and the script will proceed to the next line.

We then check its value.

If the digit is 1 we jump (`goto`) to label `::SECOND_MENU::`.

If it's 2, we use the construct `session:execute()` to run a dialplan application; in our case, we use the transfer app to exit the script and re-enter the default dialplan at extension `5000`.

If it's 3 we use `session:streamFile` to play an audio file (classical guitar music, recorded at low volume). After playing the music, the script continues to the next step; here, we don't jump away as in the previous two cases.

```
    if (digits == "4") then
      stamp("FIRST_MENU: 4",whichline(),logfile,call_uuid,this_call_caller_id)
      session:execute("bridge","sofia/external/888@conference.freeswitch.org")
    end
    if (digits == "5") then
      stamp("FIRST_MENU: 5",whichline(),logfile,call_uuid,this_call_caller_id)
      break
    end
    if (digits == "6") then
      stamp("FIRST_MENU: 6",whichline(),logfile,call_uuid,this_call_caller_id)
      local api = freeswitch.API()
      isready(session, whichline(), logfile,call_uuid,this_call_caller_id)
      local utc_hours_right_now = api:execute("curl",
        "http://www.timeapi.org/utc/now?\\H")
      isnil(utc_hours_right_now, whichline(), logfile,call_uuid,this_call_caller_id,
        session)
      isready(session, whichline(), logfile,call_uuid,this_call_caller_id)
      local utc_minutes_right_now = api:execute("curl",
        "http://www.timeapi.org/utc/now?\\M")
      isnil(utc_minutes_right_now, whichline(), logfile,call_uuid,this_call_caller_id,
        session)
      isready(session, whichline(), logfile,call_uuid,this_call_caller_id)
      session:speak("U T C hour is " .. utc_hours_right_now ..
        ", while U T C minute is " .. utc_minutes_right_now .. ".")
    end
```

The code in the preceding screenshot starts at **line 99**.

If the digit is 4, we `session:execute()` the dialplan application bridge. In this case, the bridge app will originate an outbound SIP call to the remote `FreeSWITCH.org` conference server, and if this newly originated call is successfully connected to the server, the same bridge app will join it to our original incoming call (the incoming call that spawned this script). This will hopefully result in a bidirectional audio stream between the original call (**A leg** in this context) and the newly originated call (**B leg**). This bidirectional connection between two remote end parties is what end users understand as a call, while for us VoIP gurus, it's two calls bridged together.

If the digit is 5, we break out from the `while session:ready()` loop. In our case, this brings us to the end of the script. Arriving at the end of the script is the standard way to exit a LuaIVR script in FreeSWITCH. When a Lua script ends, the default action taken is to hang up the call. If you want instead to continue with the next dialplan action, then you must `session:setAutoHangup(false)`. In our case, we have not set it, so the call is hung up.

If the digit is 6, we make a couple of HTTP transfers via FreeSWITCH's internal `curl`, then combine those transfers results into a text that will be read to the caller by TTS. Let's see the details.

First, we create a local `freeswitch.API()` object and name it `api`. This object is a direct connection to the FreeSWITCH console command line (`fs_cli`). We can use it to get the result of the command we send.

Then, because an HTTP transfer can take time (for example, until `curl` timeout, or HTTP server timeout), and because an `api` call is blocking (for example, script wait for command result), before executing it we use our `isready()` function to check if call is up. `isready()` is just a glorified `session:ready()`, we'll see later about it. We'll see later how to have a non-blocking HTTP transfer. We `api:execute()` a `curl` command, exactly as if we were typing on `fs_cli`. In our case, we are getting the UTC hours and minutes in two local script variables.

`isnil()` checks if the variable is equal to NIL (for whatever reason). Because Lua scripts aborts if a NIL value is concatenated to form a string, we use the `isnil()` function to check the variable's value, and handle it nicely if the variable is NIL. We'll see later how this `isnil()` function works.

Eventually, `session:speak()` will use TTS to read the caller a string concatenated with the curl results:

```
if (digits == "7") then
   stamp("FIRST_MENU: 7",whichline(),logfile,call_uuid,this_call_caller_id)
   local dbh = freeswitch.Dbh("sqlite://voicemail_default")
   if dbh:connected() == false then
     freeswitch.consoleLog("WARNING", "welcome.lua cannot connect to database\n")
     isnil(nil, whichline(), logfile,call_uuid,this_call_caller_id,
       session)
   else
     freeswitch.consoleLog("WARNING", "welcome.lua connected to database\n")
   end
   local cid_number = nil
   dbh:query("select cid_number from voicemail_msgs", function(row)
       cid_number = row.cid_number
     end)
   isready(session, whichline(), logfile,call_uuid,this_call_caller_id)
   isnil(cid_number, whichline(), logfile,call_uuid,this_call_caller_id,session)
   freeswitch.consoleLog("WARNING",string.format("Message from %s",
       cid_number))
   session:speak("Message from. " .. cid_number .. ".")
end
if (digits == "8") then
   stamp("FIRST_MENU: 8",whichline(),logfile,call_uuid,this_call_caller_id)
   local dbh = freeswitch.Dbh("pgsql://hostaddr=192.168.1.108 dbname=testdb user=te
stuser password='testpassword'")
   if dbh:connected() == false then
     freeswitch.consoleLog("WARNING", "welcome.lua cannot connect to database\n")
     isnil(nil, whichline(), logfile,call_uuid,this_call_caller_id,
       session)
   else
     freeswitch.consoleLog("WARNING", "welcome.lua connect to database\n")
   end
   local name = nil
   dbh:query("select name from test_table limit 1", function(row)
       name = row.name
     end)
   isready(session, whichline(), logfile,call_uuid,this_call_caller_id)
   isnil(name, whichline(), logfile,call_uuid,this_call_caller_id,session)
   freeswitch.consoleLog("WARNING",string.format("name = %s", name))
   session:speak("name is. " .. name .. ".")
end
```

The code in the preceding screenshot starts at **line 124**.

If the digit is 7 we'll create a FreeSWITCH internal DB handle for querying the SQLite database FreeSWITCH uses as default persistence for voicemail metadata (for example, just for the information about voicemails; actual audio messages are by default stored as .wav files on the filesystem).

We pass the filename of the SQLite database we want to open or create to freeswitch.Dbh(). We can prepend the filename with an absolute directory path (for example, sqlite:///tmp/test). If we do not prepend it, the filename will be in the default FreeSWITCH core SQLite directory (if you compiled from source, it is /usr/local/freeswitch/db). Pay attention; if the db file is not there, it will not report an error. Instead, the db file will be created empty — if the directory exists, and is writable.

Then we check if our DB handle was not able to connect to the file, dbh:connected()==false, in which case we pass nil to the isnil() function (because in Lua, false is different to nil) to nicely handle connection failure.

If all is good, we dbh:query() the database handle and get a row of results in a local script variable. In our case, we ask for the caller ID number of a voicemail message. We then read it by TTS.

If the digit is 8 we again create an internal FreeSWITCH DB handle, this time to query a remote PostgreSQL database server. It works exactly as in the previous, 7, case.

FreeSWITCH can create internal DB handles for SQLite, PostgreSQL, and for ODBC connections. DB handles are pooled and managed in a very efficient way by FreeSWITCH, and are the recommended way to interact with databases.

If the digit is 9, we do an asynchronous, non-blocking HTTP transfer. We'll see this later.

Second and third voice menus

The code in the following screenshot starts at **line 170**.

```
::SECOND_MENU::
stamp("SECOND_MENU",whichline(),logfile,call_uuid,this_call_caller_id)
while (session:ready() == true) do
  local digits = session:playAndGetDigits(1, 1, 3, 3000, "#", "say:This is the second
menu. We are showing nested menus using dreaded gotos. Yes, you can use various nested
loops instead, if you like. To call music on hold, press 1. To go to the first menu, p
ress 2. To go to the third menu, press 3.","say:You have not pressed a key between 1 an
d 3!","[1-3]", digits, 3000, "operator")
  if (digits == "1") then
    stamp("SECOND_MENU: 1",whichline(),logfile,call_uuid,this_call_caller_id)
    session:execute("transfer","9664")
  end
  if (digits == "2") then
    stamp("SECOND_MENU: 2",whichline(),logfile,call_uuid,this_call_caller_id)
    goto FIRST_MENU
  end
  if (digits == "3") then
    stamp("SECOND_MENU: 3",whichline(),logfile,call_uuid,this_call_caller_id)
    goto THIRD_MENU
  end
end
goto END

::THIRD_MENU::
stamp("THIRD_MENU",whichline(),logfile,call_uuid,this_call_caller_id)
while (session:ready() == true) do
  local digits = session:playAndGetDigits(1, 1, 3, 3000, "#", "say:This is the third
menu. Again, nested menus. To call Lenny, the telemarketers punisher, press 1. To go to
the first menu, press 2. To go to the second menu, press 3.","say:You have not pressed
a key between 1 and 3!","[1-3]", digits, 3000, "operator")
  if (digits == "1") then
    stamp("THIRD_MENU: 1",whichline(),logfile,call_uuid,this_call_caller_id)
    session:setVariable("effective_caller_id_name", "Giovanni Maruzzelli")
    session:setVariable("effective_caller_id_number", "14158781565")
    session:execute("bridge",
      "{absolute_codec_string=pcmu,pcma}sofia/external/13475147296@in.callcentric.com")
  end
  if (digits == "2") then
    stamp("THIRD_MENU: 2",whichline(),logfile,call_uuid,this_call_caller_id)
    goto FIRST_MENU
  end
  if (digits == "3") then
    stamp("THIRD_MENU: 3",whichline(),logfile,call_uuid,this_call_caller_id)
    goto SECOND_MENU
  end
end
goto END

::END::
freeswitch.consoleLog("WARNING",
  "The End (https://en.wikipedia.org/wiki/The_End_%28The_Doors_song%29)\n")
stamp("***ENDED***",whichline(),logfile,call_uuid,this_call_caller_id)
```

The second and third menus are actually just a demo of how to use previous techniques to jump in and out of different voice trees. The only interesting thing is that with option 1 of the third menu, we bridge the call to Lenny, a beautiful honeypot/torturer for telemarketers, where an IVR will keep a telemarketer busy by simulating an old and chatty person. We first set `effective_caller_id_name` and `effective_caller_id_number`, because Lenny's server only accepts non-anonymous incoming calls. Then, we bridge to the SIP URI, prepending the setting of a channel variable to `dialstring`.

By the way, you definitely want to check Lenny's recorded sessions on YouTube at `https://www.youtube.com/playlist?list=PLduL71_GKzHHk4hLga0nOGWrXlhl-i_3g`.

Fourth menu – asynch! Nonblocking! Fun with threads!

The code in the following screenshot starts at **line 211**.

```
::FOURTH_MENU::
  stamp("FOURTH_MENU",whichline(),logfile,call_uuid,this_call_caller_id)
  while (session:ready() == true) do
    local digits = session:playAndGetDigits(1, 1, 3, 3000, "#", "say:This is the fourth
menu. Press 1 for a back ground asynchronous web query using threads. Press 2 to check
the web without threads. To go to the first menu, press 3.","say:You have not pressed
a key between 1 and 3!","[1-3]", digits, 3000, "operator")
    if (digits == "1") then
      stamp("FOURTH_MENU: 1",whichline(),logfile,call_uuid,this_call_caller_id)
      local api = freeswitch.API()
      session:setVariable("from_luarun_end_moh", "0");
      api:execute("luarun", "LuaRunMoh.lua "..log_filename.." "..call_uuid.." "..
        this_call_caller_id);
      stamp("MOH BACKGROUNDED",whichline(),logfile,call_uuid,this_call_caller_id)

      local utc_hours_right_now = LuaRunWeb(session, log_filename,
        "http://www.opentelecom.it/cgi-bin/test.cgi")
      isnil(utc_hours_right_now, whichline(), logfile,call_uuid,this_call_caller_id,
        session)
      local utc_minutes_right_now = LuaRunWeb(session, log_filename,
        "http://www.opentelecom.it/cgi-bin/test.cgi")
      isnil(utc_minutes_right_now, whichline(), logfile,call_uuid,this_call_caller_id,
        session)
      stamp("utc_hours_right_now="..utc_hours_right_now.." utc_minutes_right_now=" ..
        utc_minutes_right_now,whichline(),logfile,call_uuid,this_call_caller_id)

      session:setVariable("from_luarun_end_moh", "1");
      stamp("kill the moh",whichline(),logfile,call_uuid,this_call_caller_id)
      api:executeString("uuid_break "..call_uuid)-- stops moh
      api:execute("msleep", 300) -- pause a third of a second
      session:speak("U T C hour is " .. utc_hours_right_now ..
        ", while U T C minute is " .. utc_minutes_right_now .. ".")
    end
```

There are times when you want that something more. Normally just does not cut anymore.

Enter threads! In the fourth menu, by pressing 1, we can observe two usages of threads: the first one lets you play music or announcements to the caller while you do something else (originate another call leg, check the Web, query a database, or whatever). The second thread lets you check the Web while being shielded from the blocking and hangup aspects of Lua scripting. For example, the call is actually destroyed in FreeSWITCH immediately after hangup, while your Web checks (or db query, or whatever) continue unabated.

If the digit is 1, we begin by creating an API connection with FreeSWITCH. Then we set to zero a channel variable named from_luarun_end_moh".

At this point, we execute the **luarun api**. luarun starts a separate Lua interpreter in its own thread, passing to it all arguments. So, the first argument to luarun will be the name of the script to run, and the arguments that follow (if any) will be arguments to that script.

Let's check in the preceding screenshot how that script, LuaRunMoh.lua, works:

```lua
dofile("/usr/local/freeswitch/scripts/utils.lua")

--local moh_wav_file = "/usr/local/freeswitch/sounds/music/8000/suite-espanola-op-47-l
eyenda.wav"
local moh_wav_file = "/usr/local/freeswitch/sounds/en/us/callie/ivr/8000/ivr-thank_you
_for_holding.wav"
local orig_logfile = argv[1]
local call_uuid = argv[2]
local this_call_caller_id = argv[3]

local my_logfile = orig_logfile .. "_moh"
local logfile = assert(io.open(my_logfile, "a"))

local api = freeswitch.API()
local session = freeswitch.Session(call_uuid)

stamp("***BEGIN***",whichline(),logfile,call_uuid,this_call_caller_id)

stamp("moh_wav_file="..moh_wav_file,whichline(),logfile,call_uuid,this_call_caller_id)

if (not (session:ready() ) ) then goto goodbye; end
from_luarun_end_moh = session:getVariable("from_luarun_end_moh")
while(from_luarun_end_moh == "0") do
        stamp("START MOH",whichline(),logfile,call_uuid,this_call_caller_id)
        session:streamFile(moh_wav_file)
        api:execute("msleep", 300) -- pause a third of a second
        from_luarun_end_moh = session:getVariable("from_luarun_end_moh")
        if (not (from_luarun_end_moh == "0" )) then goto goodbye; end
end

::goodbye::
stamp("***ENDED***",whichline(),logfile,call_uuid,this_call_caller_id)
logfile:flush()
logfile:close()
```

After including the `utils.lua` file, we set which audio file will be played. Then the first three script arguments are assigned to local variables. We then open a `logfile` with the same name as the main script logfile plus an added suffix.

At this point, we get to the session from the `call_uuid` string we were passed as argument. That's the power of uuids! `session = freeswitch.Session(call_uuid)` give us a valid session object!

If `session:ready()` and call is still up, we check the channel variable `from_luarun_end_moh`. If it's `0` then we proceed to play the audio file to the caller. After a brief pause, if the variable has not changed, we play it again forever, in a loop.

Going back to the fourth menu in previous picture, we just *backgrounded* music on hold (MOH) to the caller. We then call the `LuaRunWeb()` function twice (we'll see its contents later) to check a value via the Web. Those two HTTP transfers (they could be `db` queries) will be executed even if the call has been hung up, because they run in an external thread of execution.

Those HTTP transfers incur a 15 second delay each, so you can test what happens if you hang up the call. You can see the CGI content in the following screenshot; it just sends `11` after a 15 seconds delay:

```
#!/bin/bash
echo -en "Content-Type: text/plain\n"
echo -en "\n"
sleep 15
echo -en "11"
```

After the second HTTP transfer we set the `from_luarun_end_moh` variable to `1` (this variable controls if MOH continues to loop after finishing the current play).

Then we interrupt the current playing by issuing a FreeSWITCH API break to the call leg `api:executeString("uuid_break "..call_uuid)`. This will immediately stop the audio stream.

Eventually we read the user the information we received via HTTP.

For your reference, if instead of `1` we pressed `2` at the fourth menu, we go to a non-threaded version of the same steps (without MOH, obviously). You can check there what happens if you hang up (hint: blocking). Pressing `3` brings you back to the first menu.

Let's check how the function we use to start an HTTP transfer in a different thread, `LuaRunWeb()`, works in the following screenshot:

```lua
function LuaRunWeb(session, logfilename, query)
  local api = freeswitch.API()
  session:setVariable("from_luarun_end_query", "0")
  api:execute("luarun", "LuaRunWeb.lua "..logfilename.." "..
    session:getVariable("call_uuid").." "..session:getVariable("this_call_caller_id")
      .. " "..fs_urlencode(query))
  local from_luarun_end_query = session:getVariable("from_luarun_end_query")
  local return_value = "CURL ERROR NO_SESSION"
  while(from_luarun_end_query == "0") do
    if (not (session:ready() ) ) then
      goto goodbye
    end
    api:execute("msleep", 300) -- pause a third of a second
    from_luarun_end_query = session:getVariable("from_luarun_end_query")
  end
  return_value = session:getVariable("curl_response_data")
  ::goodbye::
  return return_value
end
```

First we create a local API object, then we set a `from_luarun_end_query` channel variable to `0`.

Then we run `api:execute luarun`, and pass to it the script name `LuaRunWeb.lua` and other arguments for that script.

Because we need to have normal strings without spaces or special characters, to pass to the script as arguments, we URL-encode the last argument (the HTTP query) so we can use any complex URL. We'll see `fs_urlencode()` later, in the *Utility functions* section.

luarun returns immediately because `LuaRunWeb.lua` is spawned in its own new thread. So, while `LuaRunWeb.lua` is running, we spin in a loop, checking if it has finished. This loop spinning is interruptible both by hangup and by setting `from_luarun_end_query` to 1. We set a default return value `CURL ERROR NO_SESSION` to be returned if the caller hangs up before `LuaRunWeb.lua` returns the value grabbed from HTTP. And now, let's have a look at `LuaRunWeb.lua` in the following screenshot:

```
dofile("/usr/local/freeswitch/scripts/utils.lua")

local orig_logfile = argv[1]
local call_uuid = argv[2]
local this_call_caller_id = argv[3]
local query = fs_urldecode(argv[4])

local my_logfile = orig_logfile .. "_query"
local logfile = assert(io.open(my_logfile, "a"));

local api = freeswitch.API();

stamp("***BEGIN***",whichline(),logfile,call_uuid,this_call_caller_id)
stamp("query="..query,whichline(),logfile,call_uuid,this_call_caller_id)

local curl_response = api:execute("curl", query)
local session_exists = api:execute("uuid_exists", call_uuid)

if( not (session_exists == "false")) then
  local session = freeswitch.Session(call_uuid);
  session:setVariable("curl_response_data", curl_response)
  session:setVariable("from_luarun_end_query", "1")
end

stamp("session_exists="..session_exists,whichline(),logfile,call_uuid,
  this_call_caller_id)
stamp("curl_response="..curl_response,whichline(),logfile,call_uuid,
  this_call_caller_id)

::goodbye::
stamp("***ENDED***",whichline(),logfile,call_uuid,this_call_caller_id)
logfile:flush();
logfile:close();
```

We begin by including the `utils.lua` file. Then the first three script arguments are assigned to local variables.

The fourth argument is the URL we passed `urlencoded`, and we `urldecode` it before assigning it.

We then open a `logfile` with same name as the main script `logfile` plus an added suffix. After creating a local FreeSWITCH API object, we execute the (blocking) `curl` API command on the URL and gather the transfer result into a local variable. In our case, this will take 15 seconds because of the delay in CGI.

We then check if the string we get passed as the second script argument `call_uuid` still represents an existing FreeSWITCH session (that is, whether the call leg was not already hung up and destroyed).

If `call_uuid` is still valid, we create a session object from it and set two channel variables: `curl_response_data` to what we get from HTTP, and `from_luarun_end_ query` to 1.

This will break the spinning loop in the `LuaRunWeb()` function, and that function will proceed to grab the HTTP transfer from the `curl_response_data` channel variable, and return it to the main script. Wheeeeee!

After hangup

Let's go to the actual beginning of our main script, `welcome.lua`, in the following screenshot:

```lua
if(env) then
  -- we are in api_hangup_hook, after call ended
  local call_uuid = env:getHeader("call_uuid")
  local mduration = env:getHeader("mduration")
  local billmsec = env:getHeader("billmsec")
  local progressmsec = env:getHeader("progressmsec")
  local answermsec = env:getHeader("answermsec")
  local waitmsec = env:getHeader("waitmsec")
  local progress_mediamsec = env:getHeader("progress_mediamsec")
  local flow_billmsec = env:getHeader("flow_billmsec")
  local log_filename = env:getHeader("this_call_log_filename")
  local this_call_caller_id = env:getHeader("this_call_caller_id")

  freeswitch.consoleLog("WARNING", "ACCOUNTING in MILLISECONDS:\nmduration=".. 
    mduration.."\nbillmsec=".. billmsec.."\nprogressmsec="..progressmsec..
    "\nanswermsec="..answermsec.."\nwaitmsec="..waitmsec.."\nprogress_mediamsec=".. 
    progress_mediamsec.."\nflow_billmsec="..flow_billmsec.."\n")

  local logfile = assert(io.open(log_filename, "a"))
  stamp("ACCOUNTING in MILLISECONDS:\nmduration="..mduration.."\nbillmsec=".. 
    billmsec.."\nprogressmsec="..progressmsec.."\nanswermsec="..answermsec..
    "\nwaitmsec="..waitmsec.."\nprogress_mediamsec="..progress_mediamsec..
    "\nflow_billmsec="..flow_billmsec.."\n", whichline(),logfile, 
    call_uuid,this_call_caller_id)

  local dat = env:serialize()
  freeswitch.consoleLog("WARNING", "DUMP BEGINS\n"..dat.."\nDUMP ENDS\n")
  stamp("DUMP BEGINS\n"..dat.."\nDUMP ENDS\n", whichline(),logfile,call_uuid, 
    this_call_caller_id)
else
```

After including the `utils.lua` and `LuaRunWeb()` function, we check the env object.

If env is a valid object, the script has been called a API Hangup Hook.

The call leg has already been destroyed, so the session object is not valid any more. But we have in `env` a copy of all channel variables. In addition to all those variables, we have also the definitive values and the only reliable source of valid accounting timers available via FreeSWITCH scripting (you have all of them via ESL, but that's another chapter).

We repeat: if you want to do accounting from scripting, API Hangup Hook is the only way to have ready-made accurate durations for all call phases.

We use `env:getHeader()` to assign some of those values to local variables, then we print it on FreeSWITCH's console as a warning message.

Then we reopen the same filename that was opened, written, and closed the first time this script was run (answering the incoming call), and append to it our logging. This technique is useful for keeping all logging neatly organized by `call_ids`.

Then we get a local variable with `env:serialize()` value, so actually we dump in `urlencoded` format all the contents of `env`, and then print it both on the FreeSWITCH console and in the logfile.

Utility functions

We've used a lot of self-written functions. It's time to have a look at them. Let's open the top half of the `utils.lua` file, in the preceding screenshot.

The first three functions serve mainly to build the fourth function, `stamp()`, that we use throughout our scripts to do structured logging.

`shell()` is an example of a typical Lua interaction with an operating system. It executes a command, and returns the output as a string. We use it in `stamp()` to obtain the result of the command `date`.

`trim()` uses Lua native string manipulation, and is equivalent to the `chomp()` command in Perl, and many similar others in different languages: it deletes the trailing newline in a string, if it exists, and returns the string without the newline.

`whichline()` comes from the debug package. It returns the current line number in the script, for example, like `__line__` in C.

`stamp()` is our logging workhorse; it takes the string we want to log (our log message), a string (returned by `whichline()`) representing where we are in the script file, an open filehandle to append to, the `uuid` string identifying the call we're logging about, and the call's `callerid` string as arguments. The function pretty prints all its arguments to the file, adding the current `datetime`.

fs_urlencode() and fs_urldecode() use the FreeSWITCH API to encode and decode a string as per the URL W3C standard. We use it in LuaRunWeb() to pass URLs and HTTP transfer results back and forth.

```lua
function shell(c)
  local o, h
  h = assert(io.popen(c,"r"))
  o = h:read("*all")
  h:close()
  return o
end

function trim(s)
  return (s:gsub("^%s*(.-)%s*$", "%1"))
end

function whichline()
  return debug.getinfo(2, 'l').currentline
end

function stamp(string,whichline,logfilehandle, uuid, callerid)
  local logfile=logfilehandle
  local local_date = shell("date");
  logfile:write(local_date);
  logfile:write("call_uuid="..uuid.."\n");
  logfile:write("caller_id="..callerid.."\n");
  logfile:write("line="..whichline.."\n");
  logfile:write("\n\n");
  logfile:write(trim(string).."\n\n");
  logfile:write("=========\n\n");
  logfile:flush();
end

function fs_urlencode(s)
  local fsapi = freeswitch.API();
  return fsapi:execute("url_encode", s)
end

function fs_urldecode(s)
  local fsapi = freeswitch.API();
  return fsapi:execute("url_decode", s)
end
```

Let's look now at the bottom half of `utils.lua`file in the following screenshot:

```lua
function isready(session, line, logfile,call_uuid,this_call_caller_id)
  if (not (session) ) then
    error()
  end
  if (not (session:ready() ) ) then
    stamp("HANGUP: SESSION NOT READY at LINE: "..line.."\n",whichline(),logfile,
      call_uuid,this_call_caller_id)
    freeswitch.consoleLog("WARNING",
      "The End (https://en.wikipedia.org/wiki/The_End_%28The_Doors_song%29)\n")
    stamp("***ENDED***",whichline(),logfile,call_uuid,this_call_caller_id)
    error()
  end
end

function isnil(variable, line, logfile,call_uuid,this_call_caller_id,session)
  if (variable == nil) then
    stamp("ERROR: VARIABLE IS NIL at LINE: "..line.."\n",whichline(),logfile,
      call_uuid,this_call_caller_id)
    session:speak("We are sorry, an internal error has occurred, this call will be ter
minated. Please pardon and call again.")
    freeswitch.consoleLog("WARNING",
      "The End (https://en.wikipedia.org/wiki/The_End_%28The_Doors_song%29)\n")
    stamp("***ENDED***",whichline(),logfile,call_uuid,this_call_caller_id)
    error()
  end
end

function input_callback(session, type, obj, arg)
  freeswitch.consoleLog("WARNING", "CALLBACK: type: " .. type .. "\n")
  if (type == "dtmf") then
    freeswitch.consoleLog("WARNING", "CALLBACK: digit: [" .. obj['digit'] ..
      "]\nduration: [" .. obj['duration'] .. "]\n")
    if ( (obj['digit'] == "*") or (obj['digit'] == "#") ) then
      freeswitch.consoleLog("WARNING", "CALLBACK: got " .. obj['digit'] ..
        " let's break out of blocking operation\n")
      return "break"
    end
  end
end

function myHangupHook(session, status, arg)
  local mduration = session:getVariable("mduration")
  local sip_received_port = session:getVariable("sip_received_port")
  if(mduration == nil) then mduration="N/A" end
  freeswitch.consoleLog("WARNING", "myHangupHook=" .. status .. " hangupCause="..
    session:hangupCause().." mduration="..mduration.." sip_received_port="..
    sip_received_port.."\n")
end
```

The first two functions, `isready()` and `isnil()`, help us manage situations where we expect a condition vital for the continuation of the script to be true, specifically the `call to be up` (not already hung up) and a variable to be non-nil.

`isready()` will print in the logfile at which line the session was found to be already hung up, and then aborts the script execution with an error.

`isnil()` shields us from a quirk of Lua's that I found most disagreeable: if you try to concatenate a variable that has a `nil` value, the script aborts. `isnil()` gives us an orderly script shutdown, printing a log line and playing the caller a *we're sorry, there is an error, please call again* TTS audio stream.

The last two functions have much more active roles.

`input_callback()` is the DTMF interpreter we set very early in our `welcome.lua` incoming call processing section. When there is not another DTMF processor active (for example, when we are not executing a `PlayAndGetDigits()` menu), `input_callback` will listen to keypresses from the caller, and act accordingly. In our case, we react to * and #, *breaking* out from blocking operations. For example, if the caller presses star or pound while listening to an audio file playing, the playback will be interrupted immediately, and the script proceeds to the next step.

`myHangupHook()` is a function that is called during incoming call processing when the call is hung up, as the last step before the session is destroyed. At this stage, no accounting timers and values are available yet (that you get in the post hangup API hook), but you still have the session, and you can do other kinds of useful last moment things.

Summary

In this chapter we delved right into the middle of a moderately complex LuaIVR.

We saw an example of how to implement different Lua FreeSWITCH techniques: logging, nesting, multiple files, setting and getting channel variables, accounting, asynchronous execution, web access, database access, error handling, post-hangup execution, functions, and more.

First, we introduced how to create interactive voice menus with `PlayAndGetDigits()`, the workhorse of FreeSWITCH LuaIVR scripting.

At the same time we showed TTS usage with `say()`, which is very useful both for prototyping and for reading arbitrary messages to the caller.

Then we originated a new call leg and connected the incoming call to the outbound leg, bridging them in an end-to-end call.

We used the basic `curl()` API function to access the Web, and used the power of FreeSWITCH's Dbh to access both local and remote databases.

We switched back and forth between different menus using the despised `gotoLua` construct.

Then we showed you some techniques to try, techniques that allow nonblocking and asynchronous concurrent execution of various tasks, such as playing music to the caller while accessing the Web or a database, or while connecting outbound calls.

We closed the chapter with a description of the utility functions we used that you can customize and recycle.

11
Write Your FreeSWITCH Module in C

Modules are where you add functionalities to FreeSWITCH.

Is not very easy to write or modify a module, but neither is rocket science (by the way, as in real life, it always depends on what kind of rocket you want to build). And you can always find professional help by contacting the core FreeSWITCH developers.

This chapter will lay down all of the basic techniques needed to develop a new module:

- Reading XML configuration
- Adding a dialplan application
- Adding an API command
- Adding an event hook
- Adding a channel state change hook
- Firing an event

What is a FreeSWITCH module?

FreeSWITCH proper, the core FreeSWITCH, is a switching and mixing fabric with some message queues and a lot of very abstract APIs that define concepts and actions. The only possible interaction with the core is via those APIs and message queues; there is no access whatsoever to internal data, structure, functions, and so on. Everything is completely opaque and protected; there is no way to harm the stability and performance of core. From the outside, core is a blackbox able to accept commands and return results via APIs.

All functionalities are implemented in modules.

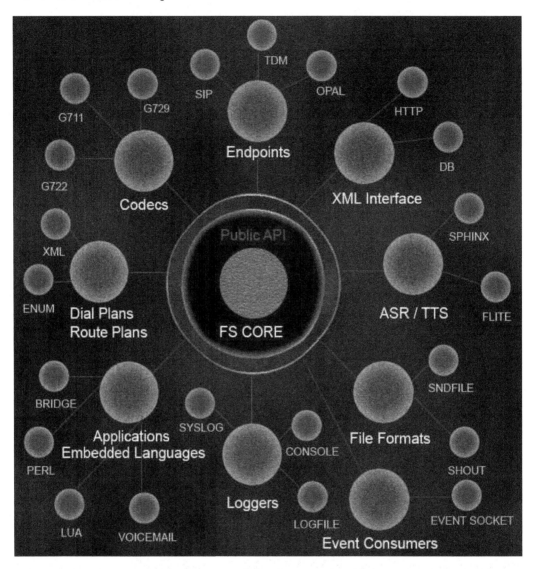

A FreeSWITCH module is a shared library to be loaded by core. A module provides additional features, APIs, and implementations. Usually, a module is the low-level plumbing needed to interact with the real world.

In core you have the concepts of channel, session, call, message, codec, and many others. These are just concepts, well thought-out and articulated abstractions useful to describe real-time communication entities at their interoperability plane.

In modules you have actual implementations of a, let's say, SIP channel, or voicemail system, or G711 codec. Modules make the bytes go around.

Modules are roughly categorized by the features that they bring to FreeSWITCH, and as such they are organized into `src/mod/*` subdirectories, for example, endpoints (modules that implement actual communication protocols or devices, such as SIP, TDM cards, Skype, and many more) are under `src/mod/endpoints`, formats (the ability to read data from a specific kind of file) are under `src/mod/formats`, and so on and so on (to quote Zizek).

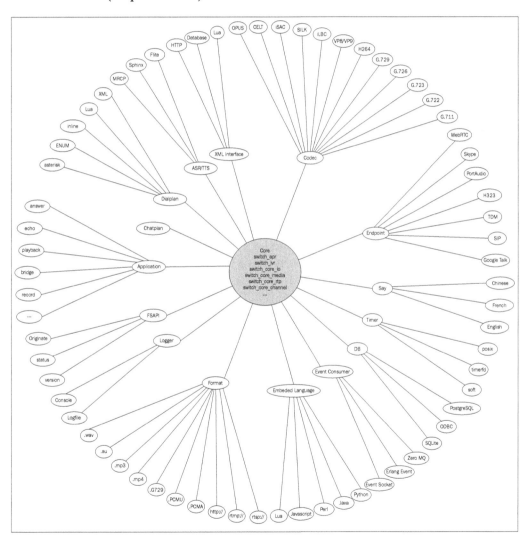

In each of those subdirectories you find all that's needed to compile a module, its source file(s), its makefiles, and all ancillary stuff.

Developing a module

As we commoners always do, and which sets us apart from Jedis such as Anthony Minessale II, we start developing our new FreeSWITCH module by copying from a working one.

You can start by copying the one I'm presenting here, `mod_example`. I have started copying `mod_skel`, removing complex things from it, then I added simple things. I like simple things.

You copy the entire directory and rename it, you delete `Makefile.in` and `Makefile` (for example, you only leave and edit `Makefile.am`) and you rename all occurrences of the same name in each of the files contained in that directory. In my case, `mod_skel.c` was renamed `mod_example`, and all instances of `skel` were modified to `example` inside all other files. At the end of this process, if you `grep` in the new directory, you don't find any more mention of `skel` (the original module name).

You then go in the main FreeSWITCH sources directory, edit `modules.conf` file, and add a line for your new module. After that, from that same main sources directory, you issue `make mod_yourmodulename-install`, and hopefully the Makefile will be created and your module will be compiled and installed. In my case, that command was as follows (notice the difference between a dash and an underscore):

```
# make mod_example-install
```

Copy the `config` file, `example.conf.xml`, into `conf/autoload_configs/`. Then from FreeSWITCH's console, or `fs_cli`, type this command:

```
> load mod_example
```

To unload it, use the aptly named command:

```
> unload mod_example
```

Hopefully, you'll be greeted by `Successfully Loaded` (the errors are expected, we'll talk about them later), and then by a `Runtime!` line, repeated each 5 seconds, until you type the following:

```
> example
```

```
freeswitch@freeswitch-src-01> load mod_example
+OK Reloading XML
+OK

2016-06-22 07:32:49.957101 [INFO] mod_enum.c:880 ENUM Reloaded
2016-06-22 07:32:49.957101 [ERR] mod_example.c:136 Integer must be an integer, but is 3
0a
2016-06-22 07:32:49.957101 [ERR] mod_example.c:144 Unknown attribute ciao
2016-06-22 07:32:49.957101 [INFO] switch_time.c:1415 Timezone reloaded 1750 definitions
2016-06-22 07:32:49.957101 [CONSOLE] switch_loadable_module.c:1538 Successfully Loaded
[mod_example]
2016-06-22 07:32:49.957101 [NOTICE] switch_loadable_module.c:292 Adding Application 'ex
ample'
2016-06-22 07:32:49.957101 [NOTICE] switch_loadable_module.c:338 Adding API Function 'e
xample'
2016-06-22 07:32:54.957160 [NOTICE] mod_example.c:296 Runtime!
2016-06-22 07:32:59.957142 [NOTICE] mod_example.c:296 Runtime!
2016-06-22 07:33:04.957142 [NOTICE] mod_example.c:296 Runtime!
freeswitch@freeswitch-src-01> |
```

Mod_Example outline

mod_example has been written to be, huh, an example, so I tried to stuff in it many useful features, in the simplest way. You can use it as a base, adding and subtracting features:

mod_example.c code layout:

- Declarations:
    - The module's mandatory three functions (example_load, example_runtime, example_shutdown)
    - Module definition
    - A data structure (globals) we'll use to keep state and configuration
    - The function (example_on_state_change) we'll execute when channel state changes
    - The table (example_state_handler) describing which function to execute at which state change

- Implementations:
    - The function (example_on_state_change) we'll execute when channel state changes
    - The function (do_config) we use to read values from config file and initialize the globals data structure

- ° The function (example_api) we use to implement an API command
- ° The function (example_event_handler) we use to implement reactions to events
- ° The function (example_app) we use to implement a dialplan application
- ° Modules' mandatory three functions (example_load, example_runtime, example_shutdown)

Mandatory functions

Each FreeSWITCH module must at least declare three functions, LOAD, RUNTIME, and SHUTDOWN:

```
#include <switch.h>

SWITCH_MODULE_LOAD_FUNCTION(example_load);
SWITCH_MODULE_RUNTIME_FUNCTION(example_runtime);
SWITCH_MODULE_SHUTDOWN_FUNCTION(example_shutdown);
                                                   2,0-1        Top
```

The LOAD and SHUTDOWN functions must be implemented, and are called at startup and when unloading the module. In LOAD you create and initialize the module's data structures, get values from the configuration file, and get your module ready for work. In SHUTDOWN you do any housekeeping needed to happily forget about your module, and in particular you release any resources you may have locked or allocated during module initialization and lifespan.

RUNTIME function implementation is not mandatory. For example, you must declare it, but you can avoid implementing it. If you implement it, the RUNTIME function will be executed in its own thread after the LOAD function has finished execution, for example, when the module has been successfully loaded by FreeSWITCH.

RUNTIME is often (not always) implemented as a looping function that will continue to run until module unloads.

Load function

Let's see what's inside our implementation of the LOAD function.

```
/* Macro expands to:
switch_status_t example_load(switch_loadable_module_interface_t
        **module_interface, switch_memory_pool_t *pool) */
SWITCH_MODULE_LOAD_FUNCTION(example_load)
{
        switch_api_interface_t *api_interface;
        switch_application_interface_t *app_interface;

        /* connect my internal structure to the blank pointer passed to me */
        *module_interface = switch_loadable_module_create_module_interface(pool,
                modname);

        do_config(SWITCH_FALSE);

        globals.looping = 1;
        globals.print = 1;

        SWITCH_ADD_API(api_interface, "example", "this command fires an event of " \
                "type TRAP, and toggle printing on/off from module's runtime function",
                example_api, "");

        SWITCH_ADD_APP(app_interface, "example", "prints <num> log lines",
                "prints <num> log lines, 5 as default, min 0, max 1024", example_app,
                "<num>", SAF_NONE);

        switch_event_bind("mod_example", SWITCH_EVENT_ALL,
                SWITCH_EVENT_SUBCLASS_ANY, example_event_handler, NULL);

        switch_core_add_state_handler(&example_state_handler);

        /* indicate that the module should continue to be loaded */
        return SWITCH_STATUS_SUCCESS;
}
                                                          271,0-1        84%
```

After declaring an api_interface and an app_interface pointer (we'll use them later) we allocate an interface structure from the memory pool that was given to us, and let module_interface point to it. Being allocated from an automatically managed memory pool, there will be no need to free the interface structure when unloading.

do_config() implements the important task of reading values from the XML config file and initializing the globals data structure where we decided to store module state and configuration. We'll look into this function later.

We then set two integer members of the `globals` data structure, looping and print, to 1 (structure names and members are just a convention; they can be whatever you like). We use them to control the `RUNTIME` function behavior.

Then we register with FreeSWITCH core both an API and an APP function, `example_api` and `example_app`, with their names, invocation, help description, and arguments. They will then become available respectively as an API command (you'll be able to invoke it from the console, `fs_cli`, and ESL connection) and as a dialplan application (you'll be able to invoke it as an `action` tag). We'll see these two functions later.

`switch_event_bind` will subscribe our `example_event_handler` function to all kinds of events, while `switch_core_add_state_handler` will register that function with FreeSWITCH core.

Eventually we return with success, telling FreeSWITCH core this module loading phase is finished, and can proceed further.

Runtime function

If the module's `RUNTIME` function has been implemented, it will be executed into a new thread as soon as the `LOAD` function returns successfully. It is often implemented as a loop that runs until the module is unloaded. You can also use a nice feature of FreeSWITCH core related to this kind of function: if the function returns anything different from `SWITCH_STATUS_TERM`, core will execute it again (if the module is still present, for example, if it was not unloaded).

```
/* Macro expands to: switch_status_t example_runtime() */
SWITCH_MODULE_RUNTIME_FUNCTION(example_runtime)
{
        while(globals.looping)
        {
                switch_yield(5000000); // 5 seconds
                if(globals.print)
                        switch_log_printf(SWITCH_CHANNEL_LOG, SWITCH_LOG_NOTICE,
                                "Runtime!\n");
        }
        switch_log_printf(SWITCH_CHANNEL_LOG, SWITCH_LOG_NOTICE, "Exit Runtime!\n");
        return SWITCH_STATUS_TERM;
}
                                                        284,57          95%
```

In our implementation, `example_runtime` runs in a loop until the looping member of `globals struct` tests as `true`. In each loop, it sleeps for 5 seconds, then tests the `print` member of `globals`, and if `true` it prints a log line.

If looping tests `false`, the function exits and returns `SWITCH_STATUS_TERM` because we chose not to use the runtime function restart feature of FreeSWITCH core.

Shutdown function

In the `shutdown` function you must clean it all and restore the situation as it was before the module loaded. You free allocated memory and other resources, and unregister all interfaces from FreeSWITCH core.

```
/* Macro expands to: switch_status_t example_shutdown() */
SWITCH_MODULE_SHUTDOWN_FUNCTION(example_shutdown)
{
        globals.looping = 0;
        switch_core_remove_state_handler(&example_state_handler);
        switch_event_unbind_callback(example_event_handler);
        switch_safe_free(globals.string);
        return SWITCH_STATUS_SUCCESS;
}
                                              273,58        90%
```

In our implementation, `example_shutdown` as its first step sets looping to `false` so the runtime function will exit at the next loop. Then it unregisters the event subscription and handler from FreeSWITCH core.

We use `switch_safe_free` to free the memory we allocated to store a string read from configuration (see later). When we unload the module, or when FreeSWITCH shuts down, we can see `example_shutdown` is executed.

```
freeswitch@freeswitch-src-01> unload mod_example
+OK

2016-06-22 10:01:21.197125 [NOTICE] switch_loadable_module.c:1055 Deleting Applicatio
n 'example'
2016-06-22 10:01:21.197125 [DEBUG] switch_loadable_module.c:1057 Write lock interface
 'example' to wait for existing references.
2016-06-22 10:01:21.197125 [NOTICE] switch_loadable_module.c:1110 Deleting API Functi
on 'example'
2016-06-22 10:01:21.197125 [DEBUG] switch_loadable_module.c:1112 Write lock interface
 'example' to wait for existing references.
2016-06-22 10:01:21.197125 [CONSOLE] switch_loadable_module.c:2012 Stopping: mod_exam
ple
2016-06-22 10:01:21.197125 [NOTICE] switch_event.c:2100 Event Binding deleted for mod
_example:ALL
2016-06-22 10:01:21.197125 [CONSOLE] switch_loadable_module.c:2028 mod_example stoppi
ng runtime thread.
2016-06-22 10:01:25.457213 [NOTICE] mod_example.c:297 Exit Runtime!
2016-06-22 10:01:25.457213 [NOTICE] switch_loadable_module.c:115 Thread ended for mod
_example
2016-06-22 10:01:25.457213 [CONSOLE] switch_loadable_module.c:2032 mod_example unload
ed.
freeswitch@freeswitch-src-01> freeswitch@freeswitch-src-01>
```

Configuration using XML

FreeSWITCH uses XML to represent its configuration, because XML lends itself perfectly (and directly) to a tree representation in which you can add and delete branches and leaves and easily locate sections, parameters, and values. Optimized XML routines are able to parse, create an in-memory representation, and manipulate that representation.

So, you'd better stop whining and learn to love XML.

There are many advanced facilities to help parse FreeSWITCH's configuration files; check syntax; associate settings, parameters, names, descriptions, allowed values' ranges; and many more.

In our implementation we keep it simple to the max (we love kisses), and only use the most basic XML related functions.

```
static switch_status_t do_config()
{
        switch_xml_t xml_root_node = NULL, settings = NULL, param = NULL, node = NULL;

        memset(&globals, 0, sizeof(globals));

        if ((xml_root_node = switch_xml_open_cfg("example.conf", &node, NULL))) {
                if ((settings = switch_xml_child(node, "settings"))) {
                        for (param = switch_xml_child(settings, "param"); param;
                                param = param->next) {
                                const char *name = switch_xml_attr(param, "name");
                                const char *value = switch_xml_attr(param, "value");

                                // Ignore empty/missing attributes
                                if (switch_strlen_zero(name)) {
                                        continue;
                                }
                                if (switch_strlen_zero(value)) {
                                        continue;
                                }

                                if (!strcmp(name, "string")) {
                                        // allocate memory in "globals" and copy string
                                        switch_strdup(globals.string, value);
                                } else if (!strcmp(name, "integer")) {
                                        int nodigit=0, i;

                                        for(i=0; i<strlen(value); i++) {
                                                if(!isdigit(value[i])){
                                                        nodigit=1;
                                                }
                                        }
                                        if(nodigit) {
                                                switch_log_printf(SWITCH_CHANNEL_LOG, S
WITCH_LOG_ERROR, "Integer must be an integer, but is %s\n", value);
                                        } else{
                                                globals.integer = atoi(value);
                                        }
                                } else {
                                        switch_log_printf(SWITCH_CHANNEL_LOG, SWITCH_LO
G_ERROR, "Unknown attribute %s\n", name);
                                }
                        }
                }
        } else {
                switch_log_printf(SWITCH_CHANNEL_LOG, SWITCH_LOG_ERROR, "Failed to load
 example's config!\n");
        }
        return SWITCH_STATUS_SUCCESS;
}
                                                                108,0-1        39%
```

We create our XML pointers, then we raze the `globals` data structure we'll use to store state and configuration (you'd better do this razing, or you'll end up with stale values if you unload then reload the module).

`switch_xml_open_cfg()` will read our XML configuration file and insert (or substitute, if already present) its parsed content as a branch into the in memory XML configuration tree.

Then we are able to begin querying the configuration, looping into sections, subsections, parameters, and so on. We put two values into the `globals` data structure. One we convert to an integer and assign directly to a structure member. The other we want to store as a string, and so we use `switch_strdup()` to safely allocate memory to the `globals` pointer member and duplicate the string. Memory will be freed by the SHUTDOWN module's function.

Reacting to channel state changes

FreeSWITCH channels are always, deterministically, in one specific state of a finite state machine. There are rules for going from one state to another, and you can ask FreeSWITCH core to alert your module whenever a channel changes state.

There are 12 states a channel can be in (`init`, `routing`, `execute`, `hangup`, `exchange_media`, `soft_execute`, `consume_media`, `hibernate`, `reset`, `park`, `reporting`, `destroy`), plus the state `none`, which a channel is supposed to never assume.

State changes are important moments, particularly for billing and accounting (start of media flows, hangup), but you may want to trigger some procedures in other cases too, for example, when a channel is parked.

```
switch_state_handler_table_t example_state_handler = {
        /* on_init */ example_on_state_change,
        /* on_routing */ NULL,
        /* on_execute */ NULL,
        /* on_hangup */ example_on_state_change,
        /* on_exch_media */ NULL,
        /* on_soft_exec */ NULL,
        /* on_consume_med */ NULL,
        /* on_hibernate */ NULL,
        /* on_reset */ NULL,
        /* on_park */ NULL,
        /* on_reporting */ NULL,
        /* on_destroy */ NULL
};

static switch_status_t example_on_state_change(switch_core_session_t *session) {
        switch_channel_t *channel = NULL;
        const char *change_count;
        switch_channel_state_t state;
        char chan_state[64];

        channel = switch_core_session_get_channel(session);

        change_count = switch_channel_get_variable(channel,"change_count");
        if(change_count){
                int number = atoi(change_count);
                number++;
                switch_channel_set_variable_printf(channel,"count","%d", number);
        }else{
                switch_channel_set_variable(channel,"change_count","1");
        }

        state = switch_channel_get_state(channel);

        switch (state) {
                case CS_HANGUP: /* Deactivate and end the thread */
                        sprintf(chan_state, "CS_HANGUP");
                        break;
                case CS_INIT:           /* Basic setup tasks */
                        sprintf(chan_state, "CS_INIT");
                        break;
                default:
                        break;
        }

        switch_log_printf(SWITCH_CHANNEL_LOG, SWITCH_LOG_ERROR, "STATE CHANGED to %d (%
s), change_count is %s call_state is %s\n", switch_channel_get_state(channel), chan_sta
te, switch_channel_get_variable(channel,"change_count"), switch_channel_callstate2str(s
witch_channel_get_callstate(channel)));

        return SWITCH_STATUS_SUCCESS;
}
```

Our implementation first declares which state changes we want to deal with (LOAD function will register this table with FreeSWITCH core), INIT, and HANGUP.

Then it defines the function we'll use to react to those changes (you can have different functions for each state). Inside the function, you must deal with all state changes.

We use one only function for all state changes, example_on_state_change(). It gets the channel object from the session object has been passed to it, then reads and sets a variable on that channel, checks the state we're in, prints a log line, then calls it a day and returns successfully.

Receiving and firing events

Events are FreeSWITCH's nervous system. They carry around information, commands, and feedback.

Tapping into the event flow will give your module a complete and real-time view of what's happening in each of the many components and subsystems of FreeSWITCH, from channels to reporting.

Firing events enables your module to actively participate in this flow, making information available that other modules can act upon in real time, or sending API commands as if typed in the console.

Events come in various types and subcategories. Each module can subscribe to ALL events or only to a certain subset, and then further filter to which event to react to based on the content of the event's oh so many fields:

```
void example_event_handler(switch_event_t *event)
{
      switch(event->event_id) {
            case SWITCH_EVENT_CHANNEL_OUTGOING:
                  switch_log_printf(SWITCH_CHANNEL_LOG, SWITCH_LOG_ERROR,
    []                      "A channel named \"%s\" is OUTGOING\n",
                              switch_event_get_header_nil(event, "channel-name"));
                  break;
            case SWITCH_EVENT_CHANNEL_CREATE:
                  switch_log_printf(SWITCH_CHANNEL_LOG, SWITCH_LOG_ERROR,
                              "A channel named \"%s\" is CREATED\n",
                              switch_event_get_header_nil(event, "channel-name"));
                  break;
            case SWITCH_EVENT_CHANNEL_DESTROY:
                  switch_log_printf(SWITCH_CHANNEL_LOG, SWITCH_LOG_ERROR,
                              "A channel named \"%s\" is DESTROYED\n",
                              switch_event_get_header_nil(event, "channel-name"));
                  break;
            default:
                  break;
      }
}
                                                          162,2-16      61%
```

In our implementation, we subscribed to ALL events during the LOAD function.

Then, in the example_event_handler(), function we filter the events flow based on event_id (the specific kind of event), and if the event is suitable, then we get a particular header (for example, field) from it, and print a log line.

We'll describe how to fire events later, see the *API command* section in this chapter.

Dialplan application

Modules can add applications to those available to be called in dialplan.

Applications in dialplan are invoked as actions and can have arguments in the data string. An example of application and arguments is the `bridge` app, which takes the dialstring as the argument to be used to originate the call leg to be bridged to:

```
SWITCH_STANDARD_APP(example_app)
{
        switch_channel_t *channel = switch_core_session_get_channel(session);
        const char *arg = (char *) data;
        int loops, i;

        if (zstr(arg)) {
                loops = 5;
        } else {
                loops = atoi(data);
        }

        if (loops < 0) {
                loops = 5;
        } else if (loops > 1024) {
                loops = 1024;
        }

        for(i=0; i<loops; i++) {
                switch_log_printf(SWITCH_CHANNEL_LOG, SWITCH_LOG_ERROR,
                        "=>[%d] I was called with argument \"%s\" on channel \"%s\"\n",
                                i, arg, switch_channel_get_name(channel));
        }
}
                                                        197,0-1        71%
```

In our implementation, we registered a dialplan app with FreeSWITCH core during the LOAD function. Here, we'll have a look at how we implemented the actual application's inner workings.

We get the channel object from the session object we were passed.

Then we check if the `arg` string we were passed is empty (zero length). If it's empty, we assign a default value to how many loops we'll execute. If it's not empty, we convert it into a number, assigning a default in case of error, and enforcing value boundaries.

For each loop we then print a log line that pretty much displays all the entities we used.

From dialplan, you invoke this application as follows:

```
<action application="example" data="7"/>
```

API command

API commands are the way to interact in real time with FreeSWITCH. You can use API commands to originate a call, to answer, to gather statistics, to write accounting data, to shutdown the entire system, and more.

API commands are commands you can type while you're connected to FreeSWITCH's console, or via `fs_cli`. You can send API commands by firing events, both from a module and via an ESL TCP connection.

Modules can add new such functionalities; actually, pretty much all API commands come from modules:

```
SWITCH_STANDARD_API(example_api)
{
        switch_event_t *event;

        if (switch_event_create(&event, SWITCH_EVENT_TRAP) == SWITCH_STATUS_SUCCESS) {
                int x = 0;

                switch_event_add_header_string(event, SWITCH_STACK_BOTTOM,
                        "testing", "true");
                switch_event_add_header_string(event, SWITCH_STACK_BOTTOM,
                        "foo", "bar");

                for (x = 0; x < 5; x++) {
                        char name[128];
                        switch_snprintf(name, sizeof(name), "test-header-%d", x);
                        switch_event_add_header(event, SWITCH_STACK_BOTTOM, name,
                                "value-%d", x);
                }

                //DUMP_EVENT(event);

                switch_event_fire(&event);
                switch_event_destroy(&event);
        }

        if(globals.print) {
                globals.print = 0;
        }else{
                globals.print = 1;
        }

        stream->write_function(stream, "EXAMPLE: Event Fired, Runtime Log Toggled!\n");

        return SWITCH_STATUS_SUCCESS;
}
                                                    122,0-1        49%
```

We registered our API command during the LOAD function, as per the dialplan application.

example_api() is the function that implements the API command. We use it as a demonstration of how to send an event from a module.

First, you create the event pointer, then you give it an earthly existence with switch_ event_create(), passing the event-specific kind as an argument.

At this point you have an empty event, a skeleton event with only the standard minimal headers (fields). You can flesh it out adding additional arbitrary headers, with names and values as you deem fit.

You can add a body to the event too, such as an attachment (like the SDP in SIP, if you like those apple to orange comparisons), but usually you don't.

Then you can use the DUMP_EVENT macro to print the event in the log (to see in the console what the result would be), or fire it.

Don't forget to destroy the event to release the memory associated with it.

Eventually, our implementation toggles the value of the print member in the globals data structure, which is read by the RUNTIME function, and determines if a line will be printed each 5 seconds.

We give the console user a feedback, then exit with success.

Wow, so much ado for nothing!

Summary

In this chapter, we gave you a complete and detailed view of the module development process.

We described the approach we take (copying an existing, working module, and then modifying it) and then guided you through the various sections of the new module's source code.

We saw how to implement the load, runtime, and shutdown functions that are the foundation of every module. In those functions we initialized our data structures and registered hooks and callbacks in FreeSWITCH core.

Then we implemented all functionalities with simple and straightforward code that will serve you well as a base for building your own modules.

If your new module does something that could be useful to others, don't forget to contribute it back to the FreeSWITCH project, for mainline inclusion. Many useful modules were born this way!

12
Tracing and Debugging VoIP

Troubleshooting is a big part of working with FreeSWITCH and VoIP. There are so many moving parts, and so many of them are outside your control, that you will soon become fluent in debugging failed calls.

Usually you have a patchwork LAN where your users hook different phone models, then your FreeSWITCH server, then one or more ITSPs and/or DID providers. Interspersed, you have firewalls, routers, ADSLs, T1/E1s... And you often have direct control only of your FreeSWITCH server! Ouch!

This chapter will give you first the big picture, how it works and why it breaks, and then will introduce you to the latest and best tools for troubleshooting VoIP.

We're very lucky that FreeSWITCH is so reliable, predictable and well-documented. But the ecosystem of VoIP extends far into uncharted territory.

For a comprehensive view of the problem, I would recommend *VoIP Deployment for Dummies*, Wiley— it's not for dummies at all, and (even though it was published in 2009) will give you a complete general course 400 pages long (covering topics including SIP, LAN metrics, dealing with ITSPs, and many more).

In this chapter, we will cover:

- Signaling and media
- Why they break
- Network trace, capture and analysis tools
- Audio analysis and manipulation tools

What can go wrong?

There are two completely separate flows in telecommunication: Signaling and media. They often take completely unrelated paths from caller to callee that is, their IP packets traverse different gateways and routers. Also, the two flows are managed by separate software (or by different parts of the same application) using different protocols. Signaling and media have nothing to do with each other; each one can work or fail independently from the other flow. But you need both to work correctly for your user to have a complete communication session.

Signaling is a flow of information that defines who is calling whom, taking which paths, and which technology is used to transmit which content. The most used signaling protocol in telecommunication is SIP. It defines the caller's IP address and port, the callee's IP address and port, and the IP addresses and ports of all intermediate servers that the signaling is sent through, and it also announces the various phases of call (begin, ring, hangup, busy, and so on). SIP uses SDP (transmitted as part of SIP packets) to define the kind of content (audio, video, file or desktop sharing, and so on), the codecs to use, the IP addresses and ports of the next "media server", for each communication direction (that is, from caller to callee, or from callee to caller). You can think of SDP as an integral part of SIP, although technically it is a separate protocol.

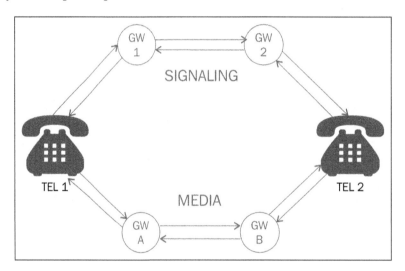

Media proper is exchanged mostly via RTP protocol, through paths defined by SDP in SIP. RTP packets contain, for the most part, audio or video streams in binary encoded samples.

So, we have at least four flows (signaling from caller to callee, media from caller to callee, signaling from callee to caller, media from callee to caller, and possibly additional media streams) that go through various possible intermediate servers.

Any one of those flows can fail independently of others. So it's pretty usual to have failures where you have one way audio, or where you cannot hang up, and, obviously, you can have failures where you cannot initiate calls, but you can receive them, or vice versa. Firewalls, especially "smart", "dynamic" firewalls, can block IP packets in subtle ways, selectively by protocol, after a time period, intermittently, and so on.

What else can go wrong? (NAT problems)

Reality is actually much much more complex than that. We described how each step in each path is represented by an IP address and port. That would be good and easy, but most of those addresses are "fake": They are a particular kind of address that resides only in the private Local Area Networks of users, and are not recognized in the public Internet. This comes from the very success of the Internet: From a finite pool, available IP Internet addresses were assigned at an ever-increasing pace to users, and, after a while, the entire pool would have end up assigned: No more Internet expansion.

To avoid that "end of the Internet", a technique was invented where, instead of each device having its own address, each Internet "entity" would be given only one address to face the public Internet (as the only contact point). All other (internal) addresses of the "entity" (such as an individual with three devices, or a corporation with tens of thousands devices) are translated back and forth to/from that one public Internet address.

This is called **Network Address Translation** (**NAT**), and is usually performed automatically by routers, firewalls, ADSL modems or other "edge" devices that sit between the public Internet and the private LAN of the "entity".

NAT does a lot of magic, associating the origin's IP address/port and the destination's IP address/port in a table, so it can route (translate) packets from the Internet back and forth to the right device in the local network. This NAT method is transparent for, say, web browsing (because only the physical packet is to be translated) but it is a nightmare for VoIP, and can go wrong in an almost endless number of ways.

The problems that NAT causes for VoIP come from the very distinction between SIP and SDP, and, at the end of the day, between signaling and media: SIP IP physical packets are translated automatically by NAT (in same way as HTTP/WEB IP packets), and so they materially reach their intended destinations. But those SIP packets contain text that describes the media origination addresses and ports (in SDP), and each device will write its own "idea" of its own media address there, often an internal LAN address non-reachable via the Internet. Those media addresses and ports contained in SDP are pure text (that is, they are not part of the physical packet), and are not automatically translated by NAT. They're like words in a web page: They are parts of the content and will be delivered by NAT "as is", but they're not part of the physical packet.

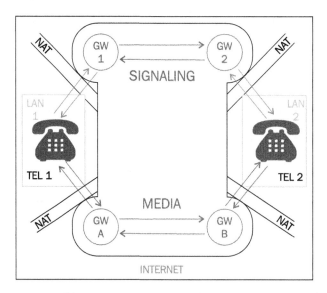

Additional, smarter translation is necessary to change SDP media addresses/ports to public Internet addresses/ports (in accordance with NAT tables), and this function can be performed by the client software (for example, the phone itself), or by the PBX, or by the server, or by a "smart" NAT (for example, ADSL routers with ALG). Any one of these possible "translators" can go wrong, particularly ALG devices.

So, anything can happen to those SDP addresses/ports described by the text contained within the SIP packets: They can stay as private addresses and no media will flow between the parties (private addresses are unreachable from the Internet), and they can be modified by client software in many ways, ways that can match or not match an open path (address/port couple) in the NAT between LAN and the Internet. Yes, that's a nightmare, and this description is way simplified.

"VoIP is FUN!"

Other things can go wrong too

Until now, we've reviewed how VoIP packets can take wrong paths. Those are all network problems, and make up a fair part of the problems you will encounter.

But let's assume packets will find the correct path and will reach their destination and will contain reachable media addresses. Now the problem becomes: Is the content delivered by those packets working as expected in the end user environment?

You can have lags and delay, echo (especially from PSTN adapters), distortion, clipping, or altogether no sound and no call because of incompatible codecs, or you can encounter timing issues that make your call (or your audio, or your video) fail. Especially with WebRTC, with Skype, with anything that's not entirely managed by FreeSWITCH, you need to be aware of their internal working, and, most of all, of timing problems that arise from too much loading, IRQs-sharing, VM simulation and overhead, and so on, and which can cause failures in timing sync, making the stream fail.

And you have to take into account the transducers, the physical path taken by audio from analog to digital and vice versa. Will the soundcard, or the microphone, or that specific hardware phone model work well with the rest of the environment? Will that feature, or button function, be correctly translated from that hardware phone to FreeSWITCH to that other hardware phone? Will that computer be powerful enough to decode and display that video sent via SIP? Will the browser version be able to properly render WebRTC streams?

You will need bandwidth, a lot more bandwidth, if you're to run video and HD audio on your network. And bandwidth problems are easier to show off in your LAN than in your Internet pipe. That's because, for a while at least, you will rarely route videos and HD audio to the Internet (and if you do, you will surely check you have a pipe big enough).

All in all, you need to develop a holistic approach to debugging and troubleshooting your FreeSWITCH installation, and related communication infrastructure. Everything is interacting and affecting everything else, the micro with the macro. At the end of the day, users will judge you by the audio and video quality and reliability, and that depends on oh so many coggles and wheels.

"VoIP is A LOT of FUN!"

SIP, RTP, SDP, RTCP, OH MY!

To troubleshoot VoIP you need to understand at least a little bit of SIP and related protocols. That's the sad truth. You will get nothing from packet-capture and analysis if you don't understand the basics of the protocols.

You can certainly send the file containing the captured packets to someone who's more SIP conversant. If you want to take that option, read the following section about the tools you can use to generate a pcap file with all the relevant info.

The other option is to learn it yourself before problems occur, using sipgrep and sngrep (they make for a colorful, easy and complete toolset) to visualize protocol packets, and one of the many books/tutorials out there as reference. Do test calls and watch what happens. You'll see that there are regularities and meanings, and after a while you'll know most patterns and what to look for. You'll be ready when the time comes.

Tools

Telecommunication can be seen as being comprised of the two elements of signaling and media, and so can the tools to debug and troubleshoot it.

But this comes with a caveat: Anything that runs in a server, or through wires, is just packets of data. So, for media too, we will have to get the stream of data describing our audio (or video, or fax), then convert it into a playable format, and hear what the end user experience was.

Bottom line: Packet capture, analysis, conversion, editing, archiving, slicing and dicing is the bread and butter of diagnosing VoIP for all that concerns codecs, routing, networking, infrastructure, and the like, while media replaying (say, listening or watching captured RTP packets) has in itself a lesser role. But actual end user experience can only be understood via media replaying (are there audio artifacts? Low volume? Echo? Noise? Clipping?). Understanding end user experience "in their own words" is fundamental for a smooth support assistance ("*then, since I started talking about that meeting, suddenly I was hearing noise and an echo*", not "*240 milliseconds after that Re-Invite, jitter started shooting*").

Many tools out there can do almost anything: They have features added on a continuous basis, have command line switches for almost any low case *AND* capital letter, and their man pages are longer to read than a Nordic Saga.

We'll focus here on the most typical, specialized, and popular, usages for each tool, with a "toolbox" approach.

Firewall

Firewalls are the evil stars of VoIP debugging: They block packets. We want packets to flow. If they block them, the packets do not flow.

Maybe they block packets right away. Maybe after a while (30 seconds, anyone?). Maybe in just one direction. Or intermittently.

Maybe there is no separate firewall on the customer's premises, nor on their pbx, but a firewall is running on their ADSL router. Or on their client machines.

Firewalls: They are out there, they are between us, they are inside us.

From a security and network-management standpoint, packet-filtering (firewalling) is the best line of defense, and an invaluable and flexible tool.

But when you're troubleshooting a new installation, or sudden lack of audio, or one way audio, or an inability to hang up a call (or to call altogether), then disable all the firewalls involved and recheck.

If it works out, then you know it is a problem of misconfigured firewall rules, and you can focus on fixing it, or call the security personnel in charge of it.

On a Linux machine, to disable all firewall rules, as root do:

1. Create a shell script (`iptables_flush.sh`) and copy-paste the following lines:

```
#!/bin/sh
echo "Flushing iptables rules..."
sleep 1
iptables -F
iptables -X
iptables -t nat -F
iptables -t nat -X
iptables -t mangle -F
iptables -t mangle -X
iptables -P INPUT ACCEPT
iptables -P FORWARD ACCEPT
iptables -P OUTPUT ACCEPT
```

2. Make the file executable:

```
chmod +x iptables_flush.sh
```

3. Run the script:

```
./iptables_flush.sh
```

 NB: Please pay attention to creating the script and then execute it all at once! DON'T execute it line by line: You can lock yourself out from the machine, requiring a manual hardware reboot.

FreeSWITCH as SIP self tracer

The first line of inquiry will be from fs_cli, the command line interface to FreeSWITCH; you can enable SIP packet display per single profile (sofia profile internal siptrace on) or per all profiles at once (sofia global sip trace on).

This can be useful both as a quick way to check for a problem, and as a way of obtaining added information recorded permanently on logfile.

For having a complete picture of each call, complete with FS debug info and SIP packets, input the following:

```
<param name="uuid" value="true"/>
```

In `/usr/local/freeswitch/conf/autoload_configs/logfile.conf.xml`, set siptrace:

```
<param name="sip-trace" value="yes"/>
```

Inside profile definition in `/usr/local/freeswitch/conf/sip_profiles/ internal.xml` and `/usr/local/freeswitch/conf/sip_profiles/external.xml` and:

```
<param name="tracelevel" value="DEBUG"/>
```

Inside the global setting in `sofia.conf.xml`. When you run `fsctl loglevel 7` you'll have complete info on logfile.

You can find a tool for call_uuid-SIP packet correlation at `https://github. com/2600hz/community-scripts/blob/master/FreeSWITCH/sipify.sh`, invaluable for finding out exactly what's happening.

Tcpdum – the mother of all packet captures

tcpdump is a utility that writes out all the stuff that passes by a network interface (for example, eth0, the first Ethernet card). It writes it all in a format that can then be easily parsed out and analyzed by other software.

tcpdump (that's not limited to tcp, as the name would suggest) is a command line utility with little dependencies (usually just libpcap and libssl) that you can easily install on any remote machine you're debugging (it's packaged ready to install on almost any operating system, and it's called "windump" on Windows).

tcpdump is able to get all that touches the network interface (and also stuff that's not directed to the local machine, but simply transits through the wire). Capturing all network traffic passing by is called "promiscuous mode". Today, with switched networks, it is seldom useful, because the packets that touch the network interface are almost always those from and to the local machine. But in old Ethernet networks (with "hubs" instead of "switches") it can be very useful. In modern switched networks, advanced switches have a special port on them where all traffic passes by (not only the one directed at the attached machine), and if you can connect to that special port you'll enjoy the promiscuous sweetness of being able to dump traffic between any third machines. For being promiscuous, leave out the -p parameter.

In its most simple invocation, you connect the traffic you want to dump via ssh to the machine and input the following:

```
tcpdump -w trace.pcap -p -nq -s 0 -i eth0
```

This will write into the `trace.cap` file anything that passes by the interface eth0, in the most efficient and complete way. On a testing server, where there is no traffic apart from your testing, this invocation is appropriate; you'll get it all, including things that you didn't know you wanted. On a busy server, let's say with an almost saturated Gigabit Ethernet card, this will blow your hard disk(s) in minutes).

You may want to discriminate what to write in the file, and tcpdump has its own way to specify just that. The following invocation will dump traffic that "has to do with" ports 5060 and 5080 (both to and from local and remote ports):

```
tcpdump -w trace.pcap -p -nq -s 0 -i eth0 port 5060 or port 5080
```

Those two ports happen to be the standard SIP port (5060), so it will probably be the public SIP port you use to connect to your ITSP, and both the internal (5060 used by your internal phones) and external (5080 used for receiving incoming calls) ports used by default by FreeSWITCH profiles. That is to say, this invocation will dump all the signaling SIP traffic that goes back and forth from your FreeSWITCH server in default configuration, and will produce very little, but complete, pcap files (it's only signaling, no media).

If you want to add the media dump to the previous invocation and still try to capture only VoIP traffic (for example, no HTTP, SMTP, or whatever else), run it like this (we're adding the default range FreeSWITCH uses for media, and restricting dump to UDP only):

```
tcpdump -w trace.pcap -p -nq -s 0 -i eth0 udp and port 5060 or port 5080
or portrange 16384-32768
```

The following invocation will save into file all the traffic (signaling AND media) between the local machine (that is, FreeSWITCH) and two remote addresses, for example, the addresses of your ITSP's SIP server and Media server:

```
tcpdump -w trace.pcap -p -nq -s 0 -i eth0 host 167.233.44.34 or host
167.233.44.36
```

```
gmaruzz@lxle-BIG: ~                           −  +  ✕

freeswitch@internal> sofia status profile internal user 1010@self.gmaruzz.org

Registrations:
==========================================================================
=================
Call-ID:      GmCu-kmCDs
User:         1010@self.gmaruzz.org
Contact:      "" <sip:1010@192.168.1.203:5090>
Agent:        Linphone/3.8.1 (belle-sip/1.4.0)
Status:       Registered(UDP)(unknown) EXP(2015-05-14 19:06:05) EXPSECS(3369)
Ping-Status:  Reachable
Host:         vz125
IP:           192.168.1.203
Port:         5090
Auth-User:    1010
Auth-Realm:   192.168.1.125
MWI-Account:  1010@self.gmaruzz.org

Total items returned: 1
==========================================================================
=================

freeswitch@internal> █
```

Another neat trick is to capture all traffic between a registered user (phone) and our FreeSWITCH server. Let's assume our phone is registered as user 1010. From fs_cli we get the phone's IP (address), then we exit fs_cli and start tcpdump:

```
tcpdump -w trace.pcap -p -nq -s 0 -i eth0 host 192.168.1.203
```

Infinite tcpdump options are possible, but here you've got the most important ones.

ngrep – network grep

ngrep is based on the same libpcap like tcpdump, and so can use the same packet filters and read/write pcap files. It is almost certainly available as a package for your operating system.

What ngrep brings to your toolbox is the popular grep's regular expression matching with the packets' payload. The invocation takes the format `ngrep [options] [regex] [filter]`. Remember: regex before filter. Also, remember regex is applied to the entire packet content, not to the single lines that comprise it. It captures and displays packets in real time, so you can monitor a machine looking for something to happen:

```
ngrep -qt -W byline "393472665618" port 5060
```

The first example will display all packets on port 5060 (respecting their newline characters) that contain 393472665618.

```
ngrep -qt -W byline "^INVITE|^BYE|^CANCEL" port 5060
```

The second invocation will display all packets for methods that initiate or terminate a call leg. If you don't put the caret anchoring the match to the beginning of the line, almost all SIP packets would match because of the "Allow" header, which contains all the methods supported by the packet sender.

```
ngrep -qt -W byline "CSeq: [0-9]* INVITE" port 5060
```

This third invocation will display in real time all INVITE methods and all INVITE related responses (for example, 100, 180, 183, 407, 487, 200, and so on).

tshark – pure packet power

tshark is Wireshark in a terminal, that is, you can run it remotely on the server via ssh, without a remote desktop. It can do an awful lot of things, like Wireshark itself, but why you would want to use it?

On the one hand, you can use it to write pcap files using the same filter grammar used by tcpdump (they both use libpcap as a capturing backend). This is very efficient, but why not use tcpdump? Pcap style capture filter is defined by the f option.

On the other hand, it's got the r option. With it you can define "Display (Read) Filters", which are less efficient than pcap filters, but allow you to drill down to the subtle nuances of the protocols. Then, you can dump the packets in a pcap file for later inspection and analysis (for example with Wireshark), or you can see the results in real time, both for packets and as comprehensive statistics, printed on terminal. Use the "z" option for getting statistics.

(T | Wire) shark (Display | Read) filters can pinpoint, isolate, evaluate, aggregate (and so on) any known field in protocols, and if you invest time in understanding their logic, they'll repay you with sheer power (and wow factor with collegues). The main docs are at `http://www.wireshark.org/docs/dfref/`; look for sip, sdp, rtp, rtcp, t38, and so on.

```
### Filter in real time on RTCP packets displaying any packet loss or
jitter over 30ms:
tshark -i eth0 -o "rtcp.heuristic_rtcp: TRUE" -R 'rtcp.ssrc.fraction>= 1
or rtcp.ssrc.jitter>= 30' -V
### Capture SIP, RTP, ICMP, DNS, RTCP, and T38 traffic in a ring buffer
capturing 100 50MB files continuously:
tshark -i eth0 -o "rtp.heuristic_rtp: TRUE" -w trace.pcap -b
filesize:51200 -b files:100 -R 'sip or rtp or icmp or dns or rtcp or t38'
### Display STUN packets in real time:
tshark -Y stun
```

pcapsipdump

pcapsipdump is like tcpdump, and can use the same filters, but it listens to the network interface(s) and writes one pcap file for each SIP session (call). Generated pcap files can contain RTP (media) flow or only signaling (SIP+SDP).

It is easy to compile, and you can find the latest version at `http://pcapsipdump.sourceforge.net`.

It's incredibly useful to keep your SIP traffic monitored while looking for intermittent problems reported by users. If you have a busy server, dump it on a big and fast hard disk, and don't forget to delete the files you don't need anymore.

sngrep – the holy grail

This maybe the latest tool to come out from the ingenious people in the open source VoIP community, and, with sipgrep, they're my preferred packet utilities. Hands down. Wholeheartedly.

This single tool allows for both the capturing and visualizing of live (and in real time) SIP dialogs for each call, and visualizes live flow graphs, drilling down to the details. Also, you can select more than one call (for example, A leg and B leg of a bridged call) and see them both in one comprehensive flow.

It is based on libpcap, so it accepts all the standard filters like tcpdump and can write pcap files (it can also load standard pcap files). It supports IPv6, and, if compiled with openssl, is able to read and display TLS-secured SIPS (given the keyfile). If compiled with pcre, it gives you the complete "perl" regular expressions.

And you can do all of this server side, in a terminal, via ssh, without downloading or streaming pcaps to your desktop, actually without any software on your side, just an ssh terminal.

Sngrep justifies filling an HD monitor with a maximized xterm (you still chat and browse in that second monitor, don't you?).

At the time of writing this, sngrep is too new to be included in distros, but it is very easy to download and compile from sources, and installable packages are available for `Debian/Ubuntu/CentOS/RedHat/OSX`. Have a look at `http://github.com/irontec/sngrep` for latest version.

You start sngrep from the command line, similar to tcpdump:

```
sngrep -d eth0 -O trace.pcap host 192.168.0.50 port 5061
```

This will filter and display all SIP packets to/from port 5061 and host 192.168.0.50 and write them in `trace.pcap` file.

At the start you'll find yourself in the call list window, where the dialogs will be listed. On a busy server, you'll see that it immediately begins to populate. In this window *any* dialog that satisfies the command line filter will appear, not only call legs, but registrations, pinging options, and so on. If you only want to visualize dialogs starting with the method INVITE (that is, call legs), use the -c command line argument.

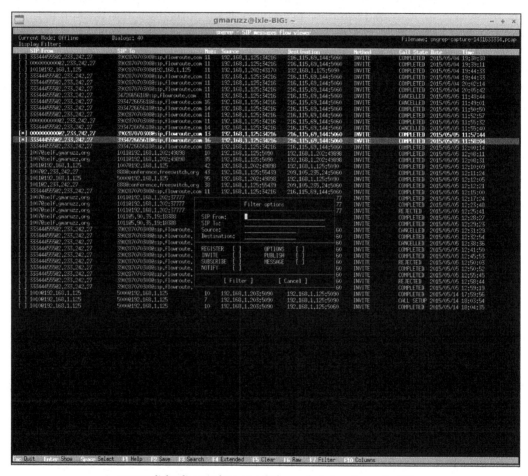

sngrep dialog list window, two dialogs selected, and pressing F7

You can filter the list by general criteria with *F7*, or you can search for specific dialogs with F3. You can choose which "columns" to show in the list, in which order, and save the layout as default.

From this window you can press enter on a dialog to see its flow, the individual messages that comprise the SIP transactions. Also, you can select (pressing space bar) more than one dialog, and when you hit *Enter* you'll see their collective flows (for example, a bridged call).

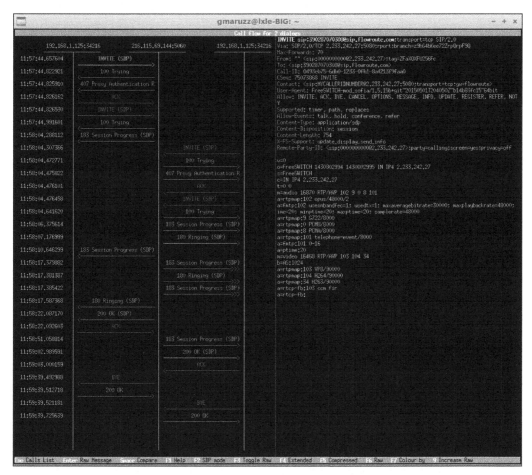

Flow of two legs of a bridged call, colored by transactions

With UP and DOWN arrows you browse through messages that are visualized in the right pane. Pressing *F2* will show the flow with SDP in the graph. Pressing *Enter* on a message will show it raw; this is useful to copy and paste from terminal. With space bar you can select two messages (for example, an Invite and a re-Invite); pressing *Enter* will show them side by side, with differences highlighted.

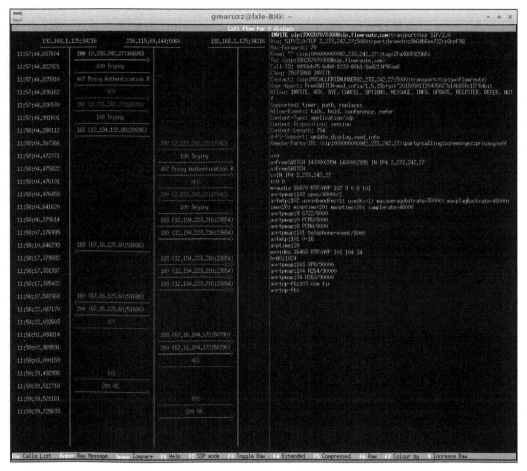

Flow of two legs of a bridged call, colored by transactions, showing SDP in graph

Pressing *F7* in the call flow window will change the coloring of messages, for example, from transactions to CSeq, or CallId.

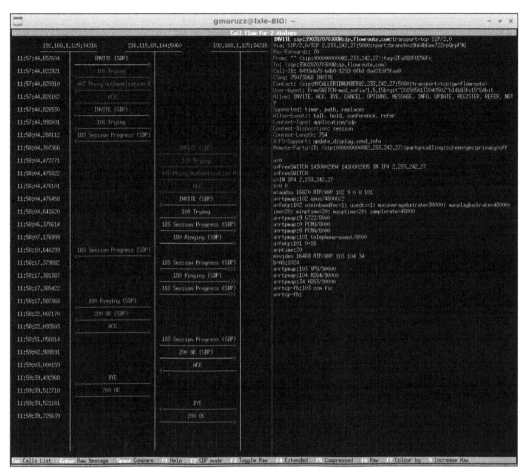

Flow of two legs of a bridged call, colored by Cseq

Sipgrep, Ngrep on steroids for VoIP

The fine people that brought Homer into this world (Homer being an open source SIP capture and monitoring system, database-centered, carrier-grade, http://www.sipcapture.org), see next chapter gave us a new sipgrep.

The previous sipgrep incarnation was a Perl script, wrapping, parsing and coloring the output of ngrep. This new incarnation is a self-standing tool written in C, starting from a ngrep codebase and adding the smorgasbord of VoIP options.

It's a relatively new tool, so you probably won't find it prepackaged by your distro (that version may be too old). Go straight to `http://github.com/sipcapture/sipgrep`; there is easy info on how to build and install it.

Start sipgrep with the `-f` or `-t` option to visualize dialogs where From: or To: matches an expression, and add `-G` option if you want a report with statistics:

```
gmaruzz@lxle-BIG: ~                                    - + x
root@vz125:~# sipgrep -t 347266 -G
interface: eth0 (192.168.1.0/255.255.255.0)
filter: (ip) and ( portrange 5060-5061) or (udp and ip[6:2] & 0x3fff != 0)
match: (To:|t:) (.*)347266(.*)

U 2015/05/16 18:21:51.236707 192.168.1.203:5090 -> 192.168.1.125:5060

INVITE sip:3934726656180192.168.1.125 SIP/2.0.
Via: SIP/2.0/UDP 192.168.1.203:5090;branch=z9hG4bK.NbhgrKuo";rport.
From: <sip:10100192.168.1.125>;tag=G6oDzdl7o.
To: sip:3934726656180192.168.1.125.
CSeq: 20 INVITE.
Call-ID: 3DetG"FVOH.
Max-Forwards: 70.
Supported: outbound.
Allow: INVITE, ACK, CANCEL, OPTIONS, BYE, REFER, NOTIFY, MESSAGE, SUBSCRIBE, INF
O, UPDATE.
Content-Type: application/sdp.
Content-Length: 511.
Contact: <sip:10100192.168.1.203:5090>;+sip.instance="<urn:uuid:5aa8879f-a1c0-44
17-94a7-e738348c2fe2>".
User-Agent: Linphone/3.8.1 (belle-sip/1.4.0).

v=0.
o=1010 3433 1411 IN IP4 192.168.1.203.
s=Talk.
c=IN IP4 192.168.1.203.
t=0 0.
a=rtcp-xr:rcvr-rtt=all:10000 stat-summary=loss,dup,jitt,TTL voip-metrics.
m=audio 7078 RTP/AVP 96 0 8 101 97.
a=rtpmap:96 opus/48000/2.
a=fmtp:96 useinbandfec=1; stereo=0; sprop-stereo=0.
a=rtpmap:101 telephone-event/48000.
a=rtpmap:97 telephone-event/8000.
m=video 9078 RTP/AVP 96 97 98.
a=rtpmap:96 VP8/90000.
a=rtpmap:97 H264/90000.
a=fmtp:97 profile-level-id=428014.
a=rtpmap:98 MP4V-ES/90000.
a=fmtp:98 profile-level-id=3.

U 2015/05/16 18:21:51.237147 192.168.1.125:5060 -> 192.168.1.203:5090

SIP/2.0 100 Trying.
```

sipgrep looking for To: in dialogs, and preparing stats

In this example, we started sipgrep with the option for statistics, then made a call from a SIP client to a callee that matched the `-t` option we gave to sipgrep. We generated from Linphone an A leg incoming to the server, and FreeSWITCH generated an outbound B leg to the callee, then FS bridged the two legs in a complete call.

Sipgrep visualized all the packets related to the two dialogs (legs), with nice colorization. Then, at the call end, after hangup, we hit *Ctrl + C* to interrupt sipgrep, which gave us its report on both dialogs that were part of the call.

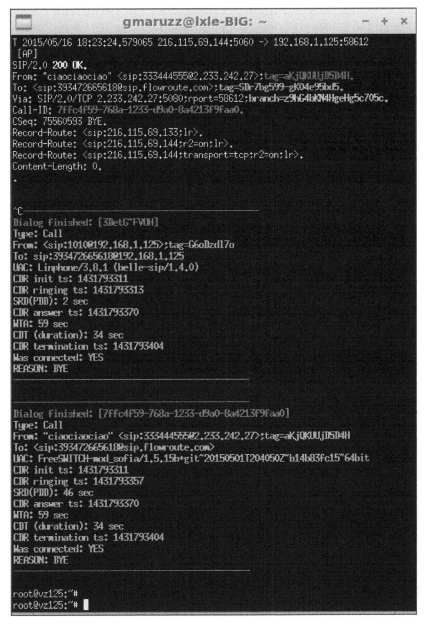

sipgrep statistics results

The -M option will disable multiline matches, while -m will disable dialog matching (that is, it will match only specific messages, not entire dialogs).

Another intriguing feature of sipgrep is activated with -J option: It will automatically send a packet-of-death (a combination able to crash the remote software) to any "friendly scanner" probing/flooding your SIP server (use -j to customize the user agent of the scanner).

It can read and write pcap files, of course, and has nice features for managing file sizes, rotation, time duration, among many other things.

Wireshark – "the" packet overlord

Wireshark is "the" network packet analyzer. It can analyze LAN performances, HTTP and NFS, USB traffic, BlueTooth, WiFi signals. It's got everything and the kitchen sink. There are books about it, and specific books about its use in VoIP.

Wireshark can be installed on most operating systems, and can then act as a real-time network analyzer (for example, by capturing packets from the network interface, or by receiving a stream by a capture utility) or can read pcap files.

To use tcpdump on a server (server has 192.168.1.125 ip address), and receive the capture in real time with our desktop Wireshark, using the -U (unbuffered) tcpdump option, we first create a named pipe (and we exclude port 22 from capture because we're using ssh to stream it):

```
$ mkfifo /tmp/sharkfin
$ wireshark -k -i /tmp/sharkfin&
$ ssh root@192.168.1.125 "tcpdump -U -w - -p -nq -s 0 -i eth0 'not tcp
port 22'"> /tmp/sharkfin
```

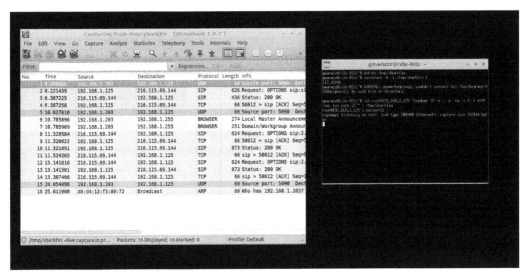

Remote tcpdump to local wireshark

Or you can install wireshark on a remote server, execute it there, capturing locally, and display it remotely on your desktop (via VNC, ssh -X, etc). Installing Wireshark on a Linux server does not install or run on the desktop; only just enough X stuff to permit remote display. It does not add load to your server.

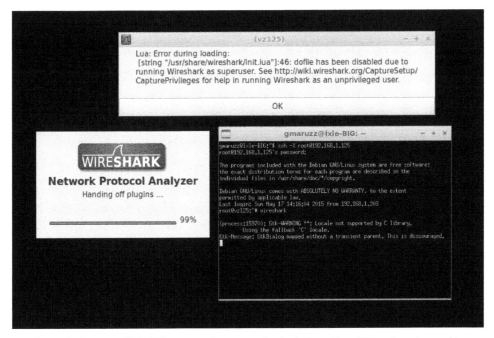

Perform ssh -X on FreeSWITCH server and execute wireshark there. Press OK, and you're good to go

OK, so you're capturing now. Make a call or two, then open menu **Telephony |
VoIP Calls**.

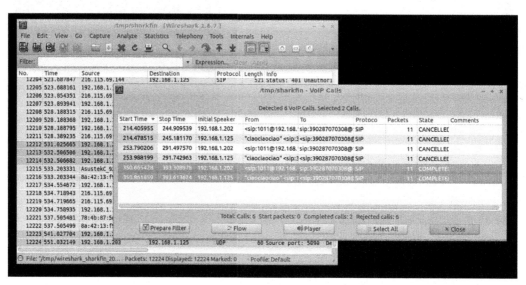

Select the call legs you want to analyze (you can select two legs to analyze the flow of a complete bridged call).

(from **Telephony | VoIP Calls** menu, selecting two legs of a call)

Then you select **Flow**, and a graph will appear with our whole (two-legged) call.

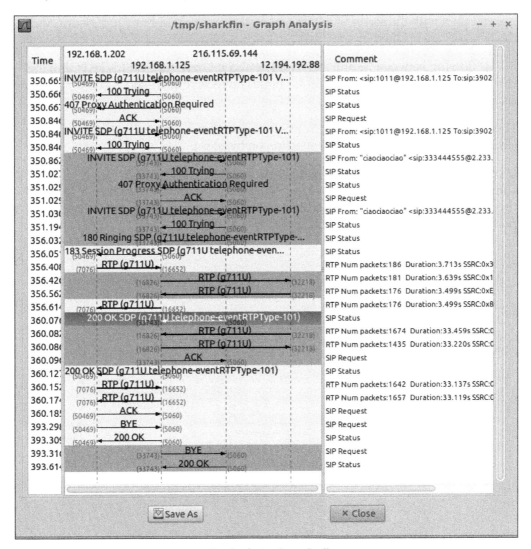

Graph of a two legged call

It can seem intimidating at first. Actually, it's not.

Linphone is calling a PSTN number via FreeSWITCH. FreeSWITCH uses an ITSP as PSTN gateway. Columns: final 202 is Linphone client, final 125 is FreeSWITCH server, final 144 is our telephony provider (ITSP) SIP signaling server, final 88 is our ITSP's RTP (media) server.

There are back and forth INVITE between Linphone and FreeSWITCH, and then between FreeSWITCH and ITSP, until with "200 OK" the call leg from FS to ITSP is up, and then with the second "200 OK" the call leg from Linphone to FS is up, and the two legs are bridged by FS.

RTP is flowing between FS and ITSP, and between Linphone and FS. FS is "mixing" (bridging) the two RTP flows, and Linphone can receive and send audio to/from the remote PSTN phone.

The call is terminated by a "BYE" from Linphone, that is relayed by FS to the ITSP (ITSP will tear down the PSTN connection on his side).

If you click on an element in the graph (let's say the first "200 OK"), the corresponding packet(s) in the main window are selected. You can then inspect them. In our case we're showing both the message headers (for example, the SIP part) and the message body (for example, the SDP content).

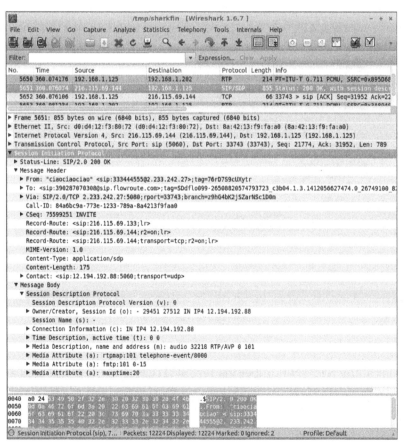

Visualizing a SIP packet, and its SDP body

From "VoIP Calls", after selecting the legs you can click on "Player", and if you have captured RTP too (that is, not only signaling, but media too) you'll be able to hear the audio streams that were exchanged.

You have four streams, for a bridged call: From Linphone to FS, from FS to Linphone, from FS to ITSP, from ITSP to FS. Select one or two of those streams, and click **Play**. If you selected two streams, one will be on the right audio channel, other one on the left (you'd better use stereo headphones, or listen to one stream at time).

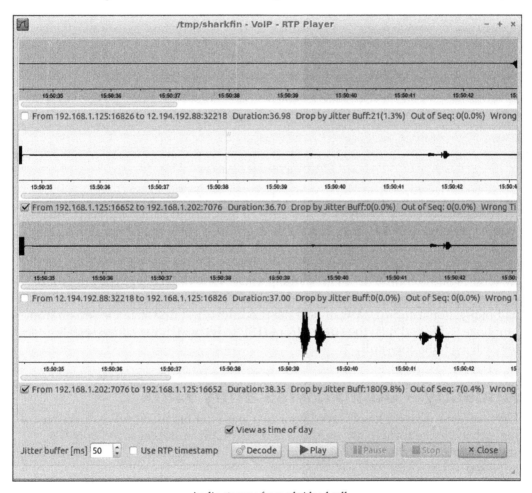

Audio streams from a bridged call

You can have advanced statistics on RTP by selecting one or more streams from **Telephony | RTP | Show All Streams**, and then **Telephony | RTP | Streams Analysis**.

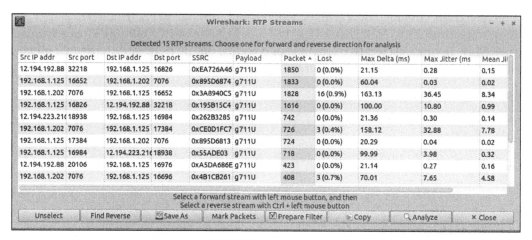

RTP All Streams window

Also, from here you can save the decoded audio as `.raw` or `.au` format. Order the "All Streams" window for "packet"; clicking on the column name, will help you identify the streams with most packets, such as those of the longest duration. Select the RTP stream of one call leg and click "Find Reverse", then "Analyze", then "Save Payload", then save as ".au""both" channels. Repeat for the other leg. You now have two copies of the complete call, from the point of view of each leg. They're probably more or less the same, if the call was successful (for example, if both caller and callee had bidirectional audio). Now, repeat the procedure, but first save the stream from Linphone to FS, and then the stream from ITSP to FS (watch the addresses!), saving for each leg only "forward".

Audacity – audio Swiss army knife

Let's say with wireshark you saved your two legs (combination of two directions for each leg in .au format) as LegAboth and LegBboth, and then saved only the stream going from the endpoint (Linphone or ITSP) to FreeSWITCH as LegAfwd and LegBfwd.

You can now finely analyze them with Audacity. Audacity is a complete tool for analyzing, editing, and modifying audio files. It is open source, and runs on any operating system.

Open the LegAboth file, then, from the menu **File | Import | Audio**, open LegBboth file. You'll see they're very similar, and also that the speakers were speaking in turns. That's expected. They've both got incoming and outgoing audio.

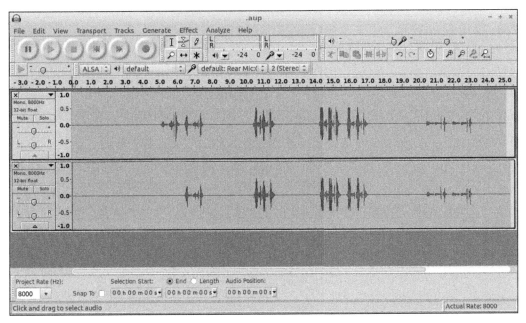

Complete audio from both directions, two legs of a call

Now open LegAfwd and then import LegBfwd.

You'll see only the audio sent from the endpoints to FreeSWITCH. The combination of both makes the complete call (assuming FreeSWITCH has correctly bridged the two legs, and there are no network problems in the RTP paths between endpoints and FreeSWITCH).

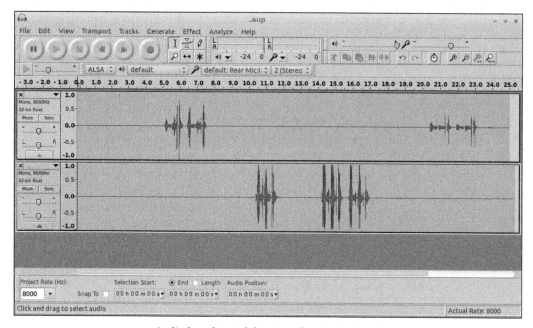

Audio from forward direction of two legs of a call

SoX – audio format converter

When talking about Audacity, it is almost natural to mention SoX too, because often you'll need to convert from one audio format to another, change sampling rate, combine channels into mono, and so on. With these, SoX is your friend.

If you know what codec will be used by your calls, then convert all your IVR prompts and music to that format, so FreeSWITCH will not waste CPU processing doing the conversion in real time for each call.

Sometimes MP3 support for SoX is packaged apart from SoX main program, for example, in Debian 8 Jessie you need to install libsox-fmt-mp3 on top of it.

If you know you'll receive an incoming call from an ITSP via G711 a-law (in US would be u-law), you want to convert your stereo MP3 music and your prompts into mono PCMA at 8khz sampling. FreeSWITCH's mod_native_file, compiled and installed by default, will use them directly, without conversion.

```
sox -V music.mp3 -r 8000 -c 1 -t al -w music.pcma
```

But you would also often need the converse, for example, to let people "hear" from web or email files recorded by FreeSWITCH callers. They prefer receiving MP3:

```
sox -V /usr/local/freeswitch/recordings/2015-05-17/test.wav test.mp3
```

Summary

In this chapter we first had a 10 thousand mile overview of how VoIP works and why it is complex to diagnose (separation between media and signaling, firewalls, and NATs).

Then we looked at the various ways our flows can be interrupted, mostly due to internal LAN addresses wrongly sent as Internet reachable addresses, mismatching in configurations, packet-filtering and security devices not allowing network traffic.

A big part of the chapter was devoted to illustrating the practical usage of the best and latest network-tracing tools, both for capturing and visualizing VoIP packets.

Now you have all the tools and insights of the pros; now's the time to accumulate experience!

13
Homer, Monitoring and Troubleshooting Your Communication Platform

Homer is your NSA, your friendly GCHQ, where all of your signaling, statistics, and metadata belongs. If something happened anywhere in your realm, something you want to know, you ask the blind poet Homer about it. He'll immediately recount the whole story, from beginning to end. Think about it as data-warehousing for **Real-Time Communication** (**RTC**), like a time machine able to pinpoint for you any moment in the past from any location in your network.

Homer is invaluable in any VoIP installation of a sizable dimension, and is your only way (OK, your only open source way) to give your customer base the support they deserve (and pay for).

In this chapter, we will cover:

- Homer installation
- Setting Capture Agents to feed data to Homer
- Querying for Call Signaling
- Feeding and checking Media Quality Reports
- Correlating call legs, logs and events

What is Homer?

Homer is the user interface part of the open source SIPCAPTURE stack. SIPCAPTURE as a whole provides a real-time modular monitoring and troubleshooting framework comprised of Capture Agents and Capture Servers.

User Interface (Homer proper) interrogates the Capture Server. The Capture Server stores the data sent to it by one or more Capture Agents. A Capture Agent gets data by listening to the network (like `ngrep` or `tcpdump`) or from the file system (like the *tail* Unix utility) or interacting with the OS, then in real time it repackages those data and sends it to the Capture Server.

Homer is a Php-JS-Angular-D3 browser application that runs out of a web server. Homer queries a database (MySQL or PostgreSQL), and displays the data back to you, in a tabular or graphical (charts) arrangement.

A Capture Server is a SIP proxy (OpenSIPS or Kamailio) using a special module for receiving and massaging HEP packets, instead or in addition to SIP packets, and then storing the data contained in those HEP packets in a DB.

A Capture Agent can be a stand-alone dedicated program, or a feature in a more complex application, able to get data and transmit it to a Capture Server using HEP/EEP.

The HEP **Extensible Encapsulation Protocol** (EEP) provides a method to duplicate an IP datagram sent to a collector by encapsulating the original packet and its relative headers within a new IP packet transmitted over UDP/TCP/SCTP for remote collection. The format was initially designed by Alexandr Dubovikov and Roland Hänel at QSC AG, joined by Lorenzo Mangani and QXIP Research & Development.

The Capture Agent feature has been integrated into most popular open source RTC servers and tools, including:

- FreeSWITCH
- RTPEngine
- OpenSIPS
- Kamailio
- Asterisk
- SnGrep
- SipGrep

If you happen to use a recent release of one of the supported applications, activating the integrated HEP/EEP Agent is as simple as editing a few lines of configuration. The main advantage of native agents is having direct access to the guts of your RTC servers, and their ability to capture and forward packets from *inside*, so you'll get unencrypted data straight out the core, even in the case of TLS or WSS!

A stand-alone Capture Agent comes in handy when you do not want (or cannot) modify in any way the settings of your communication platform, or when you operate using closed source, legacy, or outdated systems.

Project CaptAgent (part of the **SIPCAPTURE** stack) can be installed on a host or device connected on your network, and will take care of passively sniffing and filtering data from its network interfaces and sending it to the Capture Server.

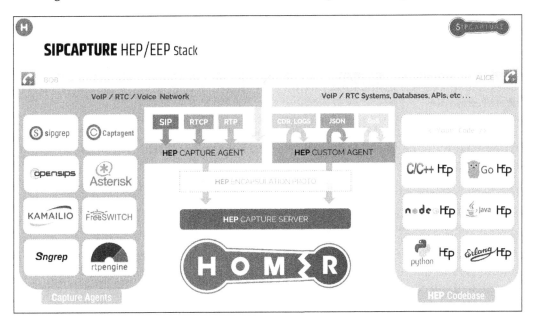

Other stand-alone Capture Agents available in the SIPCAPTURE stack are HEPipe. js and HEPpipe-ESL.js. The first one is a generic tool for monitoring log files in real time, and sending lines to the Capture Server(s), automatically extracting a session correlation-ID for each line. HEPipe-ESL is an extension of the same framework connecting directly to the FreeSWITCH Event-Socket, subscribing to various kinds of events correlated to SIP sessions and sending them a Capture Server. Forthcoming versions will extend to use AMQ for additional flexibility and ability to provide dedicated logging queues into Homer.

SIPCAPTURE stack is completed by HEP/EEP bindings, libraries, examples, and code snippets for most programming languages, enabling a quick route for developers interested in adopting the encapsulation format in homegrown or custom applications.

So, the money quote: You set up some Capture Agents in your servers and/or on your network, they send signaling and logs to the Capture Server(s), the Capture Server(s) do some massaging, then store that info in a database, and you use Homer to query that database.

SIPCAPTURE stack is extremely scalable and solid, used by first tier telecom and cable carriers worldwide, and commercially backed by its core developers at QXIP.NET.

Installing Homer and the Capture Server

Each SIPCAPTURE stack element is open source and available from GitHub, accompanied by full installation instructions and an active Wiki containing several useful examples.

Because there are a lot of different moving parts that need to fit together, to get acquainted with the stack, it is much easier to help yourself with one of the different ready-made offerings from SIPCAPTURE.

In a basic or testing installation, all elements can co-exist on the same host or system: Capture Server, database, web server, user interface. For large setups, each component can be installed (and scaled) separately.

At the moment of writing, SIPCAPTURE project provides Docker images (one single container, and one multi-container) and a Puppet recipe producing a complete system with all core elements preconfigured.

For those (like this humble writer) who are a little bit more traditionalist, there is an automated shell script that installs it all from pre-built packages on both Debian and CentOS (RHEL).

Let's use the installer script method. It's important to start with a clean, minimal and fresh OS installation. The script will take care to install and modify all that it needs, but assumes it is being executed on a basic and empty, just-installed machine. A virtual machine will do, no problem.

So, fire that Debian Jessie or CentOS 7 VM, ssh in it, install the little prerequisites (`wget`, `curl`, `git`, `flex`, `bison`, `libpcap-dev`, and a few others: Check the beginning of the installer script for latest info), download and execute the script.

```
# cd /usr/src
```

```
# wget https://cdn.rawgit.com/sipcapture/homer-installer/master/homer_installer.sh
```

```
# bash ./homer_installer.sh
```

During (semi) automated installation, please resist the temptation to customize the results with your own passwords, usernames, and the like. Yes, I know the script is asking you to choose, but... Just hit *Enter*, always, to accept the default choice. It is the easiest and safest option, and always works. Let's shoot for instant gratification; you'll do your tweaking in future installs.

The most complex part, at the time of writing, is the creation of the SSL certificate request for the Homer website (which will then be automatically self-signed from an internal dummy Certification Authority), but you have probably been there before. Just remember to use as **FQDN (Fully Qualified Domain Name)** something like `homer.dummy.com`. You then insert the same name with the corresponding Homer server IP address into your browser machine's hosts file (last time I checked Windows had it, too), and you're gold to connect.

Default browser login and password are `admin` and `test123`.

Feeding SIP signaling from FreeSWITCH to Homer

If you followed the previous installation instructions, you're now logged into an empty Homer, as we have no Capture Agents sending data to the Capture Server. No data rows have been written to database.

Reach for your nearby FreeSWITCH (you do have a FS server, don't you?) and start editing its configuration.

Modify `autoload_configs/sofia.conf.xml` to read (uncomment the line and substitute your Capture Server address):

```
<param name="capture-server" value="udp:192.168.10.202:9060;hep=3;cap
ture_id=200"/>
```

Then, inside your SIP profiles (for example, `sip_profiles/internal.xml` and more) `settings` section, edit or add this line to read:

```
<param name="sip-capture" value="yes"/>
```

Reload `mod_sofia`, or restart FreeSWITCH altogether, and you're ready to roll.

Searching signaling with Homer

After you configured and started the Capture Agent inside FreeSWITCH, make a call.

Then, log into your Homer, set the Time Range to **Today**, select **calls** as **transaction kind**, and click **search**.

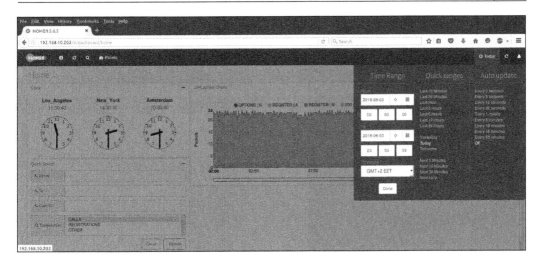

You'll be greeted by a tabular view of the SIP signaling comprised in your call. If you get no results, check the `homer_data` database if `sip_capture_call_2016*` table has been created for today. If not, execute as root `/opt/homer_rotate`.

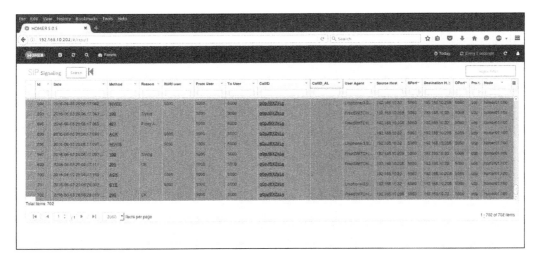

If you click on the **Method** name, a popup springs up showing the whole message, with nice coloring.

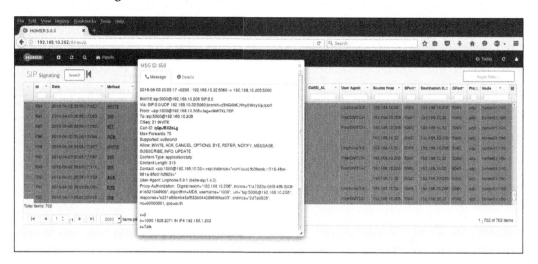

If you click on the **CallID** field, you can peruse the entire end-to-end Call-Flow, in sngrep/wireshark style.

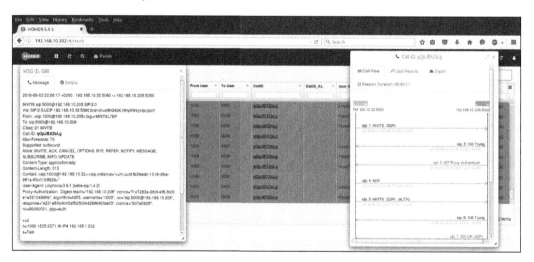

Clicking on a method inside the Call-Flow popup shows a new popup with that whole message.

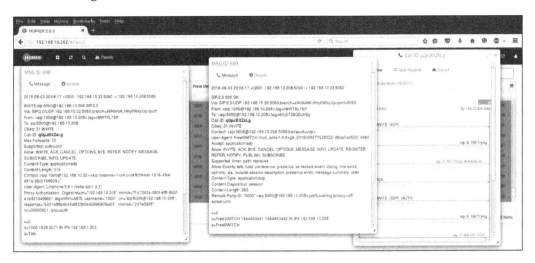

Feeding SIP signaling, QoS, MOS and RTP/RTCP stats from CaptAgent to Homer

At the moment of writing, all media-related reports (RTP, RTCP, Quality of Service, Medium Opinion Score, and so on) have not yet been added to the Capture Agent integrated as features in FreeSWITCH.

We'll take the opportunity to see the usage of CaptAgent, the universal stand-alone Agent for the SIPCAPTURE stack.

Let's start building the latest version:

```
# cd /usr/src
# git clone https://github.com/sipcapture/captagent.git captagent
# cd captagent
# ./build.sh
# ./configure
# make && make install
```

Now head to `/usr/local/captagent/etc/captagent/` and feel the pain! Configuration is complex, and distributed in many files. Be tenacious; you'll be rewarded. Start by checking all paths in `captagent.xml`. Then, edit `captureplans/sip_capture_plan.cfg` and uncomment the entire `if(sip_has_sdp())` block.

Enable `true` RTCP in `socket_pcap.xml`. Then edit `transport_hep.xml` and insert the IP address and port of Capture Server.

Leave all the rest to default values. CaptAgent is now configured and ready to feed the Capture Server.

Before starting CaptAgent, let's temporarily disable the Capture Agent feature integrated into FreeSWITCH, so we don't send double signaling into Homer. From `fs_cli` (or console) input:

```
> sofia global capture off
```

Let's run CaptAgent, and then do the same call as before, again.

```
# /usr/local/captagent/bin/captagent
```

Search for calls in Homer, and click on the CallID of the new call. Then, in the Call-Flow popup, click on **QoS Reports** tab.

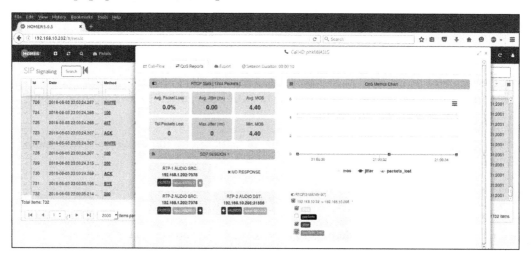

Here you have all the info on media and user experience, both as average and max packet loss, jitter, and MOS-estimation (MOS is the perceived audio quality as judged by users).

Also, on the right side, you have a graphic with the time series of those values. The panel is completed by the codecs used in the call (the SDP contents that were agreed upon).

Correlating A-leg and B-leg

As we have seen many times in this book, because FreeSWITCH is a **B2BUA (Back to Back User Agent)**, when a user makes a call via FS, FS actually originates a completely independent new call (to callee), and bridges the two calls' audio streams. The streams then flow from caller to FreeSWITCH to callee (and back). In this context, the first call (from caller to FS) is named "A-leg", while the second (from FS to callee) is named "B-leg".

From the point of view of the user, what she experiences as *a call* is what for us VoIP geeks is *two calls*, or a *bridged call*, or *A-leg and B-leg*.

It's obviously very useful to be able to visualize and debug a complete bridged call, made by the two legs. This gives us the complete picture of what was experienced by the end user.

We have at least two sides to configure: We need FreeSWITCH to introduce into SIP packets a correlation ID that will tag two calls as two legs of a bridged call, and we need to instruct the Capture Server to use that Correlation ID.

In FreeSWITCH, we edit `dialplan/default.xml` and add it to the beginning of the file, just inside the `context` section:

```
<extension name="x-cid" continue="true">
<condition >
<action application="set"><![CDATA[sip_h_X-cid=${sip_call_id}]]></
action>
</condition>
</extension>
```

With this extension, we set the channel variable `sip_h_X-cid` on the incoming (from the caller) call. We assign to that variable the value of the call CallID. This variable will be acted upon by FreeSWITCH into adding an X-Header to the `INVITE` SIP packets of the outbound call (the B-leg) that will be originated and bridged to the caller. For example, the newly originated B-leg call (from FS to callee) INVITE packets will contain an X-cid header that will bring along the CallID of the incoming (from the caller to FS) call. This X-cid header will be the tag which correlates A-leg and B-leg.

Then, we must configure the Capture Server to use that X-cid SIP Header. On the Homer machine, edit `/var/www/html/api/preferences.php` to read:

```
define('BLEGCID', "x-cid"); /* options: x-cid, b2b */
```

Then, edit `/etc/kamailio/kamailio.cfg` and add:

```
modparam("sipcapture", "callid_aleg_header", "X-cid")
```

to the section where SIPCAPTURE parameters are set. To be on the safe side, restart both Kamailio and Apache2, and you're good. Try a test call again, and then bridge it (that is, call the 5000 FreeSWITCH default IVR, then press *1* on dialpad to be bridged to the FreeSWITCH Conference).

Log into Homer, do a search, and this time you will see two different calls (A-leg and B-leg) with two different CallID. But beware! The CallID_AL field of the B-leg INVITE is populated with A-leg CallID.

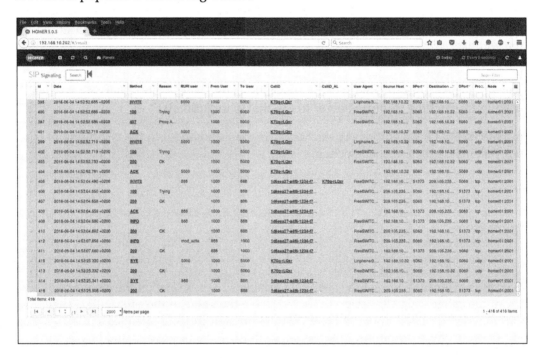

Click on that **CallID_AL** (our correlation ID, the X-cid we inserted) and the complete Call-Flow to the bridged two legs will pop up.

In the picture example, you can see on the left the incoming call (A-leg) from Linphone to FreeSWITCH 5,000 extension (default IVR), then on Linphone we press *1* to be connected to a remote Weekly Conference Call. A new call (B-leg) is originated on the right.

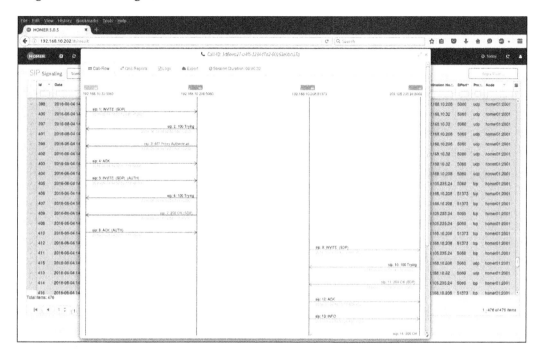

You can then click on the **QoS Reports** tab of Call-Flow to display combined media reports of A-leg and B-leg.

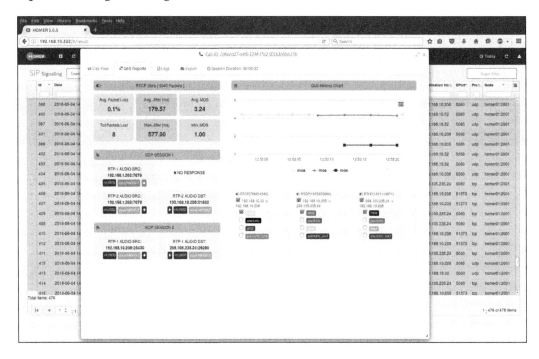

Feeding logs and events to Homer

Now that a basic flows and B2BUA correlation is done, maybe you want to add something else to complement your session investigations and take them to the next level. How about sending the Capture Server all sorts of info you deem related to a call, so it'll be instantly available, in the same Call-Flow popup? OK, I know you want it. As an example, let's set FreeSWITCH to provide two different sets of call-related data, one from dialplan, and one from **CDRs** (**Call Detail Records**, the accounting info written at the end of a call).

Logs to Homer

On the FreeSWITCH machine, edit the file `autoload_configs/cdr_csv.conf.xml`, and modify the `example` template (or the template you are using, if different from `example`), adding the SIP CallID as first field:

```
<template name="example">"${sip_call_id}","${caller_
id_name}","${caller_id_number}","${destination_
number}","${context}","${start_stamp}","${answer_stamp}","${end_stam
p}","${duration}","${billsec}","${hangup_cause}","${uuid}","${bleg_
uuid}","${accountcode}","${read_codec}","${write_codec}"</template>
```

From `fs_cli` or console, activate the changes by `reload mod_cdr-csv`.

Edit `dialplan/default.xml` and, inside the extension `x-cid` we added before, add the following action, which will print a line into standard logfile with a lot of info, the SIP CallID, and a tag (`tohomer`).

```
<action application="log" data="INFO 'tohomer ${sip_call_id}
${sip_full_from} ${sip_full_via} ${sip_full_from} ${Channel-Name}
${Caller-Context} ${FreeSWITCH-Switchname} ${toll_allow} ${callgroup}
${endpoint_disposition}'"/>
```

From `fs_cli` or console, activate the changes by `reloadxml`.

FreeSWITCH will now provide all the info we wanted, each set correlated with the call SIP CallID. Obviously, we have FS to dump all kind of variables and arbitrary values of our choice. We need a way to transmit this information to the Capture Server.

Enter `HEPipe.js`. It is a Node.js program that allows for the monitoring of files (like `tail` does), match lines on regular expressions, encapsulate them in HEP format, and send the matching lines to the Capture Server.

Download and install `HEPipe.js` on the FreeSWITCH machine from `https://github.com/sipcapture/hepipe.js` (npm install), then edit `config.js` and be sure to set your Capture Server IP address and port, with the correct regular expressions, and the location of your logfiles. If you followed our examples, you can copy from the image.

```
// HEPIPE-JS SETTINGS (please configure)
// ---------------------------------------------------
var config = {

        // Address and Port of your HEP Server
        HEP_SERVER: '192.168.10.202',
        HEP_PORT: 9060,
        // the HEP ID and Authentication for this Agent
        HEP_ID: '2099',
        HEP_AUTH: 'HEProcks',
        // the Logfiles to monitor
        LOGS: [
                {
                  tag : 'cdr-csv',
                  host : '127.0.0.1',
                  pattern: '"([^"]*)",.*', // escape backslashes!
                  path : '/usr/local/freeswitch/log/cdr-csv/Master.csv'
                },
                {
                  tag : 'log',
                  host : '127.0.0.1',
                  pattern: '.*mod_dptools.c.*tohomer\\s(\\S*).*', // escape backslashes!
                  path : '/usr/local/freeswitch/log/freeswitch.log'
                }

        ]
};

// ---------------------------------------------------

module.exports = config;
                                               1,1          All
```

In the `pattern` field you match the CallID between parentheses. Run `HEPipe.js` with `nodejs hepipe.js`. It will monitor the files in real time, as lines are added to them. If an added line matches the regex, that line will be sent to Capture Server, and will be correlated to the call identified by CallID.

In Homer you then click on the **Logs** tab of the Call-Flow popup to peruse all the info.

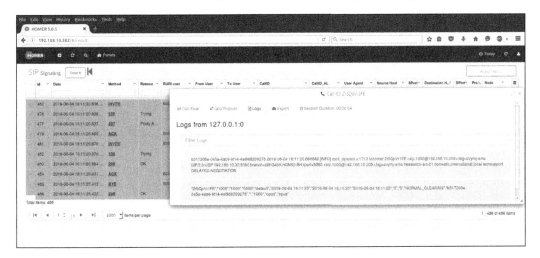

You can use this same technique to monitor any kind of file, not only FreeSWITCH-generated files.

FreeSWITCH events to Homer

HEPipe is a generic tool, and has been modified to uniquely interface with the FreeSWITCH event system.

HEPipe-ESL.js (https://github.com/sipcapture/hepipe.js/tree/master/esl) will connect to the ESL TCP socket, subscribe to *all* events (you'd better modify it to only subscribe to the events you're interested in), filter/extract/correlate key details based on the event type, and send them to the Capture Server. Also, when the call ends, HEPipe-esl.js will create a QoS media report leveraging the internal media session details released by FreeSWITCH.

As per previous examples, modify the HEP_SERVER and HEP_PORT values inside HEPipe-esl.js to reflect those of your Capture Server, then execute with nodejs hepipe-esl.js (or using *run forever* once you decide to make it permanent).

Make a test call, then check the **Logs** tab of the Call-Flow popup.

This time you'll find plenty of info, too much actually, but this is just a demo. Received log rows can be filtered in real time using Strings or Regex directly from the **Logs** tab.

Summary

In this chapter we gave you a good hint of what Homer can do for your organization with minimal setup and configuration effort. Homer is able to store and display in real time millions of minutes' worth of call signaling, correlate call legs, webRTC signaling, media statistics and reports. It can be the deck of your communication support team, letting them immediately pinpoint any customer complaint. We followed through from installation of the user interface (Homer proper) to the care and feeding of the Capture Server, and the setup of Capture Agents. Building on our examples, you can customize your entire platform network for end-to-end centralized monitoring and troubleshooting.

Index

rxgain parameter 100

S

Sangoma ISDN stack
about 95
reference 95
screen sharing
about 158, 159
dialplan extension 159
SDES
(S)RTP, encrypting via 69, 70
SDP 229
Session Border Controller (SBC) 12
Session Description Protocol (SDP) 116
Session Initiation Protocol (SIP) 27
Session Initiation Protocol (SIP) stack 4
signaling
about 224
searching, with Homer 260-263
signaling modules
about 91
analog modules 92
cellular GSM / CDMA (ftmod_gsm) 93
ISDN 91
MFC-R2 protocol 92
SS7 92
Simple Network Management Protocol
(SNMP)
about 34
and FreeSWITCH 35
configuration, on Linux 35, 36
installation, on Linux 35, 36
SIP
about 229
encrypting, with TLS (SIPS) 68, 69
SIPCAPTURE 257
sipgrep
about 241-244
URL 241
SIPp, testing with
load testing 30
scenarios, running 27-30
SIP signaling
feeding, from CaptAgent to
Homer 263, 264
feeding, from FreeSWITCH to Homer 260

SIPS (SIP Secure) 68
sngrep
about 237-241
reference 237
Sofia 4
SoX 252
SS7 92
system configuration, FreeTDM
about 97
DAHDI 99
FreeSWITCH configuration 102, 103
FreeTDM library configuration 99-101
operation 104-106
Wanpipe 98

T

T38
about 165, 168
gateways 169
terminals 169
tcpdump 233, 234
Text to Speech (TTS) 81
time domain multiplexing (TDM) 88
TLS (SIPS)
SIP, encrypting with 68, 69
tools, for troubleshooting
about 229
Audacity 250
firewall 230
FreeSWITCH, as SIP self tracer 232
ngrep 234, 235
pcapsipdump 236
sngrep 236-241
SoX 252
tcpdump 232-234
tshark 235
wireshark 244
traditional telephony codecs
constrain audio 74
troubleshooting
about 223
media 225
NAT 225, 226
signaling 224
VoIP packets 227, 228
trunk_type parameters 100

tshark 235
txgain parameter 100

U

User Agent Client (UAC) 27
User Agent Server (UAS) 27
utility functions
  about 197
  fs_urldecode() 198
  fs_urlencode() 198
  input_callback() 200
  isnil() 200
  isready() 200
  myHangupHook() 200
  shell() 197
  stamp() 197
  trim() 197
  whichline() 197

V

Value Added Services (VAS) 10
Verto 127
video conference
  about 151
  configuration 151, 152
  managing 160, 161
  mux profile settings 152
  performances 161
  screen layouts 153-158
Voice Response (IVR) 4
VoIP encryption
  new frontiers 71

W

Wanpipe drivers
  about 93
  reference 94
WebRTC
  about 115-117
  browsers 116
  encryption 122, 123
  FreeSWITCH 127
  gateways and application servers 124, 125
  legacy on Web 125, 126
  mod_verto, configuring 128
  to communication networks
    and services 123
  under the hood 117-119
welcome.lua
  structure 180, 181
wireshark 244-250

Z

ZRTP
  (S)RTP, encrypting via 70

Lightning Source UK Ltd.
Milton Keynes UK
UKOW07f0157010816

279624UK00001B/35/P